THE JUDGEMENT

The Judgement

Inside Story of the Emergency in India

Kuldip Nayar

VIKAS PUBLISHING HOUSE PVT LTD

New Delhi   Bombay   Bangalore   Calcutta   Kanpur

VIKAS PUBLISHING HOUSE PVT LTD
5 Ansari Road, New Delhi 110002
Savoy Chambers, 5 Wallace Street, Bombay 400001
10 First Main Road, Gandhi Nagar, Bangalore 560009
8/1-B Chowringhee Lane, Calcutta 700016
80 Canning Road, Kanpur 208004

ISBN 0 7069 0557 1

1V02N0807

First impression, June 1977
Second impression, June 1977
Third impression, June 1977
Fourth impression, June 1977
Fifth impression, June 1977
Sixth impression, June 1977
Seventh impression, June 1977
Eighth impression, June 1977

Printed at Dhawan Printing Works, 26-A, Mayapuri, New Delhi 110064

To

the people of India

the only ones who

could and did

Preface

IT WAS midnight on 25 June 1975, when the telephone woke me up. The caller said that he was speaking from Bhopal. Streets there were teeming with police and could I find out why? I said sleepily I would and he hung up. But as soon as I put the telephone down, it rang again. It was from a paper in Jullundur and the caller said that the police had seized the press and all copies of the day's paper. This was followed by a call from my office, the *Indian Express*, reporting that the electricity to all newspaper offices in Bahadur Shah Zafar Marg, New Delhi's Fleet Street, had been cut off and unofficial sources said that it was not likely to be restored "in the near future."

Frankly I saw no connection between these events. I thought that the bureaucrats were up to their tricks once more. Many months earlier the supply of electricity to newspaper offices in Delhi had been cut off at the time of the bus drivers' strike; it was restored only after ten hours. Perhaps the authorities did not want newspapers to report JP's rally on 25 June at which he had given a call for a Satyagraha.

But then came a call from Irfan Khan, then working in *Everyman's*, a weekly started by JP. He said that he had received reports of wholesale arrests of leaders, including JP, Morarji and Chandra Shekhar. The announcement of the emergency and censorship followed within a few hours; a nation had been trussed and gagged.

For a newsman nothing can be more frustrating than to gather news that he knows cannot be printed. It was soon evident that the emergency operation was a "success" and it appeared that for democracy it would be a night without end. But, however faint the hope of a dawn, the idea of keeping notes and writing a book one day came to me as I went round to find out the reasons for the emergency. It was hard to collect information.

Such was the atmosphere of terror and intimidation that few would talk. I did get some facts but I was arrested on 26 July. It was only after my release, seven weeks later, that I could pick up the thread again.

Even after the relaxation of the emergency on 18 January, when the elections were announced, there were few who would talk to me. But things changed after the elections and I have been able to talk to Sanjay Gandhi, R.K. Dhavan, H.R. Gokhale, Chandrajit Yadav, Ruksana Sultana, Mrs Fakhruddin Ali Ahmed and top officials in the police and other departments. All these people did not want anything attributed to them, and I have kept my promise. But they have been frank in their talks and most of the story of the emergency that I have reconstructed is based on what they told me. I approached Mrs Gandhi for an interview at least six times but she did not accede to my request.

I also travelled through most of the country twice during the emergency, once in October-November 1975 and again in the middle of 1976. On these trips I met a large number of people and collected a lot of material. I also got some "underground" publications that appeared during the nineteen months of terror.

I do not claim that everything about the emergency is in this book. For one thing, it is too long a story to be told in a hundred thousand words, for another I have not been able to check the many charges and rumours that followed the lifting of the emergency or to break through all the veils of secrecy covering the misdeeds during the emergency. But whatever is contained in the book has been checked and rechecked for veracity.

I know that certain things which I have gleaned may not be to the liking of some and these people are likely to contradict them. I do not want to join issue with them. I have only done my job of reporting events truthfully, with malice towards none. To the best of my ability, I have remained objective.

One thing that I have observed during my tours and interviews is that, however submissive almost everyone was, very few people had accepted authoritarian rule. There was fear, obedience, but not acceptance. Who were the people who instilled that fear and why did practically nobody in the government or elsewhere try to withstand the pressure? There should be an open debate on these questions.

I am thankful to S. Prakasa Rao and V. Achutha Menon,

once my colleagues in the *Statesman*, for making useful suggestions, to Kedar Nath Pandita of the *Indian Express* for having read the proofs and to Amarjit Sood, my secretary, for having patiently typed and retyped the several drafts of the manuscript.

KULDIP NAYAR

Contents

1. Towards Dictatorship

Two TELEPRINTERS clattered away in a poky little room in the prime minister's house, sputtering words endlessly. It was the night copy which the Press Trust of India (PTI) and the United News of India (UNI) were clearing during the slack morning hours. Normally, nobody ever so much as glanced at these machines, at least not so early in the day.

But on 12 June 1975, Neivulne Krishna Iyer Seshan, Mrs Indira Gandhi's seniormost private secretary, was nervously flitting from one machine to the other. There was an eerie silence in the room which even the noise of tickers and telephones did not seem to disturb.

There was news in the making and Seshan waited impatiently for it. It was the day Justice Jag Mohan Lal Sinha of the Allahabad High Court was to give his judgement on the petition which Raj Narain had filed against the prime minister's election to the Lok Sabha[1] in 1971. It was nearing 10 A.M. and only a short while before a lightning telephone call to Allahabad had brought the information that the judge had not even left his house.

Sinha, thought Seshan, was a strange person. Every man had his price, but apparently not Sinha. He could not be tempted and he would not submit to pressure.

A member of parliament from Mrs Gandhi's home state of Uttar Pradesh had gone to Allahabad and casually mentioned to Sinha whether he could do with Rs 500,000. Sinha did not respond. Later a colleague on the bench told him that he expected him to be elevated to the Supreme Court "after the judgement." Sinha merely looked at him with contempt.

Efforts to delay the judgement had also failed. Joint Secretary Prem Prakash Nayar in the Home Ministry, met the chief justice

[1]India's Lower House.

of the UP High Court at Dehra Dun and suggested to him that perhaps the judgement could be deferred till the prime minister had ended her planned visit to some foreign countries—an unfavourable judgement would be embarrassing.

The chief justice passed on the request to Sinha. The judge was so annoyed that he immediately rang up the court's registrar and asked him to announce that 12 June was the day of judgement. Sinha had already accommodated the ruling Congress party by not pronouncing judgement before the Gujarat assembly poll on 8 June so as not to influence the outcome.

Neither Seshan, nor, for that matter, anyone but the judge and his stenographer seemed to know the verdict. The intelligence bureau had drawn a blank. Some of its men had travelled all the way to Allahabad from New Delhi to try to persuade Negi Ram Nigam, Sinha's stenographer, to talk. But he appeared to be formed in his master's mould. Even threats had not worked. And from the night of 11 June, he and his wife were "missing" from their house. They had no children and intelligence men had found the house deserted.

The only silver lining for the prime minister's secretariat was that a sadhu who had been posted outside Sinha's house, knowing the judge's religious bent of mind, had reported that "everything would be all right." He, with other intelligence men, had stood behind the boundary wall of Sinha's house for days. But he could not have known what Sinha had dictated to his stenographer; the operative portion of the judgement had been typed in Sinha's presence only on 11 June, and apparently Sinha had then told his stenographer to "disappear."

Sinha had kept his findings very much to himself. During the hearing of the case also it was difficult to make out which way he was leaning. If he put two questions to one side, he saw to it that he had the same number of questions to ask the other. The hearing had taken four years, and after it ended on 23 May 1975, he had not stirred out of his house and nor would he answer the phone.

Seshan again looked at his watch as the teleprinters continued their clatter of unimportant news. It was five minutes to 10 A.M. Sinha, known for his punctuality, must be at the High Court. He was. The sparsely built judge, fifty-five years old, had driven straight to the court. As he sank into his chair in Room 24, a smartly dressed *peshkar* (court aide) announced to the packed courtroom;

"Listen, gentlemen, no clapping when the Judge Sahib announces judgement on the poll petition of Raj Narain."

Sinha, with his 258-page judgement before him, said, "I shall read out only my findings on the various issues involved in the case."

Then he added, "The petition is allowed." There was a moment of stunned silence and then a burst of applause; newspapermen ran to telephones and intelligence men to their offices.

And at 10.02 A.M. Seshan heard the bell ring on the UNI machine and saw the flash message. MRS GANDHI UNSEATED. Seshan tore the paper off the machine and ran towards the room where the prime minister was sitting. He met her elder son Rajiv, an Indian Airlines pilot, outside the room and gave him the message.

"They have unseated you," Rajiv told his mother.

Mrs Gandhi took the news without much show of emotion. Perhaps there was even some relief that the waiting was over.

All through the previous day she had been brooding; to add to her ordeal, a close friend, Durga Prasad Dhar, first a cabinet minister and then India's ambassador to Moscow, had died. But that morning she appeared more cheerful.

Another flash came that she had been debarred from holding any elective post for six years. This seemed to ruffle her and it looked as if she was hiding her emotions. Slowly she walked to the sitting room.

Sinha held her guilty of two corrupt practices in the election. The first was that she had used Yashpal Kapoor, officer on special duty in the prime minister's secretariat, to "further her election prospects." As a government servant, he should not have been put to such use. Sinha said that although Kapoor had begun electioneering for Mrs Gandhi on 7 January 1971 and tendered his resignation only on 13 January, he had continued in government service until 25 January. Mrs Gandhi, according to the judge, had "held herself out as a candidate" on 29 December 1970, the day she addressed a news conference in New Delhi and announced her decision to stand for election.

The second impropriety was that Mrs Gandhi had obtained the assistance of UP officials to build rostrums from which she addressed election rallies; the officials had also arranged for loudspeakers and electricity to feed them.

Raj Narain had lost by a margin of over 100,000 votes; these improprieties would not have materially changed the outcome. They were too thin to justify unseating a prime minister. It was almost like unseating the prime minister for a traffic offence.

But the law was the law, and it was quite clear that any assistance sought from a government servant "for the furtherance of the prospects" of a candidate's election was a corrupt practice. Sinha himself said in the judgement that he was left with no choice. There was no special provision for the PM and he could not have given any other verdict. Even the punishment for contravention of the law was fixed and the judge was left with no discretion.

The normally ebullient Sidhratha Shankar Ray, West Bengal chief minister, and roly-poly Dev Kant Barooah, Congress party president, were the first to arrive at the prime minister's house. Dismay was writ large on their faces but they kept quiet when Mrs Gandhi said that she would have to resign.

As the news spread, distraught cabinet ministers and many others started pouring in at 1 Safdarjang Road. The sitting room was full. Mrs Purabi Mukherjee, a Congress party general secretary, came in and started crying loudly. Though all those present looked like a congregation of mourners she was too demonstrative even for them. Mrs Gandhi told her with some irritation not to lose control of herself. The prime minister looked pale but calm. She knew she had no choice other than to resign.

Someone suggested that she could appeal to the Supreme Court. But that would take time. The matter was still being discussed between Ray, who claimed to be closest to the prime minister, and Law Minister Hari Ramchandra Gokhale, when there was another flash on the ticker to say that Sinha had granted a clear stay of his judgement for twenty days. The atmosphere changed; everybody relaxed. Gokhale[2] rang up Allahabad to doublecheck. It was true. Mrs Gandhi did not have to resign straightway.

But it was a near thing. Sinha had nearly rejected the stay application because he was irritated over the harassment his stenographer had undergone at the hands of intelligence men the day before. But Mrs Gandhi's lawyer, V.N. Khare, who had been flown to Allahabad from Srinagar barely twelve hours before the judgement, told Sinha that his client was not to blame for what the

[2]Half an hour later he rang up Krishna Iyer, the vacation judge, but was refused an appointment.

police did to his stenographer. Sinha accepted the explanation.

Khare's argument for the stay was that the party would take some time to elect a new leader and that administration of the entire country would be in disarray if the prime minister was asked to quit there and then.

Now the prime minister's house was full of ministers, businessmen, top officials and hangers-on. There were rude words about Sinha. At the same time there was satisfaction that he had given a stay of judgement. There was time now to plan and save the banyan tree that had for long sheltered them, as her father had done in his time.

Rajiv was near his mother in her hour of crisis. But Sanjay, Mrs Gandhi's second son, was at his factory, Maruti[3] Limited, set up to manufacture a "people's" car. In the confusion no one had thought of informing him of the crisis, though lately, unlike his brother, he had started playing an active role in politics to "protect" his mother from the communists he hated.

When Sanjay drove in his imported car to the house around noon he found a crowd outside. He knew what must have happened and went straight to his mother. He did not say anything but her face brightened on seeing him. Sanjay was only twenty-eight years old but from her experience she had known how "mature" he was in his advice.

She held a family conclave in a closed room to decide on what she should do. Both her sons, Rajiv and Sanjay, were against her quitting, even temporarily. Sanjay was the more vehement. He pointed out what she already knew—even more than the opposition she had to fear ambitious men in her own party.

She then went to the storeroom in the house, as was her wont whenever she faced a crisis. It was her refuge, it gave her time and opportunity to think.

She had much to think about. If she resigned now and came back after "exoneration" by the Supreme Court, it would silence her critics who alleged that she wanted to stick to power at any cost. But if the Supreme Court upheld the Allahabad High Court judgement, she would have to be out of office for ever with one more stigma.

She could not be certain how the court might deal with the

[3]See the full story in Annexure I.

appeal that she would file. In the past, members unseated or
disqualified by the high courts had been allowed to sit in the
House, but without the right to vote, participate in debates or
draw allowances. What if she got only a qualified stay?

Her advisers had drawn comfort from Article 88 of the Constitution which says that a minister and the attorney-general "shall
have the right" to speak and participate in debates of either
House even when not "entitled to vote." Whatever the type of stay
order, a court could not take away this right from any minister.

She would win the applause of the world if she were to resign;
her stock as a true democrat would rise so high that she could
expect to be swept back to power in any election as in 1971. But
what if the Supreme Court debarred her from seeking election for
six years? That was a long time—time enough for people to forget the good she had done, and for ambitious men, in her own
party or outside, to exhume the skeletons in her cupboard.

Sanjay was her refuge. She was confident that he would help
her in her hour of need. He was credited with having given her
the election winning slogan in the 1971 polls: "They say *Indira
Hatao* (oust Indira) but I say *Garibi Hatao* (oust poverty)." Now
he had to do more than coin a slogan. He knew his mother was
not one to give up easily, but at that time she was on the verge of
doing just that. And that must not be. He must organize public
support, not only to convince her that the country needed her but
also to keep her enemies at bay.

A dropout from Doon School and an apprentice motor mechanic
with Rolls Royce in England, Sanjay had come a long way in
"establishing" himself in politics. What fascinated him was money
and power and he was beginning to have both.

His chief aide was thirty-five year old Rajinder Kumar Dhavan,
additional private secretary in the prime minister's secretariat,
who had been a clerk in the railways on a salary of Rs 450 a
month only a little more than a decade earlier. Dhavan owed it
all to Sanjay; the two were close friends and had been together in
several escapades. He was Mrs Gandhi's Man Friday, some even
called him a second M.O. Mathai, who was Nehru's stenographer
and became one of the most influential men in his office.

Sanjay used this petty official to manipulate the entire government machinery, or was it the other way round. So powerful was
Dhavan that he could tick off any junior minister or senior official;

he spoke in the name of the prime minister. Once he took a minister to task for having sent a reminder to the prime minister's secretariat on some important matter.

Sanjay had yet another close friend, though a much older man. He was the fifty-two year old Bansi Lal, chief minister of Haryana, which he ruled as he would his fief. He was unscrupulous; means never mattered to him, only ends did. From being a briefless lawyer he had risen to be chief ministership in less than a decade, and he wanted to go still higher. It was he who gave Sanjay a 290-acre plot for the Maruti factory at a throwaway price along with a government loan to cover the amount. Sanjay in turn had brought him into the inner councils of the prime minister. Both mother and son had come to rely on him because he was ever at their beck and call, ever ready to carry out any assignment, right or wrong.

These three persons formed the triumvirate, the *Teen Murti*, around Mrs Gandhi. And she had implicit faith in them. They acted on her behalf in the government, the party and politics in general. She knew that they often employed nefarious methods, but there was no doubting their effectiveness. She allowed them to do what they wanted because it strengthened her position.

There was yet another man, quite handy, sixty-five year old Dev Kant Barooah, the Congress party's president. He was called court jester and was ever singing praises of Mrs Gandhi. It was she who had taken him out of state politics in Assam and made him governor of Bihar, then a cabinet minister, and ultimately, the Congress party's chief. He was one she could count on now.

Mrs Gandhi had known him as a friend of Firoze Gandhi, her late husband. Barooah had often interceded to patch up differences that flared up every now and then between husband and wife, both strong personalities. Barooah had flirted with right-wing communists because that gave him a veneer of ideology which went down well in an underdeveloped country. That did not please Sanjay, who called him a commie, but the common danger from the opposition brought Barooah and Sanjay together, at least for the time being.

They were soon at work to show the world that whatever a judge might say the people had no doubt that Mrs Gandhi was their elected leader and would remain so. The first step they took was to collect crowds to "prove" her popularity. This was an exercise they had gone through more than once before. Trucks were requisitioned and sent to the villages to bring people to 1 Safdarjang Road, Mrs Gandhi's residence, to demonstrate their loyalty to the leader. Government (Delhi Transport Corporation) buses were deployed with impunity to bring crowds free of charge. That after the rallies no free transport was available for the people who had to trek back home was another matter.

From the prime minister's house Dhavan rang up chief ministers of neighbouring states—Punjab, Haryana, UP and Rajasthan—to organize rallies. They too had much experience in marshalling government machinery to gather crowds. They had done so in July 1969 when Mrs Gandhi decided to nationalize fourteen major Indian banks to get herself a "progressive" image and paint Morarji Desai, her seventy-four year old rival in the Congress, as a "rightist" because he had wanted only "social control" of the banks.

Desai had twice tried to be prime minister, once in 1966 after the death of Mrs Gandhi's predecessor, Lal Bahadur Shastri, in Tashkent, and again in 1967 when the Congress party limped to power with only 285 seats in the then 520-member Lok Sabha.

Dhavan had taken upon himself the task of mustering "public support" because Yashpal Kapoor, more experienced in these things, was in the doghouse following criticism that it was he who got Mrs Gandhi into trouble on the charge of corrupt practices in the election. But Dhavan was Kapoor's sister's son and had learnt much from his uncle. Yashpal Kapoor's was also a success story. He had risen from a stenographer's chair to become Rajya Sabha[4] member and, even more important, Mrs Gandhi's political adviser and informer. Kapoor was good in image building; he had been of great help whenever Mrs Gandhi's popularity required props. He always knew which wires to pull.

For some time he had to sulk at home; he was told to stay away from the public eye because his name figured so prominently in the Allahabad judgement. Later he was allowed to come back. He coined the slogan *Desh ki Neta* (the country's leader) *Indira Gandhi.* This was improved upon by Barooah who said "Indira is India," little realizing that it would cause a great deal of embarrassment because it was much like the oath administered to Nazi

[4]India's Upper House.

youth: *Adolf Hitler is Germany and Germany is Adolf Hitler.*

It did not take the chief ministers long to get buses and men and rush them to the traffic island outside Mrs Gandhi's residence—a readymade rostrum for such demonstrations from the day of the election of V.V. Giri as India's president in 1969. At that time, the Congress party's own nominee for the post, Sanjiva Reddy, had been opposed by Mrs Gandhi and the crowds had been "organized" to show their support to her in the fight between "reaction and progress."

Politics, of course, had to be simplified for the masses. Ideology, or the profession of it, was important. The Congress party had long been pledged to "democracy" and "socialistic principles" which somehow made it slightly different from "socialism," the plan of the Socialist party. The current word in vogue was progressive as against reactionary. Mrs Gandhi was a progressive while Socialist Raj Narain was reactionary, as also the judge who had gone by some reactionary laws.

The judgement was soon made a non-event, and Mrs Gandhi made it known that she was not giving up office because "given the faith of the people," she would continue to work towards the goal of eradicating poverty and the establishment of a new society. The student wing of the Congress party, the National Students Union of India, which was later to be absorbed by the Youth Congress, Sanjay Gandhi's force, said "Mrs Gandhi is the leader of the downtrodden millions and exploited masses of India whom she leads in their struggle for a socialistic transformation of society based on justice and equality." It said not a word about the High Court verdict against her.

So crude was the exhibition of support for Mrs Gandhi that some Congress members of parliament took exception to the populist demonstrations. But her reply was, "They are spontaneous."

Support for Mrs Gandhi was also voiced by all the five chambers of commerce in the country and by top industrialists. In her, despite her "socialistic" posture, they saw the best chance of preserving their possessions and privileges. Her policies were certainly better than the socialist policies which many in the opposition professed. She had also the backing of the Communist Party of India (CPI), which adopted a resolution on 13 June which said: "The student cries of right reaction for the prime minister's resignation on so-called moral grounds cannot conceal their sinister political objectives." The party, pro-Soviet in its attitude, expected to ride on the Congress shoulders right up to the portals of a communist state.

Institutions like the Jamia Millia Islamia and the Bharatiya Depressed Classes League did not lag behind in expressing their faith in Mrs Gandhi. Over the years she and her father had tried to establish a secular society. How could they trust the opposition, which had the Jana Sangh, the parliamentary wing of the Rashtriya Swayamsevak Sangh (RSS), a Hindu organization believing in a "disciplined" society based on Hindu culture or what its *sanchalaks* (organizers) called Bharatiya culture?

That Mrs Gandhi enjoyed wide support, even without her son's rent-a-crowd operation, no one doubted. The opposition might say that the point at issue was whether a guilty prime minister should be in office, and warn the people against those out to wreck the democratic edifice of the country by challenging a judicial verdict in the streets. But its voice was almost drowned in the chorus of support for Mrs Gandhi.

Some young socialists did try to hold a counter-demonstration. When a few managed to break the police cordon outside the PM's house and started shouting, "Mrs Gandhi should resign," one of Sanjay's aides, tall, photogenic Ambika Soni, rushed out and slapped one of the boys. Thirty-five year old Ambika, who was to be president of the Youth Congress, was showing herself to be a woman of action. The police were not slow to follow her lead, the dissenters were beaten up and a few arrested.

But this did not daunt the opposition. Excepting the pro-Soviet CPI, which supported Mrs Gandhi because it believed she leaned towards Russia, all the parties in opposition declared that they did not recognize her as prime minister. They attacked her for sticking to power when a High Court judgement had held her guilty.

For them—the Congress party of the old guard, the Hindu nationalist Jana Sangh, the pro-farmer Bharatiya Lok Dal, the breakaway Communist Party of India (Marxists), CPI(M), and the Socialists—the Allahabad judgement was a godsend. They had attacked her on many points—corruption, her scant respect for democratic traditions, the trend towards dictatorship—but nothing seemed to work.

Now, what they could not achieve for years had been done for them by a court judgement. They demanded her resignation and staged *dharna* (sit-down strike) outside the house of the president, though he was away in Kashmir. They said they would take further legal action against her and ordered state party workers to step up anti-Indira rallies and demonstrations.

Among themselves the opposition did not have even sixty seats in parliament. But they had the advantage now. The issue they posed was that of morality and propriety and they sent a message to Jayaprakash Narayan, after Mahatma Gandhi the conscience keeper of the nation, to lead them.

They could not have done better than choose JP, as he was better known, to be their leader, though in 1974 they had disappointed him by not complying with his suggestion that they merge into one party to stand against the Congress. A Gandhian, and a hero of the 1942 Quit India movement against the British, he had always lent his voice to the silent majority of the suppressed and deprived. Over a period he had come to symbolize cleanliness and integrity in public life. The movement he had started in Bihar, his home state, against deepening corruption in public life, had no doubt petered out; it had got focused on a mundane thing like the dissolution of the state assembly and had forgotten the higher spiritual goals he had sought—the necessity to have a real democratic structure which was responsive to the people's needs and the cleansing of politics of opportunism. But two years later the results of the Bihar movement fructified.

In the past JP had joined issue with Mrs Gandhi for having encouraged corruption and betrayed the cause of socialism. In the Allahabad judgement, he saw an opportunity to revive the battle for moral rejuvenation, for higher standards in public life.

For long he and Mrs Gandhi had had an uncle-niece relationship and he called her Indu. But over the years, especially the previous two, they had drifted apart. He considered her the fountainhead of corruption and the destroyer of basic values. And after the Allahabad judgement he said that she had no moral right to continue as prime minister. She should quit office immediately. Her clinging to office was "against all public decency and democratic practice."

Mrs Gandhi knew JP was a force to reckon with. When he met her on 1 November 1974—a meeting arranged by D.P. Dhar

—she had agreed to dissolve the Bihar assembly on condition that he would not demand anything more. That he would not agree to.

JP received an urgent message on 17 June from the opposition parties to come to Delhi immediately to lead their rally. But he declined. He was in favour of awaiting the judgement of the Supreme Court on the appeal Mrs Gandhi had made before plunging into battle.

JP was aware of the power a united opposition could wield. The victory of the Janata Front in the Gujarat assembly election, winning 87 seats in the 182-member House, was proof enough. And six Independents had joined the Janata to give it an absolute majority. The Congress party had secured only 74 seats, as against 140 in the 1972 poll when the opposition parties were far from united.

The election had been preceded by the first campaign in JP's plan for "total revolution." JP wanted to start the Gujarat pattern in the whole of India. The time was opportune but he wanted to hear what the Supreme Court had to say on Mrs Gandhi's appeal. He was hopeful that the law being what it was the highest court of the land could not but uphold Sinha's verdict.

Mrs Gandhi also waited, and not without hope that the court would go more by the spirit than the letter of the law.

Now that the non-communist opposition parties had declared that they did not recognize her as prime minister, she could only expect the worst. A parliament session could be an embarrassment.

She had been having a hard time in parliament over a Central Bureau of Investigation (CBI) report on an import permit given to Tulmohan Ram, MP, a protege of Railway Minister Lalit Narayan Mishra, who had been assassinated on 3 January 1975, before the responsibility for issuing the permit could be pinned on anybody.

At one time Morarji had threatened to offer Satyagraha in the House if the opposition's unanimous demand to make the CBI report public was not conceded. She had vainly asked Speaker Gurdial Singh Dhillon to turn Morarji out of the House for this. Later, she was irked by the speaker's ruling that she and Morarji should meet him in his chamber. She had to suffer the slight because the speaker submitted his resignation on hearing that she had not liked his ruling, and she had to persuade him to continue in office.

There were vicious rumours that she had had a hand in getting Mishra bumped off. True, she had asked for his resignation because of the acrimonious debate over his possible involvement in the import licence scandal. But she was already repentant and had the guilty feeling that Mishra had only paid the price for aligning himself with her. Sanjay and Dhavan had Mishra's office in Rail Bhavan sealed, but that was because he had collected some papers relating to Maruti, and they did not want others to lay hands on them. She had come to know of it but she had never "interfered in the affairs" of Maruti in the past and saw no reason to do so then.

This too would come up before parliament. Mrs Gandhi considered the postponement of the July-August session of parliament. If the opposition did not allow the House to transact any business during the discussion on the import licence scandal, it would behave even worse after the Allahabad judgement. And there was no knowing how a "temporary" prime minister would react to these pressures.

By staying in office she could at least have some opportunity to direct the course of events. She could not afford to resign. But it would not do to let others know it. It would be much better to appear to be persuaded to stay by others than to be suspected of desperately clinging to office. Perhaps, knowing the answer, she asked her senior colleagues—Jagjivan Ram, Yashwantrao Chavan and Swaran Singh—whether it was proper for her to continue in office till the Supreme Court's decision on her appeal. All three told her that it would be a disaster if she were to quit. But they had different reasons for saying so.

Jagjivan Ram said that she should wait till the judicial process had run its course. But he expected the Supreme Court to give her only a qualified stay because the court had never granted a clear stay in such cases. He thought that would be the time to rise in revolt. "We can afford to wait till the Supreme Court's judgement," he told me during those days.

Jagjivan Ram's relations with Mrs Gandhi had deteriorated over the years. So much so that of late he was not being consulted even on small matters, much less important ones. She had always known that he was one of her chief rivals in the party, and had sponsored him as the Congress candidate for president in 1969 after the death of Zakir Husain, thinking that he might be tempted by that high office, where it would be safer to have him as the figurehead rather than in the cabinet.

True, she had condoned his "forgetfulness" in not having paid income tax for a decade. But he thought he had cleared the debt when he sided with her against Morarji Desai, though he was with him in the political wilderness after both were dropped from the government by her father, Nehru, in the name of reorganizing the Congress under the Kamaraj Plan in 1963. He was a clever, ambitious man and Mrs Gandhi knew it. If the Supreme Court ruled against her he would get the prime minister's mantle without the risk of leading a revolt. He could indeed afford to wait for the judgement.

For Chavan,[5] Mrs Gandhi's survival was his survival. His ambition was to be her effective number two. After voting first with the old guard during the presidential election in 1969 on the understanding that he would be made prime minister, and then rejoining her when the old guard started bargaining, his credibility with the opposition was low. He had nothing to gain from deserting Mrs Gandhi after JP[6] had made it clear that he would prefer Jagjivan Ram to him as prime minister.

Swaran Singh, with a reputation for being non-controversial, however felt the spur of ambition when he heard from one of the PM's aides that if she ever stepped down temporarily she would choose him to be prime minister for the interim period. He thought she would resign on her own, and though he advised her not to, he gave the impression that if she did she would not be doing wrong.

Mrs Gandhi's legal advisers, particularly Sidhartha Shankar Ray and Gokhale (who had made a hash of her case at Allahabad) were also against her resigning. They argued that the Supreme Court would not "play to the gallery" as the Allahabad judge had done, and she should await its verdict. Others, who had anything to do with law, pointed out that the offences for which

---

[5]Chavan was asked by the old guard, called the Syndicate, to allow Morarji to be prime minister till the elections, then due in 1972.

[6]JP told me in a press interview in 1974.

she was held guilty were only "technical."

This was reassuring. But to many in the country it was not clear where the People's Representation Act had said that some offences were technical and some material. In 1951 there used to be two types of offences—major and minor. The elections were set aside only on major counts. But in 1956, during Nehru's time, the election laws were revised and simplified. The list of offences amounting to corrupt practices was drastically cut. But the use of government servants for election purposes was retained as an offence. Many state ministers and members of parliament and state assemblies had in the past lost their seats on that ground. Mrs Gandhi herself had asked Chenna Reddy, her cabinet minister from Andhra Pradesh, to resign when he was held guilty of corrupt election practices.

If she were to go by precedent she would have to resign. She continued to ask party leaders for their advice; and this they took to be a sign that she was wavering. They started holding consultations of their own with MPs from their states.

The most important meeting was at the house of Chandrajit Yadav, a central minister of state with communist leanings. Barooah presided. Only a few trusted Congress leaders were invited; among them was Pranab Mukherjee, then only a junior minister. They discussed who should be the successor to Mrs Gandhi if she were to step down even if only temporarily.

The choice was between Jagjivan Ram and Swaran Singh. Most preferred the latter as he was considered safe and pliable. But Jagjivan Ram was the seniormost member of the cabinet and in brushing aside his claim they would be giving public expression to their private fear that he could not be trusted to make way for Mrs Gandhi even if she was exonerated by the Supreme Court. They were not clear what they should do. The way Jagjivan Ram had stood by her at the present juncture made them feel that even she would probably not hesitate to trust him. And if he were to rebel on being slighted, the party might split. They could not come to any decision. Pranab told me that if Sidhartha Shankar Ray had been at the centre,[7] he would have been the obvious choice for being inte.im prime minister. Even

---

[7]Before going to West Bengal as chief minister, he was education minister at the centre.

Jagjivan Ram perhaps would have found it hard to stand against him.

But it was an academic exercise. Mrs Gandhi was very much in office and while she held it she was sure to enjoy the overwhelming support she had always commanded.

Cabinet ministers, chief ministers and state ministers were asked to sign a pledge expressing faith in Mrs Gandhi's leadership. Good at drafting as Parmeshwar Nath Haksar[8] was, he was asked to prepare the text. He was the one who had drafted most letters sent to the other side during the Congress party's split in 1969. Haksar's draft had some veiled criticism of the judiciary and this was changed as it would not help to antagonize judges, with the Supreme Court yet to hear Mrs Gandhi's appeal. But the operative part of what he drafted remained: "Mrs Indira Gandhi continues to be the Prime Minister. It is our firm and considered view that for the integrity, stability and progress of the country, her dynamic leadership is indispensable."

There was a scramble to sign the statement, which came to be considered a bond of loyalty. Sanjay was keeping his mother constantly informed on who had so far signed it. And who had not? Newspapers carried a growing list of names.

Mrs Nandini Satpathy, chief minister of Orissa, arrive[1] late in the evening in New Delhi from Bhubaneswar to sign it, and insisted that the next morning's papers should include her name among the signatories. Men of the government's information bureau rang up editors to see that this was done. It was important to be known to be loyal to Mrs Gandhi. One minister who was late in signing the statement, despite several phone calls from the prime minister's house, was Swaran Singh. He could not simply blot it out of his mind that if she were to resign he might be the interim prime minister. And he paid the price for it months later.

Meanwhile hundreds of thousands of men paraded the streets in cities and towns in demonstrations financed and organized by state governments and the party to shout, "We will not accept the Allahabad High Court judgement." The implication was

[8]Haksar was once the prime minister's blue eyed boy but was now in the dumps, in the Planning Commission as deputy chairman, because he had tried to dissuade her from "encouraging" Sanjay and Kapoor.

that neither would they accept a Supreme Court judgement upholding it. Mrs Gandhi and her men were preparing for all eventualities; there was nothing sacrosanct about any court's judgement on "technical" points concerning an election, particularly of the prime minister—the people's expressed will was beyond the court's jurisdiction.

Mrs Gandhi also received support from an unexpected quarter. T. Swaminathan, her former cabinet secretary, whose term she had first extended and then appointed him chief election commissioner, announced that he had the power to remove any disqualification of persons holding elective posts, including that of prime minister. The rules said so, though his predecessor, Sen-Verma, had suggested in the 1971 election report that the election commissioner should not enjoy such "arbitrary powers."

Enough warning had been given that a verdict by the Supreme Court need not be considered final. But she was not, for that reason, neglecting the battle to come in the court.

She contacted a brilliant Bombay lawyer, Nani A. Palkhivala, to argue her appeal in the Supreme Court. Palkihvala had been dubbed reactionary when he had the nationalization of fourteen Indian banks struck down by the courts on the basis of discrimination and questioned the abolition of privy purses to former Indian rulers on the argument that the purse, being part of property, could not be abolished since property was a fundamental right under the Constitution.[9] But even reactionaries had their uses.

On Mrs Gandhi's summons, Palkhivala, also a senior director in Tatas, the country's biggest industrial firm, flew to Delhi. He told her that he could win the case. But what about the democratic propriety of continuing in office? But by that time she was not chary of letting everyone know that she had decided to stay on and would not step down even temporarily.

She had to make a stand because pressure to persuade her to resign was now growing. And not only from the opposition. The intelligence bureau had reported that some members of the Congress party wanted her to resign till "the cloud lifted," meaning thereby exoneration by the Supreme Court. A small,

[9]In the Golak Nath v. State of Punjab case it was held that a fundamental right was "beyond the purview" of parliament.

determined group of former Socialists, called the Young Turks, was in the vanguard. She knew their capabilities; she had once used them to demolish Morarji Desai by making official files available to a Young Turk, Chandra Shekhar, to prove Morarji's "connivance" in the doings of his son, Kanti Desai, who had begun his life as an insurance agent but was now an affluent businessman.

That the Young Turks were unhappy over Mrs Gandhi's performance in office was well known. For some time she had been trying to keep them down. Though she failed to stall Chandra Shekhar's election to the Congress party working committee, she had the president dismiss another Young Turk, Mohan Dharia, from the council of ministers because he had asked her to start a dialogue with JP.

And it was now Dharia who demanded her resignation. He suggested that she should step down in favour of Jagjivan Ram or Swaran Singh till she was exonerated by the Supreme Court. The other Young Turks were with him, and she feared that the demand would snowball.

Intelligence reports said that the Young Turks were in constant touch with Jagjivan Ram, and he was fomenting revolt. He had started saying more or less openly that the judicial judgement against the prime minister should not be taken lightly.

He had also been indulging in a game of numbers—counting how many would be with him if he were to revolt, but he found that there were not enough to back him.

Mrs Gandhi was a good tactician and floated the suggestion that if she were to decide to step down she should be allowed the right to nominate her successor. As she expected, this was a non-starter—both Jagjivan Ram and Chavan opposed it.

It was a bitter experience for Jagjivan Ram to know that when for a short time Mrs Gandhi wavered she had in mind Kamlapati Tripathi, whom she brought to the central cabinet from UP as "temporary prime minister."

Jagjivan Ram's reaction was, "We shall support Tripathi on the condition that he does not allow her to come back. All that we have to do is to start a couple of inquiries against her."

A temporary prime minister who might well turn disloyal might agree readily to the demand for inquiries that she had long resisted. An investigation would damage her reputation beyond redemption. One skeleton in the cupboard was her son's Maruti car project.

Another was that of the "heart failure"[10] of an undertrial, Rustom Sohrab Nagarwala, a retired army officer who had reportedly imitated the voice of the prime minister and of her Secretary Haksar to withdraw six million rupees from State Bank of India vaults in New Delhi. (Chief Cashier Ved Prakash who allowed this, later joined the Congress party after his exit from service.)

Not without reason did Mrs Gandhi distrust Jagjivan Ram. Already, she had to contend with the Young Turks. The growing intrigues inside the party made it essential that she should be sure of her men in parliament. She summoned all chief ministers to New Delhi so that each could take "control" of the MPs from his state. She wanted the meeting of the Congress parliamentary party, fixed for 18 June after consultations with her, to affirm solid support for her. Sidhartha Shankar Ray and V.B. Raju, a Rajya Sabha member from Andhra Pradesh, were put on the job; they were asked to get Jagjivan Ram fully committed to the resolution that they would draft.

They could be counted on to do their best. With such evidence of solid support of the Congress parliamentary party, the president should find it easy to turn aside the opposition demanding her dismissal. Under the Constitution, as long as she had the confidence of the majority party, she could remain prime minister.

At the time of the Allahabad judgement, President Fakhruddin Ali Ahmed was in Srinagar. He wanted to return that very day when he heard of the verdict, but Mrs Gandhi dissuaded him on the phone. Every day over the next three days he would check with her whether he should return, but she did not want him to cut short his tour lest the public should read more into it and imagine that he was hurrying back to accept her resignation. Outside Rashtrapati Bhavan, the president's official residence in New Delhi, the opposition had started a dharna demanding just that.

Soon after his arrival in Delhi on 16 June, Mrs Gandhi met him. It was a brief meeting, lasting less than fifteen minutes, to acquaint him with the preparations for filing the appeal in

---

[10]One of the doctors who had "something" to do with Nagarwala's body told me that symptoms of heart attack could be simulated.

the Supreme Court against the Allahabad judgement.

His meeting with the non-communist opposition leaders later in the day lasted longer. Their request to him was to "order" Mrs Gandhi to relinquish office. Ahmed appeared to consider the suggestion—he did not want to seem to be taking sides; he had the reputation of merely being Mrs Gandhi's rubber stamp to live down. He first said that they should await the outcome of the Congress parliamentary party's meeting. But then he realized that he might have said the wrong thing and might be taken to be hinting at something far from his mind. He immediately corrected himself and said what he meant was that they should await the Supreme Court's judgement. His press secretary issued a handout for clarification so that the newspapers would not get it wrong.

After meeting the president, the opposition members gave up the dharna outside his house. But they decided to intensify the agitation to make Mrs Gandhi quit. Many among them thought of establishing contacts with the Congress party members if only to appeal to them to uphold the prestige of the prime minister's office. The CPI(M) did not go with the deputation to the president, but it put its weight behind the non-communist opposition's demand that she must quit.

The opposition's meeting with the president to demand her resignation irked Mrs Gandhi the most. This had never happened before. Even when her father's stock was at its nadir, following India's defeat by the Chinese in 1962, the opposition as a body had not met the president to press for the prime minister's resignation.

She was beginning to feel hemmed in. And her main worry was not the opposition but her own party, which was beginning to seethe with discontent. Most members felt that they could not fight the next elections, due in February 1976, with her as leader. Jagjivan Ram and the Young Turks were contacting more and more MPs, arguing with them that she must step down to honour the sanctity of judicial pronouncements. It was an argument that the masses might find hard to understand but not legislators.

The strain was telling on her. She started losing her temper often. There was anger in her speeches. "I have been tolerating all kinds of allegations, lies and malicious charges against me," she would say at the rallies organized in her support.

She joined issue with Justice Sinha. Publicly she said that

Yashpal Kapoor had ceased to be a government employee on 14 January and had stopped drawing his salary from that date (Sinha had said that Kapoor was working as a government employee till 25 January) and that the building of rostrums by government officials for the prime minister's meetings was the practice even during her father's time.

More often than not in her speeches she would bring in India's victory against Pakistan in the 1971 Bangladesh war; at that time even her bitterest opponents, the Jana Sangh, had said that she was not a Congress party leader but India's leader, above all parties and creeds.

She attacked the opposition parties in every speech blaming them, as in the past, for anything that went wrong with the government's policies; they were "traitors." She said, it was the opposition that stood in the way of progress. Now she said that socialism would continue to make achievements despite "obstacles created by vested interests."

This was in sharp contrast to what her father's attitude was to the opposition. Many in the opposition recalled the days when they were consulted on national affairs and when their cooperation was sought to carry out programmes dealing with food or national integration. Now they were called in only to be informed of what the Congress party had decided. They knew that their number in parliament was small. But it had been so at the time of Nehru and despite that they were consulted and heard; he never made them feel that they had no right to question him or his government. He encouraged the right of dissent and appreciated the role set for the opposition in a parliamentary democracy.

For Mrs Gandhi the opposition was only an inconvenience. She accused the opposition of ever trying to paralyze the country for political gain and cited the example of the railway strike in 1974. Out of 1,350,000 regular employees, 350,000 on daily wages, nearly sixty-five per cent had responded to the strike call, but the government crushed it with the most repressive measures—mass dismissals, detentions, eviction of strikers' families from railway quarters, stoppage of supplies to railway fair price shops and cutting off of water and electricity to workers' colonies.

She would expatiate on the spread of anarchy and political chicanery. Indeed, some university campuses were disturbed and there was more loss of mandays in factories than ever before.

For the opposition she was an aspiring dictator to be dislodged. JP had sharpened his attack and had begun calling the central government a "one-woman government, reduced to a dictatorship under the facade of democracy." This line of argument was now faintly audible from many of her partymen.

On top of it, legal opinion was not encouraging. The best experts had told her that she could hope to get only a conditional stay from the Supreme Court, although they thought that she would be exonerated in the "final judgement." Would she be able to rule with a damaged image that a conditional stay meant?

Already "political management" had become difficult, as she told one editor. The pressure of the opposition from without— JP was already getting hundreds of thousands of people to listen to him—and the simmering revolt in her own party filled her with foreboding.

The headlines and stories on the judgement and its aftermath in the newspapers only added to this. The press had never appreciated her difficulties or achievements, she thought. One New Delhi daily had gone to the extent of associating her and her family with murder of opponents. She was sure the newspapers were biased; once she told editors that she did not read the newspapers because she knew which paper would say what.

She had a low opinion of pressmen. She knew that they were purchasable. In fact she had heard from Lalit Narayan Mishra how, through whisky, cash and suit-lengths he had kept many journalists, especially those in New Delhi, on his side. Her secretariat also had, at her instance, often used "progressive" journalists to attack her critics. Not only journalists, even owners of newspapers, she was aware, could be purchased. But now they all seemed to be ganging up against her.

She was at the end of her tether and felt surrounded by enemies. Everyone seemed to be out to pull her down, except her son, Sanjay, and his group, including Dhavan.

Agitations were increasing; her slogan to oust poverty had not improved the people's living conditions. Prices had risen a little over three per cent between 1950-51 and 1965-66. But in her regime, the increase averaged fifteen per cent. There was more vocal opposition than she had ever experienced before.

She realized that the situation as it was developing could be dangerous for her. This was the time she began to think of some drastic steps to silence her critics, both inside and outside the Congress. The opposition could swing public opinion in its favour; practically all political parties were united, and there was a threat to the Congress party from within.

She had to do "something" about the opposition which did not have even one-sixth of her party's strength in parliament. She was confident that once she decided to act she could act quickly, for she had centralized power in the prime minister's secretariat.

The process had begun with her predecessor, Lal Bahadur Shastri. His Secretary L.K. Jha began having a finger in every pie and came to be called super-secretary. Her Civil Service Secretary P.N. Haksar had improved on what Jha had done and organized the system in such a way that everything would revolve around the prime minister's secretariat. Not even a deputy secretary was appointed without its concurrence. He set up a mini government. Each officer of the secretariat dealt exclusively with almost everything in one field, whether economic, foreign or scientific. All ministries took their orders from them. But Haksar's main contribution was that he politicized the set-up, in the sense that for the first time in the country's post-independence history, government machinery came to be used for political purposes, if need be Congress party purposes. A few years later he was to rue the day he did it.

Mrs Gandhi had provided the machinery with power to control men who could provide "security." At the centre she had roughly 700,000 policemen, belonging to the Border Security Force (BSF), the Central Reserve Police (CRP), the Central Industrial Security Force (CISF) and the Home Guards. These units were independent of the police in different states (said to number about 80,000) and of the armed forces totalling one million.

The opposition, she felt, was getting ready to go to extremes; her enemies within and without her party were trying to do what they had failed to do in political battle—use the verdict of a "perverse" judge to oust her. She could also, if need be, go to extremes.

Sanjay had no doubts on that score and told her that. And

he was her chief counsellor after he had helped her come to a decision when she was torn between power and propriety after the High Court judgement. And it was he who had proved to her that the country and the people needed her.

Sanjay went on dinning into her head that she was too indulgent towards her opponents and too timid to take any action against them. This was repeated by his friend in need, Bansi Lal, who had silenced the opposition in Haryana by having his opponents beaten up, locked up or harassed by the police. "I would have put all of them behind bars," he told her. *Bahenji* (sister), give them to me and I shall set them right. You are too democratic and soft." People respected the strong, the one who could deliver the goods, as he had proved in his state.

Practically all the chief ministers also had warned her that she must do "something" if events were not to overwhelm her. She left the matter to Sanjay, who was giving her all the strength from wilting under pressure and who had told her not to resign when some of her staunchest supporters appeared to be faltering.

It was 15 June when Sanjay started working on "some plan to set things right," as he later told a friend. His idea was to restructure the government, at the political and official levels. The democratic way of functioning was not to his liking. Nor had he patience for the rigmarole of procedures. He needed time, but time was running out.

The first thing he did was to order the installation of two "secrophones" in his room. Only ministers and top officials were entitled to them, but everyone knew he was acting for the prime minister and it was promptly done. This way he could ring up anyone without the risk of going through their secretaries.

He had no preconceived notions about what he wanted to do. But he believed every opponent could be either purchased or broken. One should have no compunctions. He liked dictatorship, as he told a West German paper once, though "not of the Hitler type." Once fear was instilled in the people's mind, they would either learn to obey or at least not speak out. Sanjay wanted obedience and no method was mean enough to achieve it.

The initial plan was only to curb the press and "shut up" some leaders and important men in the opposition. This would ensure "discipline"; everyone would fall in line. The newspapers would not be able to print what was distasteful to the government and the opposition would not say what was "undesirable."

Gagging the press was important. As both Mrs Gandhi and Sanjay had often said at the family breakfast table, it was the newspapers which were to blame for lionizing their opponents and creating "an atmosphere of distrust" against the government. But they were both paper tigers and could be made to behave.

Sanjay had never been happy with the press from the day he tried to establish his factory, the Maruti. Newspapers had published too much on it and him—too much which he had not liked, even though he had sponsored editors' trips to the plant.

He put most of the blame on Information Minister Inder Kumar Gujral. Gujral, he said, was friendly to journalists but could never get them to write anything in favour of the government. In this he was unfair. It was Gujral who had built up the personality cult round Mrs Gandhi since 1969 when the fourteen banks were nationalized and he had used the government-owned radio and TV and publications to strengthen her position. He had even influenced newspapers, particularly the smaller and weaker ones by giving them advertisements—as the country's largest single advertizer, the government had much to give in patronage. After the Allahabad High Court judgement, however, Gujral did not appear to be equally enthusiastic.

Sanjay's associates, Dhavan and Bansi Lal, had also no good word either for Gujral or the press. Dhavan argued that journalists had been too pampered by Gujral and they should be cut to size. Bansi Lal told them how he had set the *Tribune* at Chandigarh right by denying it government advertisements and having the police penalize the vehicles that carried the paper to Haryana or passed through the state.

But could what was done in one small state against one paper be done all over the country to control the press as a whole? Sanjay's friend, Kuldip Narang,[11] a fledgling businessman of Delhi, supplied him with a copy of the censorship rules and details of the machinery set up to implement them in the Philippines; he had got them from his friends in the American embassy in New Delhi.

Action against JP and others had long been planned, even as

---

[11]It was in his car that Sanjay was once caught outside the graduate women's hostel at night and Narang covered up for him.

early as January. I had learnt of it from a member of the prime minister's secretariat; he said that some steps had been thought out on how to "take over." He had picked up only odds and ends here and there but though he did not know the details, they did include the arrest of JP and banning of the RSS.

At that time, being a "desk man," not a correspondent, I had the information conveyed to the *Motherland*, a Jana Sangh daily, and the *Indian Express*. The *Motherland* story said:

NEW DELHI, Jan. 30—The Government of India has decided to ban the Rashtriya Swayamsevak Sangh[12] (RSS). It has also decided to arrest Shri Jayaprakash Narayan.

The RSS is expected to be banned on the night of February 2-3 and Jayaprakash is expected to be arrested as soon as he lands in Patna on February 3.

Shri Ghafoor [chief minister of Bihar] was only announcing the PM's decision when he said: 'I will go to any length'.

The two decisions were taken by the Political Affairs Committee of the Cabinet earlier this week.

Shri S.S. Ray, Chief Minister of West Bengal—who used to draft the midnight missives for the PM in 1969—also lent his hand at drafting the ordinance.

The ordinance repeats the oft-told lie that the RSS is a secret organisation which does not believe in non-violence. And it attributes Shri L. N. Mishra's murder to the 'climate of violence' generated by the RSS and JP's movement. . . .

The *Indian Express* did not say anything about JP's arrest except to raise the possibility, but printed the rest.

NEW DELHI, Jan. 30—An Ordinance to ban the Rashtriya Swayamsevak Sangh is thought to be imminent in political circles here.

The starting point of speculation on these lines was the statement by Mr Abdul Ghafoor, Chief Minister of Bihar, during a press conference here on Wednesday that drastic action was on the way to counter Mr Jayaprakash Narayan's movement in Bihar.

[12]S.S. Ray wrote a letter to Mrs Gandhi on 8 January asking her to ban the RSS through an ordinance.

It will be recalled that Mr Ghafoor did not rule out the arrest of Mr Narayan. The arrest of the Sarvodaya leader is also considered probable by the end of this week or the beginning of next week.

The ban on the RSS will also be followed by arrests of prominent leaders in the organisation. The list of arrests may extend to several scores. ....

Mrs Gandhi's hatred for the Jana Sangh was well known. When it had planned too rganize a demonstration in Delhi in March 1974, she had personally given the Delhi inspector-general of police a list of leaders she wanted arrested. The authorities felt that the situation did not warrant such action but those were her orders. Subsequently she changed the top administration in Delhi. And this was the time when Sanjay and Dhavan moved officials who would be loyal to them into key posts in the Union Territory.

The exercise done in January came in handy to Sanjay who was working on how to "control things." Mrs Gandhi, who was consulted at every step, did not favour the arrest of JP and Morarji Desai in the beginning. But she later saw the point—it would be dangerous to allow leaders like them free to foment trouble.

Helping in the preparations was fifty-five year old Om Mehta, minister of state. Even though number two in the Ministry of Home Affairs, he had the real power because he was known to be close to the prime minister. He was often referred to as Home Mehta. Sanjay used him for any "extra-constitutional" work.

Dhavan did not like Mehta because he had direct access to Sanjay. But this was no time for personal likes and dislikes: all worked together. Dhavan was a key figure because Mrs Gandhi used to pass on instructions to officials and even to ministers through him. He had come to represent what she wanted.

Bansi Lal, in constant touch with Mrs Gandhi, was told to pass the word that some strong action might be taken against the state chief ministers assembling in New Delhi for a meeting on 18 June. Bansi Lal declined to speak to Sidhartha Shankar Ray and Nandini Satpathy, who he thought were communists. Both he and Sanjay did not like them, and so Mrs Gandhi said she would inform them herself.

They were, of course, not to be told of the details of the contemplated action. But trusted men in the bureaucracy in every state were being told what they should do. In Delhi, where most opposition leaders were present, the job was entrusted to Kishan Chand. He was a retired member of the Indian Civil Service, and Delhi's lieutenant-governor, and was beholden to Sanjay for having retrieved him from oblivion. Sanjay had direct contact with him and Navin Chawla, his Doon School mate, who was the lieutenant-governor's special assistant.

There was yet no talk of any emergency; "some action" against the press and the opposition was all that was mentioned. No one discussed what that action would be. Legal and constitutional implications were still to be worked out. But there was determination; a way to get out of trouble had to be found.

The date of action was also yet to be decided. However, Mrs Gandhi was clear in her mind that it had to be after the Supreme Court's decision on her application for a stay against the Allahabad judgement. Her lawyers were preparing to file the appeal before the vacation judge, Justice V.R. Krishna Iyer,[13] who she thought was "ideologically" on her side.

While her son and his group were preparing the "battle plan," she continued with her campaign to get full support from the party. And she seemed to be winning. Sidhartha Shankar Ray and Raju had taken the "support resolution" to Jagjivan Ram and suggested that he should move it. The resolution reiterated the party's "fullest faith and confidence" in Mrs Gandhi and belief that "her continued leadership as Prime Minister is indispensable for the nation." Jagjivan Ram made hardly any change in the draft resolution; in fact, he complimented Raju and said that he had "saved the Congress."

Mrs Gandhi also sent Jagjivan Ram a message saying that he should see that the Young Turks did not say anything against the resolution. They had told him that they were willing to support the resolution provided the last sentence saying that "her continued leadership as Prime Minister is indispensable for the nation" was deleted. They did not object to the portion "Mrs Gandhi symbolises the resurgent India of today and the aspirations of the people. Now more than ever the Congress and the nation need her leadership and guidance." But they could not subscribe to

---

[13]S.M. Sikri, former chief justice of India, had resisted Iyer's appointment in 1972 on the ground that the latter was a communist.

the preposterous idea that she was indispensable.

Jagjivan Ram could not make them change their collective mind but was able to persuade them to stay away from the meeting to avoid embarrassment in case they raised the point. The absence of the Young Turks did raise eyebrows and some whispers but did not in any way affect the 516-member parliamentary party's behaviour. It unanimously supported Mrs Gandhi. The chief ministers, each keeping a vigilant eye on the MPs from his state, applauded from the wings. Jagjivan Ram moved the resolution but dwelt more on harmony between the executive and the judiciary than on the virtues of Mrs Gandhi; Chavan, who seconded the resolution, made up for it by praising Mrs Gandhi for not only leading the country to victory in the 1971 war but also pulling the nation out of the subsequent economic crisis.

As arranged, Mrs Gandhi came to the party's meeting like a queen reviewing a guard of honour, and stayed for only a short while. What she said in her brief speech was familiar—that the present crisis had been brewing for some time and was the result of a "combination of forces" against her and the Congress, and that she derived her strength from the people.

After the adoption of the resolution unanimously, Barooah, who presided over the meeting, suggested that they troop into Mrs Gandhi's room, not far from the Central Hall of parliament where the Congress parliamentary party members were assembled. Jagjivan Ram killed the move by saying that she had already left for her house. He had gone far enough in compromising; indeed more than he should have and did not want a special show of servility after that.

With the adoption of the resolution, the question of a qualified or absolute stay by the Supreme Court lost its relevance. The prevalent mood was that come what may, she must stay. What if the Supreme Court did not allow her to vote or participate in parliamentary discussions? She would still be prime minister.

Mrs Gandhi's top advisers, both legal and political, discussed how, if the need arose, they could overcome a verdict upholding her disqualification from holding elective office for six years. They thought of legislation to remove restrictions on all disqualified members up to a particular date, say, 1 July 1975. Such a measure was once considered, to enable D.P. Mishra of Madhya Pradesh and Chenna Reddy of Andhra Pradesh to hold office, but it was not acted upon.

There was also a proposal that, to honour the Allahabad judgement setting aside her election, she could recontest the Rae Bareli seat if need be.

But strangely, whenever such suggestions were taken to Mrs Gandhi, she showed little interest in them. She looked preoccupied. Partly she was busy with the preparations of her appeal to the Supreme Court, but mostly her mind was filled with what Sanjay and his group were busy planning.

The non-communist opposition decided to press the demand for her resignation. They set 21 and 22 June for a combined meeting of the executives of the constituent members of the Janata Morcha and planned to start a countrywide movement to oust Mrs Gandhi. JP sent a message saying that he would participate in the Morcha deliberations and the rally. Raj Narain had convinced JP that they need not wait for the Supreme Court judgement before launching any action.

The opposition also pressed for the convening of the monsoon (mid-July) parliament session, and presented their demand to the speaker. Congress party leaders however had already decided against it, as the session might cause embarrassment. The Constitution, they argued, did not say anything more than that there should not be a gap of more than six months between sessions. The speaker knew Mrs Gandhi's mind and therefore did not agree to the summoning of parliament.

Left to Sanjay and his group, they would not convene the parliament session at all since to them that would be a waste of time; for example, the last session had only discussed the Tulmohan Ram case. And then, how could the government work when the better part of the year was taken up in preparing answers to parliament questions? They thought of restricting this "useless" activity.

The same thoughts were once echoed by Chandrajit Yadav, a pro-CPI Congress minister. It was the sort of remark which Shashi Bhushan, a pro-CPI Congress member from New Delhi, had made. He had said that he favoured limited dictatorship. Much later, when he was reminded of the remark, he said, "But I used the word 'limited' not 'private limited'."

By now there was a change in Mrs Gandhi. She had overcome her diffidence after the Allahabad judgement. In fact, she was now convinced that the judgement was part of a widespread conspiracy to remove her. Someone had told her that Justice Sinha was pro-Jana Sangh.

Sanjay and his group exuded confidence. Not only was Mrs Gandhi with them in the minutest detail but everything was nearly set for their operation. Lists of opposition members to be arrested were being drawn up in every state, and the Philippines-type censorship system had been spelt out to the last letter.

The time for "action" was also set; it was to be the day after the Supreme Court's order. Preparations were speeded up; the machinery to implement orders was streamlined. More officials whom they could fully trust at the time of need were being appointed to key positions.

It was decided to replace the Home Secretary Nirmal K. Mukherjee because he was "too legalistic." Rajasthan Chief Secretary Sardari Lal Khurana, considered more pliable, was picked up as his successor. Dhavan, who was from now onwards a one-man appointment board, had harboured the grievance that the administration was full of south Indians; he wanted north Indians to take over, particularly Punjabis.

The intelligence bureau chief, A. Jayaram, was moved out, Surinder Nath Mathur, inspector-general of police, Punjab, was selected as his successor—he was first appointed additional director and then director. Jayaram in any case had failed in not giving them even an inkling of what the Allahabad judgement was going to be before it was delivered.

Bansi Lal had talked to most of the chief ministers and they were only too willing to take action against the opposition and the press. Mrs Gandhi herself discussed the matter with Sidhartha Ray and Nandini Satpathy. The former, once a successful lawyer, wanted to know under which law the two steps were contemplated. He was all for them, but did not want her to stray away from the law. Of course, her own inclination was also to stay within the limits of the Constitution and she asked him to think over the methodology and ring her up from Calcutta.

The intelligence bureau reported that the opposition was getting ready to start an agitation, to march in thousands to her house and try to surround the place. They would squat on railway tracks and see that the trains did not move. The courts would not be allowed to function, government offices would not be able to work. It was an attempt to bring everything to a standstill.

This was proof, if proof was needed, that Sanjay was right in saying that the opposition had only one aim—to get her out. She was now completely dependent on him and his plans. She was confident he would come up with something to get her out of trouble. She could see him working eighteen hours a day.

At the government-managed 20 June solidarity rally in New Delhi she said she would continue to serve the people in whatever capacity she could till her last breath. Service had been her family tradition she said.

For the first time, she mentioned her family at a public meeting. The family was indeed present on the rostrum—Sanjay, Rajiv and his Italian wife, Sonia.

Mrs Gandhi said that big forces had been working not only to oust her from office but to liquidate her physically; to achieve their designs, they had spread a wide net.

Barooah was at his old job building up the Indira cult. He recited an improvised Urdu couplet: *Indira—Tere subah ki jai, tere sham ki jai, tere kaam ki jai, tere naam ki jai* (Indira—Victory to your morning, victory to your evening, victory to your action and victory to your name.)

The rally was a success. "It was the biggest in the world" as Mrs Gandhi put it. But it had not been televised, merely because it was a party rally, not a government rally. And that cost Gujral his portfolio. Sanjay had a brush with Gujral who had to tell him that he was his mother's minister, not his.

From the public meeting, as many as thirteen chief ministers trooped into Rashtrapati Bhavan to reiterate their confidence in Mrs Gandhi and to submit a one-page memorandum which said that Mrs Gandhi's resignation would lead to instability, not only at the national level "but also in various States."

Some of them were present in the Supreme Court the following Monday, 23 June, when Justice Krishna Iyer heard Mrs Gandhi's appeal. Her application had sought "absolute and unconditional" stay "in view of the position held by Mrs Gandhi." It was argued that "it is eminently in the national interest that the *status quo* should not be disturbed while the appeal is still pending."

Iyer heard the arguments of both sides for two days and came to the conclusion that Mrs Gandhi had not been convicted of "any of the grave electoral vices." He said that she could continue as prime minister but not have the right to vote in the Lok Sabha till the Supreme Court had disposed of her appeal against the judgement of the Allahabad High Court.

The stay given was conditional. But there was no bar on her participation in discussions in parliament. Iyer, however, had drawn the attention of parliament that "draconian laws do not cease to be law in court but must alert a wakeful and quick-acting legislature."

The government arranged with news agencies and, of course, radio and TV, to put across the "positive" side of the judgement. What it meant was that there was no bar on Mrs Gandhi continuing as prime minister.

The opposition leaders—by this time JP had arrived in New Delhi—did not want to join issue with the Supreme Court. They welcomed the judgement but said in a statement, "Her (Mrs Gandhi's) credibility stands destroyed, her membership restricted, her right to vote suspended. Under the circumstances, what sort of Prime Minister can she be?" They reiterated their resolve to launch a countrywide movement to make Mrs Gandhi resign.

The CPI(M) did not at this time join the non-communist opposition but reacted more or less the same way—Mrs Gandhi, as she had been proved a "liar" by the Allahabad High Court, should resign.

The CPI continued to support her. The central secretariat of the party said that she should not surrender to the "blackmail of right reaction" and that she should continue as prime minister.

Iyer's judgement upset Jagjivan Ram's plans. He was expecting a qualified stay, not a clear judicial pronouncement that she could continue as prime minister. In any case, he was late in acting because the way Barooah and others had made the moral issue a political one, the stay had become irrelevant.

Now Jagjivan Ram joined the chorus of central ministers, chief ministers and others. In a statement and a resolution they said that there was no impediment in the way of Mrs Gandhi functioning as prime minister Jagjivan Ram went a step further—it was only a legal question and no more moral and political issues were involved, he said. Morality was on Mrs Gandhi's side.

The party's parliamentary board also met to warn the nation that "some groups and elements might continue their efforts to mislead the people and exploit the situation for their partisan ends."

Among those who did not share the enthusiasm of other party-men were the Young Turks—Chandra Shekhar, Mohan Dharia, Ram Dhan, Krishan Kant and Mrs Lakshmi Kanthama—and a few others. They held a separate meeting to assess their strength. It was not much; they could count their supporters on the tips of their fingers.

"The number was not more than thirty," both Chandra Shekhar and Krishan Kant told me. "But there were many who said that they would join if need be."

The Young Turks were unhappy over the manner in which Congress leaders had thrown away any pretence of honouring democratic values to organize the pro-Indira campaign after the Allahabad judgement. Their biggest disappointment was Jagjivan Ram who, after telling them that he was with them, had welshed.

Mrs Gandhi's reaction did not bother them because they were prepared for disciplinary action by the party. They had never made a secret of their admiration for JP. Chandra Shekhar had told Mrs Gandhi more than once that she should meet him and win his cooperation for cleanliness in politics. On 24 June Chandra Shekhar hosted a dinner to JP. The intelligence bureau had reported that eighty MPs shared the views of the Young Turks. But only twenty turned up at the dinner.

What happened in the inner circles of the Young Turks, or for that matter in the Congress party, did not concern Sanjay and his group who were now putting into operation the mechanics of their plan. Sidhartha had spelt it out for them.

Two days earlier he had rung up Mrs Gandhi from Calcutta to say that the only way to go about "doing something" was to declare "internal" emergency. ("External" emergency had been in force since December 1971, when the Bangladesh war began.) He said that Article 352 empowered the president to proclaim an emergency in case there was internal disturbance. This would give the government blanket powers.

Mrs Gandhi asked him to come to Delhi immediately. For him, sudden departure from Calcutta presented no problems. A current joke was that he always had a suitcase packed and a plane ticket booked for Delhi. Ever since he left the central cabinet to become chief minister his trips to Delhi for consultations with the prime minister averaged at least two every week.

Sidhartha pursued his idea during his talks in New Delhi on 24 June. The prime minister's house hurriedly sent for a copy of the Constitution from the parliament library. A vague plan for "doing something" to silence the press and opponents of Mrs Gandhi had not only acquired firm shape but also achieved constitutional sanction—"internal emergency" was the cloak a lawyer had found for an action planned with dictatorial motives.

The prime minister's secretariat already had a note ready for imposition of emergency—one of those contingency plans which were always on the shelves. Under emergency powers the centre could give any direction to any state, suspend Article 19[14] of the Constitution or suspend the whole range of fundamental rights. Courts could be ordered not to entertain any suit seeking to enforce these rights and so on. Powers would be sweeping.

Mrs Gandhi, for whom form often appeared to matter more than substance, was greatly relieved. She would be acting under the Constitution in declaring the emergency.

How different was her attitude from that of Nehru. In October 1962, when the entire country was turning against him because of the reverses against China, Krishna Menon, then defence minister, had suggested the imposition of internal emergency. Nehru ruled it out on the ground that it would harm democratic traditions.

Now that the decision to impose the emergency had been taken, Gokhale was called in to give it legal form. But even he did not know the date of its declaration.

The time set for action was midnight, 25 June. By then, it was thought, the Supreme Court's order would be in.

Secrecy was the key point. No one but Mrs Gandhi, Sanjay, Dhavan, Bansi Lal, Om Mehta, Kishan Chand and now Sidhartha, knew of the imminent operation, though orders had started going out to hundreds of men who were set limited tasks, mostly relating to arrests.

Barooah, who smelt something cooking, was told about the emergency on 24 June. He wanted a few "progressive measures"

[14]Article 19 says: "All citizens shall have the right: to freedom of speech and expression; to assemble peacefully and without arms; to form associations or unions; to move freely throughout the territory of India; to acquire, hold and dispose of property and to practise any profession or to carry on any occupation, trade or business."

to be taken to soften the impact and he suggested the nationalization of the sugar and textile industries. He argued how the
nationalization of banks in 1969 had helped them defeat the Congress
party's official candidate in the presidential election. But Sanjay,
a firm believer in private enterprise, rejected the proposal.

Barooah made another suggestion—a dole for the unemployed.
Sanjay ruled that out also on the ground that it would cost an
enormous sum; more than twenty million were said to be unemployed.

Reddy was taken into confidence only on 25 June. But even then
he was not told who all were being arrested. Nor did he try to
know. For some time, for safety's sake, he had learnt to play
second fiddle in his Ministry of Home Affairs.

The opposition had no knowledge of what was being contemplated. Perhaps Jyotirmoy Basu, an affluent Marxist, came nearest
to the mark when he said publicly that Mrs Gandhi was thinking
of scrapping the Constitution—someone from the PM's side had
given him a hint of some drastic action. He had the windows of
his house fixed with steel bars. Biju Patnaik, former chief minister
of Orissa and a BLD leader, had the feeling that something like
that was planned, and expressed his fears. But none in the opposition believed them; the suggestion was too fantastic to be
believed.

In any case, the opposition leaders were busy preparing for the
25 June rally. The late arrival of JP, now nicknamed *Loknayak*
(the people's hero), in Delhi had delayed it by one day.

It was one of the biggest rallies Delhi had seen, but not as big
as Mrs Gandhi's rally, and her supporters took credit for that.
But the people who attended JP's rally had come on their own;
they had no government-hired lorries to bring them; it was not a
rented crowd. One after the other, opposition leaders attacked
the prime minister for clinging to power, some said that she was
being a dictator. They made it clear that they would not allow
her to function.

JP announced the formation of a five member *Lok Sangharsh
Samiti*, (people's struggle committee), with Morarji as chairman
and Nanaji Deshmukh, a top Jana Sangh leader, as secretary, to
start a countrywide agitation on 29 June to force Mrs Gandhi to
resign. There were to be nonviolent hartals, satyagrahas and
demonstrations.

JP asked the gathering to raise their hands to indicate that they, if need be, would go to jail to restore moral values in the country. Everyone raised his hand. Surprisingly, twenty-four hours later, most of them did not even protest, when protest was called for, much less offer to go to jail. JP also appealed to the police and the military not to obey any "illegal" order as their manual indicated.

Ironically, this was precisely the Congress party's own stand in the 1930s. Mrs Gandhi's grandfather, Motilal Nehru, was the moving spirit in getting the party to move a resolution urging the police to disobey illegal orders. The Allahabad High Court then upheld an appeal by those convicted of distributing leaflets reprinting the resolution. The judges of the British raj ruled that there was nothing wrong in asking the police to disobey illegal orders.

For Mrs Gandhi, Sanjay and their supporters, however, JP's appeal to the police and the military was the best propaganda ammunition they could hit upon. Now they could say that he was trying to foment trouble among the armed forces; this was something treasonable.

But that was only a pretext. Much before the rally, Sanjay Gandhi and his trusted men were getting ready for the kill. As midnight approached there was feverish activity in the PM's house. Orders had gone out to the states, and many of them wanted to know if they were to do anything more than censor the press and arrest Mrs Gandhi's opponents. The lists of leaders to be detained in Delhi and elsewhere were ready and were shown to Mrs Gandhi. In the preparation of these lists, one intelligence branch that made a significant contribution was the Research and Analysis Wing (RAW).

RAW was constituted in 1962 at the fag end of the war with the Chinese, to improve India's intelligence abroad, because during the hostilities against the Chinese there was failure of intelligence. Biju Patnaik had given a helping hand in the initial stage because he had earned a reputation of "working behind the enemy line" when, many years ago, during Dutch rule over Indonesia, he had himself flown a plane to Jakarta to rescue Sukarno, then head of Indonesia's national movement.

RAW was directly under the prime minister's secretariat. Mrs Gandhi was the first prime minister to use it for political intelligence within the country. Its advantage was its compactness and the personnel, who were chosen either for their brilliant academic record or for their relationship with a dependable top civil or police officer. RAW had built up dossiers on government opponents, on critics within the Congress party, businessmen, bureaucrats and journalists. Preparing lists of opponents was no problem; RAW had everything ready in its files.

Which law to use for detention was also not a matter for discussion. The Maintenance of Internal Security Act (MISA) had been amended only a year earlier to authorize the government to detain or arrest individuals without producing charges before a court of law. However, when this law was passed, the government had given assurance to the opposition in parliament that MISA would not be used to datain political opponents.

Bansi Lal wanted leaders in Delhi to be detained in Haryana. "I have made a big modern jail in Rohtak," he told Mrs Gandhi.

Mrs Gandhi recalled General Raina, chief of the army staff, from tour. This was just a precaution.

By this time, the top brass in the Delhi police had come to know that even people like JP, Morarji, Ashok Mehta, Congress (O) president, Atal Behari Vajpayee and Lal Krishan Advani, the two Jana Sangh leaders, were to be detained.

Under what law? Since they did not know about the emergency, they tried to find out how they could be arrested. Under section 107 of the Indian Penal Code (IPC), they were informed. But that was applicable to vagabonds. How could JP and Morarji be arrested under that section?

The Delhi list of names was still being finalized with the help of Kishan Chand. When the police wanted warrants of arrest, Sushil Kumar, Delhi's deputy commissioner, insisted on knowing the names first. Dhavan, who was informed about it, flew into a rage and made him cower. Sushil then signed blank warrants. P.S. Bhinder, a "dependable" police officer who had been brought from Haryana into the special (intelligence) branch, filled in the name on each warrant as and when the need arose.

In the states, the chief ministers, who knew what was coming, sat with their inspectors-general of police and chief secretaries to finalize the lists of those to be arrested. Though preliminary preparations had begun after the chief ministers' return from Delhi around 20 June, the idea was then vague; it was thought that only a few were to be picked up and held for a time to silence them.

Whenever chief ministers were in doubt, they would ring up the prime minister's house, called the Household or Palace. It was Dhavan at the other end who answered their queries. Some chief ministers were still not clear why there should be a new emergency when the old one was in operation. Dhavan explained the difference to them.

In UP, a model FIR (first information report) was prepared at Lucknow by police headquarters and sent to all police stations so that they had something for the file. This was a precaution even though it was known that MISA prisoners could be detained without disclosing the reason.

Sidhartha was the only chief minister staying on in Delhi and using long-distance calls to instruct officials in Calcutta. He had stayed back because Mrs Gandhi wanted him to accompany her when she went to the president with the declaration of emergency for him to sign.

Nearly four hours before the deadline, he and Mrs Gandhi drove to Rashtrapati Bhavan. It took nearly forty-five minutes for Sidhartha to explain what the internal emergency would entail. The president understood the implications quickly. He was also once a practising lawyer. Moreover, he had had some inkling of what was sought to be done from one of his assistants, K.L. Dhavan, brother of the Dhavan at the PM's house.

He did not think of demurring. He was indebted to Mrs Gandhi for elevating him to the highest position in the country. Both of them had been very close especially since 1969 when he, with Jagjivan Ram, had written to then Congress party President S. Nijalingappa that they objected to his approaching the Jana Sangh and the right-wing Swatantra to seek support for the official presidential candidate of the Congress party, Sanjiva Reddy. Ahmed remembered how they, under Mrs Gandhi's leadership, had humbled the top Congress party leadership, the Syndicate, by defeating[15] Reddy.

The proclamation of a state of emergency was signed by the president on 25 June at 11.45 P.M., fifteen minutes before the deadline. The Dhavan from the PM's house brought the draft.

---

[15]For details, read my book *India: The Critical Years*, Vikas, Delhi, 1971.

No official in Rashtrapati Bhavan retired that day before 7 A.M. "A grave emergency exists whereby the security of India is threatened by internal disturbances," the proclamation said. It authorized the government to impose press censorship, to suspend court proceedings regarding enforcement of civil rights, and so on.

It very much resembled what happened in Germany many years ago. Hitler had prevailed upon President Hindenburg to sign a decree "for the protection of the people and the State" suspending sections of the Constitution which guaranteed individual and civil liberties.

Now Mrs Gandhi had all the power to deal with the opposition and the press which questioned her legitimacy, all the power to tailor laws at will, all the power to change rules and conventions. A country which had lumbered along the path of democracy since its independence in August 1947—despite the carpings of the West whether the system was suited to the Indian genius—was now a quasi-dictatorship.

Mrs Gandhi had once said that she would like to go down in history as a strong personality, "somewhat like Napoleon or Hitler because they would always be remembered."

What her father wrote[16] about himself almost forty years earlier was beginning to be true in her case too: "A little twist and Jawaharlal might turn a dictator sweeping aside the paraphernalia of slow moving democracy. He might still use the language and slogans of democracy and socialism, but we all know how fascism has fattened on this language and then cast it away as useless lumber. . . . His over-mastering desire to get things done, to sweep away what he dislikes and build anew, will hardly brook. . .the slow process of democracy. He may keep the husk but he will see to it that it bends to his will. In normal times he would be just an efficient and successful executive, but in this revolutionary epoch, caesarism is always at the door, and is it not possible that Jawaharlal might fancy himself as a Caesar?"

Anyone knowing Nehru would know that he would not. Anyone knowing his daughter would know that she could more than fancy herself in that role. That night her son was the prompter in the wings.

---

[16]Nehru published an article, "Rashtrapati Jawaharlal ki Jai" anonymously in the *Modern Review* of Calcutta in its issue of 5 October 1937.

No one slept that night at the PM's house. After returning from Rashtrapati Bhavan, Mrs Gandhi decided to call a cabinet meeting at 6 A.M. By then she knew that the arrests of JP, Morarji and hundreds of others were going on according to plan.

The action was sudden, quick and ruthless and it had all the ingredients of a *coup*.

In Delhi, opposition leaders were woken up between 2.30 and 3 A.M., shown orders of arrest and driven to a police station, ironically not far from Parliament House. They were detained under MISA, the same Act under which smugglers were detained.

Those arrested were from all parties, the Jana Sangh on the right and the CPI(M) on the left. The only opposition party left untouched was the pro-Moscow Communist party, an ally of the Congress.

When JP was arrested he recited a Sanskrit couplet: *Vinasha kale viperita buddhi* (when a person falls on bad days, he loses his head). Two days earlier, Morarji had rejected an Italian journalist's suggestion that he might be arrested. He had said, "She will never do it. She'd commit suicide first." He and JP were taken to the Sona dak bungalow, very near Delhi. But both were lodged in separate rooms, with no communication with each other.

Most of the Delhi newspapers did not appear because the power supply to their presses was cut off before midnight; the official explanation was that the power house had developed "trouble." The *Statesman* and *Hindustan Times* in New Delhi came out because they were supplied power by the New Delhi municipality and not the Delhi municipal corporation, which alone received the orders to black out presses. In Punjab and Madhya Pradesh also presses were denied power. But newspapers appeared in cities elsewhere. On the morning of 26 June censorship was imposed on all press writings relating to the internal situation. All messages had to be submitted to the government for scrutiny.

By the time ministers arrived at 1 Safdarjung Road for the cabinet meeting, most of those on the arrest lists were in custody. The official figure given to the press was 676; the cabinet was not told even that. The proclamation of emergency was placed before them for *ex-post facto* approval. Everyone kept quiet. Jagjivan Ram and Chavan just looked at the wall facing them. The atmosphere was tense.

After a while, Swaran Singh spoke. He wondered whether the

emergency was necessary. He did not dwell on it, nor did Mrs Gandhi say anything. A little discussion followed only on what the emergency meant in constitutional terms.

But then the cabinet meeting was only a formality. Once that was over, Mrs Gandhi started working on her broadcast speech, the draft of which was ready by 4 A.M. Some Hindi equivalents for certain English words had delayed the finalization.

The *Hindustan Times* and the *Statesman* planned supplements for the following morning. By 11 A.M. the *Hindustan Times* supplement was on the streets and the rotary machine in the *Statesman* was about to be started when a flash message on the tickers announced the imposition of pre-censorship on all news and comments relating to the arrests and the internal situation. All messages had to be sent to government for scrutiny. Hurriedly the rotary was stopped. The *Statesman* sent its supplement page-proof to the Press Information Bureau (PIB) office in Shastri Bhavan for clearance. But by the time it was returned with the names of the arrested leaders deleted and their pictures crossed out, the power supply to the office was cut. The supplement could not be printed; the page-proofs remained a historical record.

And when word went round that the *Hindustan Times* copies were being sold, the hawkers were hurriedly told to return all unsold copies to avoid possible legal action.

The *Motherland*, the Jana Sangh paper, was the only one to come out with a supplement, its press was later sealed.

In a nationwide broadcast that morning, Mrs Gandhi said that the government was forced to act because of "the deep and widespread conspiracy which has been brewing ever since I began introducing certain progressive measures of benefit to the common man and common woman of India in the name of democracy." The plot, she said, "sought to negate the very functioning of democracy. Duly elected governments have not been allowed to function, and in some cases, force has been used to compel members to resign in order to dissolve lawfully elected assemblies." She referred to the murder of Lalit Narayan Mishra, insinuating that the opposition had a hand in it.

These brave words did not assuage her fears. As she told some-one later, "I did not know how the people would react."

The people were dazed; they did not know what the emergency—her diktat—meant. It gradually dawned on them that the democratic system that had functioned for more than twenty-five years had gone into eclipse. Was it permanent? they wondered.

"Now we learn of new programmes challenging law and order throughout the country with a view to disrupting normal functioning. How can any government worth the name stand by and allow the country's stability to be imperilled?" All India Radio and TV reported these words of Mrs Gandhi over and over again.

One gain of the emergency was stabilization of the prices of essential goods. Schools, shops, trains, and buses did show the effects of discipline; even cows and beggars disappeared from the streets of New Delhi.

But Mrs Gandhi did not explain why action was being taken only after the Allahabad judgement; why the enforcement of ordinary law could not put down indiscipline in factories and campuses, and why these laws could not cure whatever else was not well with the nation.

That would have been hard to explain. Perhaps she thought it was no use trying. She knew her credibility was low; she said at a meeting to condole the death of Lalit Narayan Mishra, "Even if I were to be killed they would say that I myself had got it done."

Whatever the reasons, what she did was unprecedented; it was nearly as drastic as imposing martial law—it was "police law." There was a feeling of numbness and shock in the country. No one had expected such a drastic step, no one understood its implications. It was a "Thursday massacre." The first reaction was that Mrs Gandhi would not be able to get away with it.

Most of her own partymen appeared as stunned as the others. And it was they who cowered most. The pyramid of power she had created since she came to power in 1966 had long made them tremble. Now her word was law, and no one could doubt it. From cabinet ministers and chief ministers down to the junior-most executive councillor, everyone held office at her pleasure. She had removed whoever had shown signs of revolt. Most of the remaining ones owed their political survival to her. It was not in them to protest.

The only two persons who could challenge Mrs Gandhi were Chavan and Jagjivan Ram. But they could not join hands because each wanted to be prime minister. And they were not willing to risk their position by standing against her unless they had a chance to survive. And at that moment they saw not even the ghost of a chance.

Mrs Gandhi knew the men she had to watch. And she watched them well.

When I went to see Chavan and Jagjivan Ram at their homes on 26 June, I found intelligence men noting down the car numbers and the names of people coming to visit them. Chavan was afraid even to meet me and Jagjivan Ram, who met me, only for a minute, looked nervous. All that Jagjivan Ram told me was that he was expecting his arrest; he said that after carefully taking the receiver off the telephone in the room—he knew the phone was tapped and thought that, as a further refinement, it was "bugged" to transmit conversation when the receiver was in its cradle.

There was no doubting the air of triumph in the prime minister's house on the night of 26 June. The whole operation had been painless, it was noted with satisfaction. There had been almost no resistance; "incidents" were few and quickly tackled. Except for George Fernandes, the labour leader; Nanaji Deshmukh, Subramaniam Swami, both Jana Sangh members; and a few others who had gone "underground," all important people had been arrested. (Nanaji escaped when someone rang up to inform him that the police were coming to arrest him.)

"I told you nothing would happen," Sanjay told his mother. Bansi Lal said that as he had expected not even a dog had barked. Word had been sent to Allahabad to "fix up" Justice Sinha. The police now shadowed him and all his past career was being screened and his relations harassed.

Vidya Charan Shukla who took over from Gujral, who was transferred to Planning on 28 June, reported that the censorship machinery was getting quickly into gear. Dhavan was happy that censorship was irrelevant in Delhi; he had once stopped the functioning of newspapers in Delhi by ordering the power supply to their offices cut till he gave word for it to be resumed.

Mrs Gandhi was nervous. She thought it might be too early to say that everything was all right, but every chief minister had reported "the situation is under control."

In the streets of Delhi fear hung like a pall. Jana Sangh volunteers courted arrest in groups, and there were a few incidents. But life was outwardly normal. The *Statesman* published a picture by that gifted photographer, Raghu Rai, that told all: it showed a man pushing a cycle with two children on it and a woman walking behind and scores of policemen all around. The caption said that life was normal in Chandni Chowk (an unsuspecting censor had "passed" it—he was transferred the next day).

The cyclostyled forms of MISA orders came handy to many district magistrates in UP. They put their signatures on blank forms and left the rest to the police. Arrests were carried out according to the lists prepared earlier with the help of old intelligence records. No wonder, the police raided a house in Agra to arrest a person who had died in 1968.

The press was muzzled; *Panchaa Janya*, a weekly, *Tarun Bharat*, a daily and *Rastra Dharma*, a Hindi monthly—a group of Hindi publications of the Jana Sangh—were closed down. A police party without any search warrant or order from a competent authority entered the premises of these papers, physically pushed out the press employees and put a lock on the press to stop the publication of all journals. The publishers of the papers, the Rashtra Dharma Prakashan, were hard put to find any counsel in Lucknow. Lawyers were afraid; whoever agreed was arrested under the Defence of India Rules.

At first Punjab did not take any action against the Akalis, expecting them to "side" with the government against the Jana Sangh because the two had strayed apart on the Sikh-Hindu question. But the government forgot that whatever their differences, they had got erased over the years. JP's visit to Ludhiana, where the Akalis collected an unprecedented crowd of half a million, had brought them closer to the opposition. In any case, the danger from the government's despotism was more serious than the irritation with the Jana Sangh.

Police onslaught on the papers in Punjab, concentrated in Jullundur, was ruthless. Because of convenient train timings, most Urdu and Punjabi papers were printed by midnight. The police destroyed copies of all editions, including the late night editions. The Punjab police was sent to the *Tribune* office in the Union Territory of Chandigarh, obviously on New Delhi's orders because permission of the centre is needed to enter a Union Territory. The chief commissioner objected to it. Dhavan sorted out the matter later.

In Haryana it was a normal pastime for the rulers to arrest

anyone under the MISA and DIR. No pretext was needed to detain anyone high or low, friend or foe. Besides the general crackdown on opposition leaders and workers as soon as the emergency was imposed, over a thousand people were detained on one pretext or the other. During their detention, political prisoners were treated as criminals.

The Maharashtra High Court Bar Association was the first in the country to condemn Mrs Gandhi's authoritarian rule. Ram Jethamalani, the All India Bar Association president, compared her to Mussolini and Hitler, though he had been arguing that since the Supreme Court had given her a stay it should be respected.

The bar associations in many other states followed suit, but for some reason, the West Bengal Bar Association was silent.

Gujarat escaped the wrath of the emergency because of the United Front government in the state. Chief Minister Babubhai Patel wanted to speak over the radio. He was denied the opportunity by the centre. That was his first brush with the emergency. The centre sent out instructions to states to round up Jana Sangh and other political leaders. Babubhai did not oblige, and when he finally arrested them he used DIR which allowed an arrested person to be released on bail, a recourse which was denied by law to MISA detenus.

Babubhai said in an interview that he would ensure that civil liberties remained unhampered and that he would not ban meetings and processions.

There were protests all over the state, more so in big cities. Citizens were encouraged to wear black badges, fly black flags from their homes and tack on their doors the preamble to the Indian Constitution, which stresses human rights.

Public demonstrations included silent marches, student processions, hunger strikes and sit-ins in public places. The state gradually became a refuge for hundreds of Mrs Gandhi's critics from all over India.

Navnirman student leaders would have probably suffered had there been no opposition government to shield them. They were the ones who had brought down the ministry of Chimanbhai Patel in 1974 when he set up his own candidate as vice-chancellor of Gujarat University and succeeded in having Ishvarbhai Patel in the post, defeating a nominee of the teachers, the soul behind the

Navnirman movement in Gujarat at that time.

The government did not approve of censorship and unlike in other states did not allow the state director of information to be appointed chief censor. But there was an agitation by college teachers of Ahmedabad and there was a full-day debate on the issue in the assembly. It was not clear whether the director of information acted on the advice of the government but he asked newsmen not to report the proceedings of the House that day.

Some days later, the central government appointed the local Press Information Bureau (PIB) chief as the chief censor, and he took no action to prevent newspapers from carrying reports which were embarrassing to the state government but he was prompt in suppressing all reports concerning the emergency or the central government.

Tamil Nadu defied press censorship. However, the Dravida Munnetra Kazhagam (DMK) government, headed by M. Karunanidhi, did not follow a policy of open defiance and declared that it would carry out Delhi's directives "acceptable to us." Unofficially, the DMK was all against the emergency.

In West Bengal, from ministers down to the foot constable, everyone found the emergency powers useful to settle old scores, personal or political. Two journalists, Gourkishore Ghosh and Barun Sengupta of *Anand Bazar Patrika*, who were critical of the chief minister, were arrested. Ghosh had criticized the chief minister on political grounds in a Bengali booklet, *Kalikata*, but Sengupta's attack was personal. Orders were issued for their arrest under MISA. It was easy to arrest Ghosh but Sengupta fled West Bengal and stayed in Delhi for quite some time, enjoying the protection of Sanjay—an indication of the strained relations between Mrs Gandhi's son and the chief minister. But ultimately the police arrested him, and he was badly treated in jail, mainly because the chief minister was angered by his personal attack on him.

Ashok Dasgupta, a Praja Socialist party leader, was taken in handcuffs to his house on a four-hour parole to meet his sick mother. His protests that he was a political prisoner and that it would hurt his mother to see her son handcuffed did not deter the police. There appeared to be strict instructions from the top that emergency prisoners, whenever they were taken out, should be manacled. Concessions granted to political prisoners after much agitation were withdrawn during the emergency.

Raj Krishna, a Congress (O) leader, was arrested for protesting against the increase in fares allowed by the district authorities to private bus owners. Power and Irrigation Minister A.B.A. Gani Khan Chowdhury, was known in his own district of Malda as MISA Minister. He threatened to arrest under MISA whoever he did not like.

Press censorship was used for party and personal ends. There were innumerable instances of reports of even statements by Congress leaders being suppressed merely because they did not suit Minister of Information Subrata Mukherjee. Censors were clearly told that no report against the minister's group should be allowed to be published.

In Bihar, the emergency was a period which saw the rise of many satraps. What they said was law. Some of the satraps lived in gangster style, some had rooms reserved in circuit houses and dak bungalows for their orgies. In the districts they exercised more power than the district magistrates; their writ was as good as the chief minister's and officials had very little hope of working in conformity with rules.

Every rule was twisted to serve the ends of the ruling group or the satraps' personal interests. Landholders were seriously affected by land reforms only if they were suspected to have leanings towards the opposition parties or the dissident section of the Congress.

The official publicity machinery was in high gear to build up the chief minister's image. The censor saw to it that nothing critical was published. Censorship meant non-reporting of anything that would embarrass the government or the ruling group in the Congress. Riots in Purnea and Monghyr district went unreported in Bihar and elsewhere. So also was the firing on detenus in Bhagalpur jail; they demanded basic amenities that the jail manual decreed. Over a dozen were killed by trigger-happy policemen and warders.

JP had chosen this state to build up a movement from the grassroots against corrupt and undemocratic administration all over India. The "total revolution" he was engaged in spreading was based on youth power and people's power, acting through the students' struggle committees and the people's struggle committees and on *janata sarkars* (people's governments) established at each tier of the administration, beginning at the village level. These units were not intended to build up a parallel system of national administration but to serve as watchdogs over the government machinery.

Whether Bihar, Gujarat or Delhi, the pattern all over India was the same; a show of brute force and ruthless suppression of even a flicker of defiance. And everywhere the police picked up the opponents, with or without warrants, under MISA or DIR. (Advani was served with orders after nine hours of arrest.)

What had been planned—the large-scale arrests of the opposition and the muzzling of the press—was carried out with precision and speed. The *coup* was bloodless.

People were being arrested all over India indiscriminately. The warrants of arrest said nothing except that so and so was being detained "in public interest." They were neither accused of having committed any offence under the law nor were they tried before a court of law. In most states a model first information report (FIR), a document on which action begins to effect an arrest, was cyclostyled and copies sent to district police stations to be filled in wherever needed.

Similarly, copies of expulsion order for foreign journalists were all typed and kept ready. Peter Hazelhurst of the London *Times*, who during the Bangladesh crisis had done much to tell the world of the atrocities of the Pakistan regime; Loren Jenkins of *Newsweek* and Peter Gill of the London *Daily Telegraph* were among those who received the order signed by Joint Secretary S.S. Sidhu of the Ministry of Home Affairs, saying that "in the name of the President" they could no longer remain in India, that they would be deported within twenty-four hours and that they should thereafter not enter India. Jenkins had written, "In 10 years of covering the world from Franco's Spain to Mao's China, I have never encountered such stringent and all encompassing censorship."

The mode of expulsion was the same—a knock on the door by the police, serving of the orders, a search of their papers and exit within an hour.

People abroad were shocked over the expulsion of journalists though many rationalized that India had never been a democracy and that the British parliamentary system was not suited to the Indian genius. The attitude tended to be patronizing, but there was genuine concern over the detention of people without trial and the gagging of the press which was unprecedented.

If things had turned out as expected in the country, the reactions abroad were also predictable. The West, as foreseen, was aghast at what Mrs Gandhi had done. The daughter had killed what the father had created.

But no foreign government said anything officially. It was "a domestic affair" as they put it. New Delhi was quite appreciative of it, even though it reacted with considerable indignation to the strong criticism in the Western press and by many private citizens and groups.

Obviously under pressure from within the country, the US President Ford put off indefinitely his plans to visit India. Triloki Nath Kaul, New Delhi's envoy in Washington, explained that Ford had a heavy schedule. But US officials, while acknowledging that the calendar was crowded, also said that because of the uncertain political situation in India it had been decided not to go ahead with the trip.

Subsequently, Ford said, "I think it is really very sad that 600 million people have lost what they had since the mid-1940s. I hope in time there could be a restoration of democratic processes as we know them in the US." The fact that he made this remark on the eve of his visit to China gave a handle to the government. Crude and dictatorial, Mohammed Yunus, who was appointed the prime minister's special envoy, told foreign journalists that it was amusing that Ford should have made the observation before visiting a communist country.

In Washington, an association called Indians for Democracy was formed and on 30 June a demonstration was held before the Indian embassy. Acting Ambassador Gonsalves refused to accept a petition signed by 1,200 Indians; instead, he called them Pakistani and Chinese agents.

The AFL-CIO, the American trade unions, said "India has become a police state in which democracy has been smothered." It urged the Government of the United States to withhold all aid and assistance to the Government of India until democracy was restored to its people.

England, which retains sentimental ties with India, was horrified. After all, it was the British parliamentary system that India had adopted. The death of the free press was felt all the more. The visit of Prince Charles to India was cancelled to express London's protest. The BBC, which had had its New Delhi office closed once, expanded its coverage and it was through the BBC that most people in India, even inside jail, got news about their country throughout the emergency. Subsequently, its correspondent, gregarious Mark Tully, had again to leave the country in view of New Delhi's insistence that the BBC should accept censorship on news from India.

However, opinion in the Soviet Union and the East European countries was favourable to Indira Gandhi. *Pravda* saw that the emergency had already brought positive results. The paper said, "Democratic forces approve of the arrests of leaders of the Right-wing parties carried out by the authorities, the introduction of censorship will deprive the monopoly press of the opportunity to carry on and instigating an anti-government campaign."

China was critical, as it always had been, but it was more to denigrate New Delhi than to protest against the emergency.

Zulfikar Ali Bhutto expressed satisfaction at Mrs Gandhi's conviction in court for election abuses. Later, he told a newspaper that "recent developments in other parts of the subcontinent have shown Pakistan to be an element of stability in a volatile region."

The nonaligned countries, interpreted the emergency as a movement away from an essentially democratic to a modified command system, as "further proof that democratic development models are inappropriate for the so-called emerging nations."

Mrs Gandhi did not say anything directly against the West, but her anger was plain. She said that they were biased against India. Without naming any country, she bitterly attacked the Western powers and the Western press for "trying to teach democracy" while bolstering undemocratic regimes. She indirectly accused the US of hypocrisy for speaking of democracy while it constantly backed various forms of dictatorship in Latin America and elsewhere. Mrs Gandhi lumped Western governments and the Western press together as if they were one and the same thing and alleged that foreign forces were abetting India's "underground."

She repeatedly said that the countries which had been criticizing India were the same which had supported General Yahya Khan's military rule in Pakistan and his suppression of Bangladesh. The same countries were vying with one another to come closer to China. "These countries should look at themselves rather than give sermons to us."

Foreign newspapers carrying adverse reports were barred entry. Censorship was made stricter at home under Shukla.

Press guidelines[17] were issued and barred the publication of rumours, reproduction of objectionable matter in any Indian or foreign newspaper, and printing of any article likely to arouse opposition to the government. All cartoons, photographs and advertisements which were likely to come within the purview of censorship regulations were to be submitted for censorship.

Officials were posted in the offices of news agencies so that they could cross out "objectionable" material at source. The copy beamed by foreign news agencies was screened and anything found "unfavourable," even to "friendly countries" like the Soviet Union was killed. JP's *Everyman* and *Prajaniti*, George Fernandes's *Pratipaksha* and Piloo Modi's *March of India* had to suspend publication. The Jana Sangh's *Motherland* and *Organizer* were banned and their offices sealed.

Shukla had assured Sanjay that he would "fix" the journalists, unlike Gujral who had failed to do so. He called Delhi editors to a meeting and told them bluntly that the Government would not tolerate "any nonsense"; it was there to stay and rule.

He told me that even blank space left in an editorial, article or anywhere (a common form of protest against censorship by Indian newspapers under the British) would be taken as defiance; he threatened to arrest editors. Most of them were horrified but none protested. Even more horrifying was the fact that there were a few among them who supported censorship and spoke in praise of the government in such glowing terms that anyone other than Shukla would have felt embarrassed.

It was only the whip and no carrot for the press. And to see that it would be applied well Shukla brought in K.N. Prasad of the Indian Police Service (IPS) to his ministry to serve as his right-hand man, or rather his whiphand. He invented a novel method of giving orders on the phone to the censors who in turn rang up newspapers.

But nearly a hundred journalists, including some editors, met in the Press Club of India on 29 June to protest against the imposition of censorship and urged upon the government to lift it. They demanded the release of Jagat Narain of *Hind Samachar,*

[17]See Annexure II.

Jullundur, and M.R. Malkani of *Motherland,* Delhi, who had been arrested. I sent copies of the resolution[18] to the president, the prime minister and the information minister.

Foreign correspondents could not, of course, be arrested for their news. But they could be deported. The first to be banished was Lewis M. Simons of the *Washington Post,* who had written an article "Sanjay Gandhi and his Mother." Among his observations, "Prime Minister Indira Gandhi, distrustful of even her closest Cabinet colleagues at this time of grave crisis for India, is turning to her controversial younger son, Sanjay, for help in making major political decisions.... A family friend who attended a dinner party with Sanjay and Mrs Gandhi several months ago said he saw the son slap his mother across the face 'six times'. She couldn't do a thing. The friend said: 'She just stood there and took it. She is scared to death of him'."

Sanjay was the man to decide everything for her. He had no position in the party or the government but was the "boss" in both. The entire administrative set-up in the country was at his disposal. Operating from the PM's house he gave orders to cabinet ministers, chief ministers and top civil servants, and he was obeyed. On many occasions when they wanted to discuss anything with Mrs Gandhi she would herself tell them, "Have a word with Sanjay." And he gave them directions on his own.

But Sanjay almost always told her what he was doing and what he had ordered. Every night in the early days of the emergency, Sanjay and his men—Bansi Lal, Om Mehta, Shukla and Dhavan —met in the PM's house to take stock. By that time one more man had joined the group—Yunus.[19] He was hanging around the house from the first day but was kept out of the inner councils for some time. He had been long associated with the Nehru family and Nehru chose him to be ambassador. For him Haksar was to blame for all Mrs Gandhi's troubles.

At the meetings of this "emergency council," which were attended by Mrs Gandhi, the intelligence bureau's reports, RAW's assessments, information collected by Dhavan on the phone from chief ministers and news which members of the group had

[18]More in my forthcoming book, *In Jail.*
[19]Sanjay's wedding was at his house, and Mrs Gandhi's family called him "Budhu Chacha" (foolish uncle).

gathered were discussed. They would also have before them copies
of despatches sent by foreign correspondents through the overseas
communication service.

Here it was decided what orders were to be sent to which
ministry or state, and to which official. It was very much like an
operations room during war and though Mrs Gandhi would be
there the chief of operations was Sanjay.

Between Dhavan and Om Mehta relations were often strained,
for the prime minister's personal assistant poached on Om
Mehta's home territory. Dhavan would at times act on his own
through Delhi's Lieutenant-Governor Kishan Chand and Bhinder,
Delhi's DIG of police, an officer promoted out of turn, to the
chagrin of Om Mehta and Home Secretary Khurana. The two
groups were at loggerheads, especially over the operations in
Delhi. It was Sanjay who would patch up their differences and
assign them their tasks.

Mrs Gandhi had full faith in her son and his men. She saw in
him a man of action who had saved her when she faltered. Unlike
his grandfather Sanjay was no saviour. He was sure of his destiny, he *was* the man of destiny. She was more than willing to let
him take the decisions—and not only on major matters. Even
appointments and transfers of officials, promotions for the loyal
and punishment for those who were not—all were decided by
Sanjay. At times he would interview an officer before his appointment to a vital post. He seemed to have a distrust for many of
the men who had long served his mother, especially the Kashmiris,
southerners and easterners.

Sanjay had a preference for the people of the north, particularly
Punjabis. He thought that they were the men who would be ready
to do or die for him—or at least let others die. As days went by,
the Kashmiri group, which was dominant under his mother,
changed into a Punjabi group. But it was no longer just a group.
It was the mafia.

His plan was implemented with the men he could trust about
getting other parts of "operation emergency" into position; the
screws were tightened under decrees dutifully signed by the president. The rights of Indian citizens and foreigners to seek the
protection of their fundamental rights were suspended. Under
another decree, MISA was made stricter; persons detained could
be kept in jail without disclosing to them or to the courts the

grounds for their detention. There was no court of appeal.

Mrs Gandhi claimed that she was working within the limits of the Constitution and defended her actions in the name of saving democracy. However dictatorial the regime, the democratic facade had to be kept. As Goerge Orwell said, "It is almost universally felt that when we call a country democratic, we are praising it: consequently the dictator of every kind of regime claims that it is a democracy."

After imposing press censorship, suspending fundamental rights, and detaining hundreds without trial, Mrs Gandhi could say that India remained a democracy only in the Orwellian language of Newspeak, in which the Ministry of War is called the Ministry of Peace.

The International Press Institute urged Mrs Gandhi to withdraw censorship, which "can only denigrate the image of India in world opinion."

The Socialist International decided to send a delegation on 15 July, including former West German Chancellor Willy Brandt, and Irish Posts and Telegraphs Minister Conor Cruise O'Brien to visit JP in his place of detention. But New Delhi refused permission on the ground that it would be a "gross interference in the internal affairs of India." Socialist International said in reply, "All socialists must now feel a great sense of personal tragedy at what is happening to India."

Official opinion in the West was that India had lost democracy for all time, and however painful, they might as well accept the fact and not annoy Mrs Gandhi. US Secretary of State Henry Kissinger discussed the matter in the State Department and came to the conclusion that it would be easier to deal with New Delhi now. Mrs Gandhi's policy would be "pragmatic," one of his aides said at the meeting. Kissinger remarked, "You mean, purchasable." Someone mentioned "dictator."

Perhaps even then she did not see herself as a dictator, and could feel insulted at being called one. And there were many in the country who could not believe that Nehru's daughter could turn into one: they were sure that she had assumed extraordinary powers to deal with an extraordinary situation. It would only be a temporary phase.

But there was at least one man who said clearly where she was heading. He knew that she was no democrat and had said so. And he was in jail because of that.

2. The Murk Thickens

"I HAD always believed that Mrs Gandhi had no faith in democracy, that she was by inclination and conviction a dictator," wrote JP in his diary in prison on 22 July.

Only a day earlier he had sent a long letter to Mrs Gandhi written in the same vein. He had said:

"Please do not destroy the foundations that the Fathers of the Nation, including your noble father, had laid down. There is nothing but strife and suffering along the path that you have taken. You inherited a great tradition, noble values and a working democracy. Do not leave behind a miserable wreck of all that. It would take a long time to put all that together again. That it would be put together again, I have no doubt. A people who fought British imperialism and humbled it cannot accept indefinitely the indignity and shame of totalitarianism. The spirit of man can never be vanquished, no matter how deeply suppressed. In establishing your personal dictatorship you have buried it deep. But it will rise from the grave. Even in Russia it is slowly coming up.

"You have talked of social democracy. What a beautiful image those words call to the mind. But you have seen in eastern and central Europe how ugly the reality is. Naked dictatorship and, in the ultimate analysis, Russian overlordship. Please, please do not push India toward that terrible fate."

After arrest, JP had been taken first to Sona and later to the All India Institute of Medical Sciences (AIIMS) in Delhi because he was ill. It was soon clear that he would need hospitalization for a long period. But Delhi was not the place; it was and always has been the city of rumours. Already, it was an open secret that JP was at the AIIMS, and expectant groups could be seen on the grounds outside.

He had to be taken elsewhere. The Post Graduate Institute

(PGI) at Chandigarh was selected for his detention. Bansi Lal provided hand-picked policemen as guards; it would not do to allow JP to escape, as he had done in 1942 during the Quit India movement.

Before JP was taken to Chandigarh, Mrs Gandhi thought he should be allowed to see for himself how peaceful Delhi was, though the man who had attracted hundreds of thousands to his meetings in this city, who had "mistakenly" thought he represented the people's will, was in custody. She asked the police to take him round the city to show him that none of those who had pledged themselves to resist that tyranny had lifted even a finger in protest. He was driven from one street to another. It was indeed a city that appeared uncaring for what the people had lost.

He wondered what those ladies and gentlemen in the security and comfort of their drawing rooms were saying now, those who used to tell him that he was the only "hope" for the country. Were they invoking curses on his head for bringing about "this terrible doom"? They might be saying that hemmed in as Mrs Gandhi was, she could not but act in the manner she had. His hope was that at least some people, particularly the young, were loyal to the cause he represented, if not to him personally. India would arise from the grave, no matter how long it might take.

Many did in private blame JP for giving a call for agitation without adequate preparations. Some compared his action with that of Nehru who, in October 1962, had said in public that he had asked the military to throw out the Chinese from Indian soil. The result in both cases, they argued, had been a disaster.

While JP's world lay in a shambles, Mrs Gandhi announced on 1 July the contours of her make-believe world. She had selected 20 points (originally 21) out of the 150 suggestions she had received from her ministries. There was no deep thinking behind the choice of the "points"—she picked up what she thought would be easy for people to understand, good coversation pieces at best. But many points were indeed laudable and nobody could take exception to them.

The twenty points were:

1) Scaling down prices of essential commodities and streamlining their production and distribution.
2) Economizing government expenditure.

3) Implementing agricultural land ceilings and speeding up distribution of surplus land and compilation of land records.

4) Stepping up house-site availability to the landless and weaker sections.

5) Declaring bonded labour illegal.

6) Planning for liquidation of rural indebtedness and a moratorium on recovery of debts from the landless, labourers, small farmers and artisans.

7) Reviewing laws on minimum agricultural wages.

8) Bringing five million more hectares under irrigation and preparing a national programme for use of underground water.

9) Increasing power production.

10) Developing the handloom sector and improving quality and supply of people's cloth.

11) Effecting "socialization" of urban and urbanizable land and having ceiling on ownership and possession of vacant land.

12) Having special squads for valuation of conspicuous consumption and prevention of tax evasion and summary trials and deterrent punishment of economic offenders.

13) Special legislation for confiscation of smugglers' properties.

14) Liberalizing investment procedures and taking action against misuse of import licences.

15) New schemes for workers' associations in industry.

16) National permit schemes for road transport.

17) Income tax relief to middle class—exceptional limit placed at Rs 8,000.

18) Essential commodities at controlled prices to students in hostels.

19) Books and stationery at controlled prices.

20) New apprenticeship scheme to enlarge employment and training, specially of the weaker sections.

Only a few months earlier she had done more or less a similar exercise at Narora, not far from Delhi, where she called all chief ministers, cabinet ministers and state Congress chiefs, to check JP's tide through "ameliorative steps" for the poor. She had described then the differences with him as a struggle between "the vested interests determined to thwart further progress of our society towards social justice and economic independence and the toiling masses determined to consolidate the social and economic gains that they have made and to move forward on the chosen courses.''

Mrs Gandhi had always given an economic cover to her political manoeuvres. She had done it in 1969 at the time of the Congress split and in 1971 at the time of the mid-term poll, and she had got away with it. The people had always thought that her fight was for the country's economic good and not for her own survival. This time also she believed that the twenty-point programme would hide the move to sustain herself in power. And she looked like succeeding for the time being.

The twenty-point programme came to dominate the media and every official and non-official discussion. Hoardings and posters came up everywhere, listing the points and carrying large portraits, of her. The bigger the hoarding, the better was the appreciation, until she herself ordered their dismantling because her close friends told her that she looked "hideous" in paintings on the hoardings.

It was everyone's duty to act according to the twenty-point programme or appear to be acting thusly. The Delhi administration ordered all shopkeepers and traders to display lists of stocks and prices. They had to attach price tags to practically all commodities. This order came in handy for the authorities to punish those shopkeepers who did not give money to the Congress party's, and later the Youth Congress's coffers or who did not otherwise fall in line with government thinking.

Sanjay used the price-tag order to settle scores with Haksar who had at times spoken against his actions to Mrs Gandhi. Haksar's eighty year old uncle, who owned Pandit Brothers, a departmental store in Connaught Place, New Delhi, was taken into custody for not having put a price tag on a minor item and kept in jail for three days. Aruna Asaf Ali, a local CPI leader, had to persuade Mrs Gandhi to intervene to have Haksar's uncle released.

It was a measure of Haksar's integrity that he never wavered in his loyalty to Mrs Gandhi's government. All Delhi was shocked by the incident. But this was Sanjay's or, for that matter, the government's style—to terrorize people. So many false deeds were done that Mrs Gandhi also developed a style of her own; she would plead ignorance about all such happenings, though she knew most of what her son and his henchmen were doing beforehand.

Barooah's proposal for the nationalization of sugar and textile industries had got around. Mrs Gandhi issued a statement that the government had no plans to nationalize industries or impose drastic new controls.

Mrs Gandhi also said that MISA would be used to catch smugglers. Indeed, their operations were world-wide; their headquarters were in Dubai. Banks and insurance companies had opened their offices there to finance as well as cover the risks involved in smuggling. An elaborate network of transport by sea, land and air had been built. The long coastline from Gujarat to Kerala was dotted with marked points where smuggled goods were received and then transported to numerous consumer centres in the country. Madras was a big centre of smugglers while Bangalore provided a safe retreat for them to meet and compare notes. They had their own godowns, markets, wireless—and code of conduct. There was a direct link between smugglers and black money operators.

The drive against smugglers was laudable. But Mrs Gandhi had herself removed in September 1974 a minister, K.R. Ganesh, who was doing a commendable job. His version is that most of the top smugglers had links with important people in politics and that some of them had managed to get themselves photographed with Mrs Gandhi and her chief ministers. He remembers, "During the debate on demand for supplementary grants, Madhu Limaye, a Socialist MP, insisted on knowing the names of the top smugglers. It was then quite late in the evening. Hardly a few members were present. I was on my feet. Suddenly the prime minister appeared in the House. I cut short my reply.

"Some time later the question again came up in the House and again a persistent demand was made to name the smugglers. I reeled off three names—Bakhia, Yusuf Patel and Haji Mastan.

"I was later told by one of the aides of the prime minister that I should not have named the people that way. One can imagine how powerful the smugglers had become! Some days later, when the anti-smuggling drive was at its height, a four-line letter came to me from the prime minister drawing my attention to 'a complaint' by someone from Ahmedabad that the minister used a foreign (cigarette) lighter.

"The promptness with which the prime minister communicated to me the complaint of 'someone from Ahmedabad' was unusual, to say the least. The meaning was not lost on me.

"It reminded me of another tongue-lashing by Indira Gandhi when she observed, 'Everyone wants to prove that he is clean and innocent; only I am corrupt. How can the party be run?' "

Whatever Mrs Gandhi's compulsions then, the action against smugglers was now ruthless. A good deal of black money was also unearthed and a number of traders were held under MISA for "economic offences." But not all black money operators, particularly the top ones, were arrested. And it was an open secret how many Congressmen acquired wealth trying to get "economic offenders," released on parole, in securing for officials transfers and promotions, and for businessmen contracts.

The twenty-point programme was also the political rhetoric of the ruling elite. There was no end of promises—self-sufficiency, betterment of the poor, land reforms and so on. Every political party swore by them, but putting them into practice was another matter. Land reforms, for instance, had long been on the statute books, but except in Kerala, under a coalition headed by the CPI (M) and later the CPI, no one even attempted to implement them. The number of people below the poverty line had gone up in a decade (1964-74) from forty-eight per cent to sixty-six per cent. The agrarian hierarchy was still the same—zamindars and *kamis* (workers); the disparity between the haves and the have-nots had widened and was ever widening.

There was nothing new in the "new" programme. One state said, "Give us the money and everything will be done; what is the use of mere talking." And Tamil Nadu's comment was typical—the state had already implemented nineteen out of the twenty points. Other states also did not lag behind in making similar claims, but coming from Tamil Nadu, under a DMK government, it was, for Mrs Gandhi's government, impertinence and worse.

The programme was the carrot; Mrs Gandhi also wielded the stick. The Government of India banned twenty-six political organizations on 4 July, of these only four were of any consequence. They were the Rashtryaswyam Sevak Sangh (RSS), a militant Hindu revivalist body; the Jamaat-e-Islamia-e-Hind, a Muslim religious organization; and Anand Marg, a sect of Hindu fanatics and the Naxalites (extreme leftists). They were accused of indulging in "activities prejudicial to internal security, public safety and maintenance of public order." The separatist Mizo National Front was added to the list of banned organizations on 6 August.

The Home minister said that some of the banned parties were communal. But the Law Ministry's own comment some years earlier had been that such communalism could not be legally defined. Then it was thought that it would be better to fight communalism politically but apparently the policy had changed since. For people who might not be convinced about the charge of communalism, it was given out that they had links with "foreign powers."

The banning of parties helped the government to make indiscriminate arrests. The people, who had nothing to do with the RSS or the Jamaat, or who had become inactive for many years, were picked up.

Sheikh Abdullah, who headed the Jammu and Kashmir government following an accord with New Delhi, was against the imposition of emergency. As chief minister, he would either say that it had to be imposed in Jammu and Kashmir as the state was part of India or he would explain it by saying that the promulgation of emergency was provided in the Constitution.

In an interview with me on 30 September he said that the two sides must talk between themselves to "put back democracy on the right path." However, in private, he condemned what he described as "one-person rule" at Delhi. He also criticized the opposition for having gone" too far without making any preparations."

While the Sheikh detained leaders of the outlawed organizations, he let most of them be released on parole after some time. Educational institutions run by the banned organizations were also closed down.

An evening daily, *Wadie-Kashmir* was banned during the emergency. Censorship functioned comparatively freely, so much so that the Union Government's censor would now and then point out to state authorities the "lapses" on the part of some of the newspapers.

The Sheikh was pressured by the people close to Mrs Gandhi to condemn JP, but he stoutly refused it. On one occasion, he spoke about it at a public meeting but the report of the speech was killed by the censor in Delhi.

Mrs Gandhi was keen to get at the RSS members; the arrests made till then included only a fraction of them. But the ban served little purpose; most of the cadre went underground and helped organize at least a semblance of resistance to sustain the people's hope that the government would be overthrown one day.

The underground took some time to get organized. There were two groups, one led by George Fernandes, the Socialist leader, and the other by Nanaji Deshmukh of the Jana Sangh. There was a limited coordination between the two, but limited was the operative word. On their own, each issued instructions for a civil disobedience campaign against what was described as the "Indian Fascist-Russian Axis." An eight-page cyclostyled paper was circulated with the instruction, "Read and let others read"; it called on leaders of all political persuasions to bury their differences and unite in a struggle to "restore democracy to India." It went on to warn the opposition, "There is no time for ideological quibbling or personality clashes. We have only one aim and that is to defeat fascism and to restore democracy with its fundamental freedoms and pluralist political institutions." The underground paper bitterly criticized Delhi's close relationship with Moscow, "The Russians, who were the first to welcome the fascist order in India, have also stakes in keeping India as a destitute nation, an objective Mrs Gandhi is accomplishing with ruthless efficiency."

The underground promised to set up a secret radio station and it was given out that the transmitter was lying "in a European country." But the radio station never came into being.

George Fernandes suggested in a paper, circulated surreptitiously, production and distribution of underground literature, a "whispering campaign," strikes and bandhs, paralyzing the functioning of the government and befriending the members of the police and the armed forces. He said that he did not want "to be a party to the defilement of our Constitution, to the imposition of a fascist dictatorship, to ending the rule of law in the country."

Nanaji advocated the formation of small teams to distribute leaflets and launch slogan-shouting campaigns to promote passive resistance.

The underground activity, rather limited, did keep the police on their toes and Mrs Gandhi worrying. Radhakrishnan, JP's secretary, gave a helping hand in coordinating the activity, visiting many states to string together the various groups wanting to start a Satyagraha. But he was arrested before anything could be established on the ground. The biggest blow was Nanaji's arrest during a surprise raid in a house in a south Delhi colony. His was an "Operation Takeover" but his successor, Ravindra Verma, the Congress (O) leader, gave it the name of *Aftab* (Sun).

By this time 60,000 people had been arrested. Among the arrested were Rajmata Gayatri Devi of Jaipur and the Rajmata of Gwalior. Both were detained in Delhi's Tihar jail, next to the ward I was in. The charge against Gayatri Devi[1] related to foreign exchange falsification. Both were in the female ward, along with prostitutes and female criminals, who, as Gayatri Devi later said, "were all over the place; it was like living in a bazaar with squabbling women." Gayatri Devi said, "A friend of mine from France wrote and asked what I would like as a present and I said those wax things that you stick in your ears."

The Akalis in Punjab had begun from 9 July a *morcha* (Satyagraha) with five Sikhs courting arrest at Amritsar. The morcha against the declaration of the emergency and the denial of democracy continued till the end of the emergency. Roughly 45,000 Sikhs courted arrest and the Akali top leadership, including Prakash Singh Badal and Gurcharan Singh Tohra, were detained under MISA. It was typical of Mrs Gandhi that she should think that the agitation raged because of poor "management"; she was angry with the state Chief Minister Zail Singh, on that account.

Elsewhere, the people were coming out of their initial shock and sense of disbelief. The press by and large, had begun to "behave." And there were stirrings of protest. I was arrested[2] on 26 July.

Eight Gandhites, including Bhimsen Sachar, former governor and Punjab chief minister, were arrested for having demanded removal of press censorship and "upholding the freedom and dignity of the individual." They also threatened to offer satyagraha on 7 August, "regardless of consequences to ourselves, to advocate openly the right of public speech and public association and freedom of the press, for discussing the merits and demerits of the government arming itself with extraordinary powers."

[1]Gayatri Devi was released on parole following a letter to Mrs Gandhi saying that she was no longer interested in politics and that she agreed with the twenty-point programme.
[2]More in my forthcoming book, *In Jail.*

But these were rare instances; defiance was lessening. There might be simmering anger among at least some people, but no one dared criticize the government openly. The people were cowed.

The elite's response was most disappointing. Here were the best of intellectuals—educationists, jurists, civil servants, doctors, lawyers and so on—but most of them preferred to keep quiet. Some even defended the emergency because the "life before its imposition was so insecure; there were hartals, dharnas and Satyagrahas." They now found things "peaceful and orderly."

Some argued, "We have always needed a master to make us do anything; we had the Mughals. We had the British. Now we have Mrs Gandhi. Is that such a bad thing?"

Dhavan was not surprised at the reaction. He said at one of the late night meetings of the group, "So long as you do not touch their comforts and jobs, they will be all right and rationalize even the worst of constraints."

Academic and intellectual life and the professions had not lagged behind the bureaucracy and business and industry in shaping a society around privileges, leading it towards stark consumerism.

With fear stalking the land, it was the right time to convene a parliament session. That would strengthen her hand, Mrs Gandhi thought; parliament was certain to endorse the emergency, and that would give it legitimacy in India and abroad. She decided to convene it on 21 July 1975.

However, she did not want too many embarrassing questions to be asked. Question hour should be given up. She had mentioned to her cabinet colleagues more than once before the emergency that the duration of the parliament session should be cut and procedures revised so that the ministers and government departments could do some solid work instead of wasting much time in work connected with debates and questions. The government moved a resolution saying that only "urgent and important government business" be transacted in the parliament session; questions, calling attention motions or other business initiated by private members would not be allowed.

Opposition members—most of them under detention—attacked this resolution. Som Nath Chatterjee, a Marxist, pointed out that there could not be a blanket suspension of rules. Era Sezhiyan, a DMK member, said that the House had powers to regulate its business but had to follow certain rules of procedure. Mohan Dharia said that parliament should be allowed to function in a more purposeful manner and the procedures should be business-like and not restrictive. An independent member, Raomo P. Sequiera, said that it was difficult to understand why private members' Bills had been excluded as private members had never obstructed the urgent business of parliament. He said that parliament was not meeting to legislate but to discuss the conditions in the country; since the proclamation of emergency, leaders of every opposition party had been detained. A large number of MPs had not only been detained but shifted from jail to jail. Even Indrajit Gupta, a member of the pro-government CPI, said that the motion was a *fait accompli* since the orders had been promulgated earlier.

Minister for Parliamentary Affairs K. Raghuramaiah argued in reply that the resolution to suspend the question hour was not meant to denigrate parliament. This was in the nature of self-restraint which the House put on itself.

Despite opposition protests, the motion was approved in the Lok Sabha by 301 votes to 76 and in the Rajya Sabha by 147 to 32. A resolution seeking parliament's approval for the proclamation of emergency was then moved in both Houses.

Mrs Gandhi asked Jagjivan Ram to move the resolution. Whatever his internal struggle, it was not reflected in his speech. He said that since 1967 some political parties had been making a consistent attack to denigrate the prestige of the government and create a state of unrest, which were becoming a threat to democracy. The year 1969 was a landmark in the political history of the country; not only the Congress but the entire country chose to resolve the internal conflict of struggle against disruptive forces. After the general elections of 1971, the opposition tried to organize a united front of four opposition parties, and thereafter a number of instances of arson and loot were reported in various states, particularly in Gujarat and Bihar, and sangharsh samities were organized to deter the elected members of the assemblies from attending to their political tasks. The railway strike was another effort to paralyze the government and force it to resign. Looking at the unfortunate and abnormal situation in the country, it became necessary to issue a proclamation of emergency.

The members of the Congress party spoke more or less in the

same vein. But the opposition attacked the government vehemently. Some speeches were made by the opposition leaders. A.K.
Gopalan, CPI(M), said:

This sudden declaration was not because of a real threat to
internal security but because of the judgement of the Allahabad
High Court and the verdict against the Congress in the Gujarat
election. The warning given by my party about the tendency
to totalitarian and one-party dictatorship since the last three
years had proved true with the sudden declaration of the new
emergency. By this, parliamentary democracy had been replaced
by the dictatorship of one party with full power concentrated
in the hands of one leader. This abrupt turn in the situation
and the sudden change from democracy to dictatorship was to
find a way out of the crisis to keep the ruling party in power. . . .
   The government's attitude to the RSS and the Anand Marg
which it had now banned, changed from time to time to suit its
convenience. In 1965, during the Indo-Pak war the then Prime
Minister Lal Bahadur Shastri handed over Delhi to the RSS for
civil guard duties.
   The measures taken by the government in the wake of the
declaration of emergency showed that the thrust was against
the people. The democratic rights available to the people had
been obliterated. There was not even equality before the law.
   The camouflage of the emergency being used only against
right reactionary parties had been fully exposed by the indiscriminate arrests of thousands of CPI (M) workers. The police
had been let loose on the people. In Kerala, many political
leaders and workers were beaten up both inside and outside the
jail. The attempt to create terror among the people needed to
be fully condemned.
   The threat of arrest hung over everyone who dared to
struggle against the vested interests and in defence of democracy.
These arrests were meant only to crush trade union and democratic movements.
   The movement led by Jayaprakash Narayan had accepted
the challenge of the prime minister to face elections. It was the
prime minister who developed cold feet after the verdict in
Gujarat. The factional struggle rampant in all the states had
spread to the centre too and it was no secret that after the

Allahabad judgement and the Supreme Court order there was a massive challenge to Indira Gandhi's leadership in the Congress parliamentary party itself. The threat to the Congress monopoly of power combined with the threat to Indira Gandhi's position in the party and in the government was the immediate cause for the suppression of democracy.

Mohan Dharia (Congress-I, expelled) said:

The 26th day of June 1975, the day when the emergency was declared, when my colleagues, several political workers and leaders were barbarously put behind bars, when the freedom of the press and civil liberties were surrendered to the bureaucrats, that day will be treated as the blackest day in Indian democracy and in the history of our country.

I would at the outset like to condemn this monstrous operation. I have no doubt that it is the prime minister and a few of her colleagues who are responsible for it. I am not charging the whole cabinet because I know that even the cabinet was told about it after the operation was already initiated. . . .

A systematic propaganda is being carried on that it is because of the opposition parties, it is because of the right reactionary forces, it is because of extremists that the economic programme could not be implemented. Is it true? It was possible to implement the economic programmes, the assurances made to the people in our election manifestoes of 1971 and also 1972. . . .

After the massive mandate, no one prevented us from implementing that. It is we who faltered and we are the fathers of the situation that is existing in the country today. . . .

So far as the economic programmes are concerned, it is being said that they are the programmes of the prime minister. I can understand the programmes of the party in power, the programmes of the government. But why are they creating the personality cult? It is also the way to develop dictatorship in the country. Let us not forget that.

The situation in the country is very clear today. It is because of the opposition parties coming together with more cohesiveness, not remaining only a grand old alliance, that the prospects of the ruling party have suddenly changed. Gujarat elections have amply proved that with all the use of money, power and personal prestige it will not be possible for Mrs Gandhi to acquire or retain power through democratic elections. Grand loyal exhibitions were organized through meetings and rallies to convince the people that the continued leadership of Mrs Gandhi as prime minister was indispensable for getting the contents of the petition filed in the Allahabad High Court. Without bothering much for the judgement of the Supreme Court it was announced in unequivocal terms: 'India is Indira and Indira is India. . .'.

Era Sezhiyan (DMK) said:

I am not a traitor. I belong to this country. I have been one among you, for the past thirteen or fourteen years. In my humble capacity, as a member of this side, I have also tried to help this House, and help the functioning of our parliamentary democracy. Oftentimes we may not have agreed with you but we all did agree on the functioning of democracy in this country and in this House. What has happened to that atmosphere? Why are we arraigned against each other, facing each other, to make you call us traitors, and equate us with those who are anti-national? Sir, two classes have been created. Those who support the emergency are equated with those who are supporting the economic programmes; those who are not supporting the emergency with those opposing the economic programmes. I support all the twenty points of the programme and if you want, I will add one or two more items also. . . .

When the banks were nationalized, when privy purses were abolished, we gave our full support; at the time you did not have a majority—out of 532 members or so you were only 240 in number—still we did not topple you down. We did not think of pulling down Indira Gandhi. But we gave her unstinted support because we believed in the programme of bank nationalization, in the programme of abolition of privy purses. Therefore, whenever there was a good programme we gave our support to it. Even then I may point out that in 1971 when MISA came before the House, we opposed that even though we were in friendly alliance. . . .

It may be that JP incited the army, he might have exhorted

the police and what he said might do harm to the country. I am one with you that such incitements should be severely punished. Why don't you put him before a court and say that he has committed the highest treason in the country? Expose him to the whole world, bring out the evidence, prove it to the hilt that he has done a heinous crime. However eminent he might be, however glorious his past might have been, and however popular he might have been, if he has done something against the country and against the people, put him before a court, prove the guilt and give him [whatever] punishment possible. That is the only thing we all have been pleading for throughout this day. If some organizations have been against the interests of the people of this country, take suitable action, the most stern possible action, but take it in the legal way, in the democratic way....It is very difficult to attain freedom. Once you lose it, it is still more difficult to regain it. Authoritarianism may become handy for some things, sometimes you feel this is a short-cut. Sometimes I think some of us even feel why have a parliament? Why should 500 members come here to take a decision which one person can take? That was what Hitler thought. That was what Mussolini attempted. But these systems did not work, because in a democracy if the executive does a wrong there is a check, but if a dictatorship does a wrong, there is no check, because as is said, parliamentary democracy is still the least unsatisfactory form of government possible.

Therefore, my appeal to the other side is this: I may not be in a position to make the same kind of appeal again. The same opportunities may not be available to every one of us—probably in the atmosphere that is now prevailing that may not be available. Previously what we said here was recorded and could at least be read by the people outside. But what I speak today is only for my friends here. For good or bad, for ill or well, we have been in this House. The people have elected us to run a parliamentary democracy in this country. We may be in a minority, you may be in a majority. I bow to the decision of the majority, but after due process, after due debate, taking both sides into account. Out of a hundred occasions, I may be wrong in ninety, but at least you should have the benefit of the ten occasions when we said something good for the country....

Democracy is something more than being constitutional, than being legal because of what happened to one of the best constitutions, one of the most liberal constitutions of the 20th century, namely, the Constitution of the Weimar Republic? Hitler did not subvert that Constitution. Hitler did not break the constitutional procedures laid down there. But using that very Constitution, a dictatorship arose there. By just saying that, I do not want to equate the prime minister with him. . . .

Therefore, my appeal is this: If you are meaning by parliamentary democracy only the form and the constitutional procedures, it is not going to make democracy function in this country. The spirit should also be there, not the form alone. A spirit of respect for the opposition, not merely tolerance, but positive recognition of the opinion of the opposition should be there. Unless there is a chance in our country to criticize the government without fear and to change the government without violence—that is the essence of democracy—you may retain the form and not the substance. If you think that I indulged in anything violent, by all means put me before a court and give me the sternest punishment that is possible. . . .

We had been proud that we were the biggest democracy in the world. When the freedom struggle was going on in our student days in the colleges and schools, we also fought on the side of Mahatma Gandhi: the scars left by the lathis wielded by the police of the British days are still there. . . . One of the old notes taken down by me gives a quotation from Mahatma Gandhi. It says: 'Real Swaraj will come not by the acquisition of authority by a few but by the acquisition of the capacity by all to resist authority when it is abused. In other words, Swaraj is to be attained by educating the masses to a sense of their capacity to regulate and control authority. . .'.

We all fought for that Swaraj. We all suffered. . . . But remember the day when the most precious life that human history could have seen and the man who gave us the very thought of freedom in this country was himself shot by a fanatic. Even at the gravest hour, Jawaharlal Nehru did not clamp down on the freedom of speech. Even the man who fanatically said that he killed the Mahatma in a fiendish way, was also given a fair trial.

Therefore, the same rule of law, in the name of the Father

of the Nation, in the name of Swarajya for which he fought and suffered, should be applied in all cases. Appeal to one and all that if you feel that you are right, please carry on. I wish I were wrong. Even if there is some faltering suspicion, such as I have, some apprehensions, such as I have, when some of your own colleagues have been arrested, go and ask them why they have been arrested, why they have been put in jail and what crime they have done more than the smugglers. Many of the smugglers are still at large. Many of them are still indulging in anti-social activities, but they are still at large. Law has not taken care of them. But friends, I would beg of you again, again and again, to remember that once the freedom of an individual is taken away today, the day is not far off when the freedom of everyone of us will be taken away!

P.G. Mavlankar from Ahmedabad said:

My feeling and my charge are that this emergency is unreal, that there is no threat to the security, that the threat is all imaginary, and this is a wanton abuse of the constitutional powers and that this is a fraud on the constitutional power and so it should not be approved by this honourable House. . . .

The prime purpose of parliament is the preservation of liberty of the individual, and it carries out the function, or should do so, by insisting that the executive or cabinet it produces must give adequate reasons proving that it cannot carry out its duties unless it is given further legal powers. But the minister, while moving the resolution yesterday, and the prime minister, while intervening today, have not given us adequate reasons as to why they want these vast extraordinary blanket powers. Therefore, I maintain that the power conferred under Article 352 of the Constitution on the president is a conditional power and that power can only be exercised if the conditions prescribed in that article are in existence. . . .

I want to ask specifically this question: Between 24 June afternoon and 25 June evening, what precisely happened which prompted the government to resort to this constitutional provision of declaring an emergency? Is this an internal emergency or an individual's emergency? Is this an emergency of the country or an emergency of the ruling party. . . .It is the beginning of the end of the rule of law. Since that day the Constitution had been cleverly and continuously used to destroy everything that we valued in our Constitution, more particularly the preamble of the fundamental rights. . . .

Indeed, I am sorry to say that the first republic of India is dead! Constitutional dictatorship has been launched, and that is why I say that 26 June marks the saddest and blackest day in our developing country and democracy.

Now, Mr Chairman, these last twenty-seven days or so since the declaration of emergency have been used not only to curb and curtail individual liberty but to eliminate it lock, stock and barrel. There have been large-scale arrests of leaders, arrests of MPs, MLAs and arrests of our colleagues on both sides, arrests of various parties, and, what is more, in the name of fighting against right reaction, so many leftists, socialists and other progressives have been put behind the bars. Sir, what was the fault of many of these people? They said the truth as they saw. . . . I am therefore glad that these people have been sent to prison. Let us all go to prison. . . .

The British never subjected India to this kind of humiliation which the rulers of independent India are inflicting in such an atrocious manner on all of us. Therefore, I feel that this House has a special responsibility to see that those detenus and leaders who are arrested are given fair treatment in jail.

Then I come to the question of the freedom of the press and the present censorship. This censorship is peculiar and extraordinary. Even in the British days, the worst days, when the British were fighting a second world war and they were losing battle after battle, they never subjected a dependent India to this kind of censorship which the rulers of independent India are inflicting on us. . . .

As a man believing in social justice, with socialist conviction, I do not belong to any party. . . . I want urgent economic programmes. Who prevented the government from implementing, let us know? Finally, I want to ask Jagjivan Ram, is there any point of return from today? Or are we heading towards one-party rule and then on to one person's rule? Is this not the beginning of a naked dictatorship. From the cracking of the democratic mould, are government not erecting brick by brick, a totalitarian system?. . .

S. A. Shamim from Srinagar said:

Democracy is a very inconvenient system for you. People talk against you, people oppose you but democracy has fundamental value in that ultimately the majority will prevail. But it seems that the present-day majority has taken this upon itself, not to have the inconvenience of a minority. This House is a witness to many dramas of the opposition. But the House has it on record that only that was passed which had the approval of the majority. How is it that in spite of what the opposition did, ultimately that piece of legislation has become inconvenient to you now? An illogical argument is being made that because of the emergency the efficiency has improved, the government employees attend office at 10 A.M., the efficiency in the railways has improved, and all that. By implication it means that this parliamentary system which has been there with us for the twenty-seven years has been wasting our time; by implication it means that this is a sort of 'useless organ'; by implication it means from the day you proclaimed the emergency, things have terribly improved. What is the logic of this argument? You say, let us not have this facade of a parliamentary democracy, it impedes the progress of the nation.

And then let us go to the freedom of the press. You have brought press censorship. The stalwarts who have fought for the freedom of the press and freedom of the country today are trying to give justification for censorship by saying that if a certain rumour was allowed to be spread, the country would have collapsed. Indira Gandhi yesterday in her speech said that she was told that the sword recovered from the RSS office was a wooden sword and then she said, 'Either you have a sword or you don't have a sword'. That is true also of the freedom of the press. You either have a free press or you don't have a free press. It is not that you have only a press which publishes only what you want them to publish. The essence of democracy is that both the viewpoints must be put before the people and the people in their wisdom must be allowed to judge what is right and what is wrong. You know what newspapers wrote in 1971 and yet people voted for you, they did not go by what the newspapers wrote. 'The myth and the reality' did not change the situation. How is it that today the mere suspicion of a rumour from the opposition shakes the entire government? If this particular piece of legislation, this amendment, was brought in, in good faith, I would have supported it. But this is brought in in bad faith. You have declared war on the people of this country. You have brought this in just to denigrate the judiciary and the courts and the whole world knows the reasons for this. You have no faith in the courts; you have no faith in the judiciary....

I have all the differences with Morarji Desai; I do not like one word of what he says in this House. The House has witnessed in this House that on the day when he became the spokesman of the entire opposition, I stood up and said, 'he cannot speak on my behalf'. I have said that whatever respect I had for Shri Jayaprakash Narayan, when he presided over the Jana Sangh session I did not see eye to eye with him. I never supported him the moment he attended the Jana Sangh session and after his demand for the dissolution of the Bihar assembly. But I must tell you that I will never accept that he is a smuggler. Then why has he been arrested? In the case of Morarji Desai it seems he became a security risk; he was a smuggler. That is why he has been arrested. . . .

What have you done today in the name of emergency? About the emergency, I agree that conditions were such that in truth drastic measures were called for. But against whom have you taken these measures? You have taken them against the whole nation. You have taken drastic measures against me. You have taken drastic measures against those people who are with you. You have swallowed up the freedom of those who respect the laws. It is not justice that you should snatch away the rights of anyone because someone has done something you do not like. The heads of the big people in parliament, who used to make great assaults, were cut off in 1971. The people cut off their heads. Today again, if you had gone to the country and said these people do not allow the parliamentary system to work, you would have seen that the people would once again have given you a majority and would have turned down these people. But this did not happen.

This parliament may be the last parliament of this country.

The evidence for this is that statement of Mrs Gandhi's in which it has been said that pre-emergency normalcy cannot come back now. She has named that licence. The country in which one individual decides what constitutes normalcy, what licence, what freedom, on the gateway of that country is the sign of dictatorship. Mrs Gandhi is not a dictator, but she has begun to walk the road to dictatorship. The greatest merit of dictatorship is that in the beginning principles are moulded with great care and excellence. They are moulded in beautiful words. Gradually people begin to find pleasure in them. They find quiet in them and then men tend to say that these are the principles of democracy. This happens not only here. In Russia, in Germany, in other countries where there is dictatorship, commonly the people praise democracy and take its name. I want to tell Mrs Gandhi one thing. She is a very clear-speaking woman. Whatever she wishes to say she says very lucidly. It seems to me that her belief in the parliamentary order has been lost. It would be a very good thing if she were to say clearly that today in this country there is no place for this system. Let the causes of that be what they may, I do not wish to go into them.

The CPI gave support to Mrs Gandhi. Indrajit Gupta (CPI) said that the proclamation of emergency was fully justified and everybody had supported it. However, the government should apprise the entire country of all the facts that they had got which compelled them to take this step. He said that the front formed by certain parties was under the leadership of Jayaprakash Narayan, trying for the last about one and half years to seize power in various states by means which were not entirely constitutional. There was, in fact, a very relevant international background, in the context of which these developments were taking place. The USA was playing its game.

The mover of the motion had very correctly mentioned that certain groups of newspapers were playing an active role in working up a conspiracy for seizing power. The monopoly press has the biggest circulation in the country. If they had been allowed to function freely today, by now, within twenty or twenty-five days, they would have created havoc in the country. Censorship had been imposed for the purpose of weakening the rightist and for strengthening the democratic forces. . . .

Intervening in the debate in the Lok Sabha, Mrs Gandhi accused the Jana Sangh and the RSS of conducting a "whispering campaign," and complained that the newspapers had not spoken up against the "falsehoods" which had been propagated against the government. A "massive whispering campaign," she said, was still going on about "who is under house arrest, who is supposed to be on fast, who is supposed to have died." Asserting that the opposition parties were "wedded to violence," she quoted press reports that JP had said in 1967 that he was "toying with the idea of a military dictatorship" and had suggested that because of the political instability caused by the elections in that year "the nation should call on the services of the army to fill the vacuum."

In Gujarat, she continued, members of the assembly had been forced to resign by threats to their children, and when a Congress member was lying in hospital, students had threatened to throw him out of the window. "Desperadoes belonging to criminal organizations like the Anand Marg" were still plotting to murder people. When the CPI(M) was in power in West Bengal people had not been able to walk in the streets after dark. "There can be no return to the days of total licence and political permissiveness," she went on.

"Democracy demands self-restraint from all. It is the responsibility of the government to allow the opposition to function, to allow freedom of speech and freedom of association. But it is the responsibility of the opposition not to take advantage of that to destroy democracy or to 'paralyze the government'. The words 'paralyze the government' are not mine; they were used at public meetings here in New Delhi and elsewhere. . . ."

In reply too ne of Mrs Gandhi's observations H.M. Patel (BLD) pointed out that nothing else but a "whispering campaign" and rumours could be expected when there was complete censorship of the press.

The Rajya Sabha approved the proclamation of emergency on 22 July by 136 votes to 33. After the vote, Narayan Ganesh Gorey, Socialist leader, read out a statement on behalf of the opposition announcing that they would boycott the remainder of the session as a protest against the suspension of regular parliamentary rules and the government's decision to apply the press censorship to reports of parliamentary proceedings.

The majority of the opposition members withdrew from the Lok Sabha the following day, after the proclamation had been approved by 336 votes to 59; the CPI and a number of smaller parties, including the Mulim League, Republican party, Praja Socialist party and Anna Dravida Munnetra Kazhagam (ADMK), did not, however, support the boycott.

The two Houses also passed the Constitution (39th Amendment) Bill which laid down that the president's reasons for proclaiming an emergency might not be challenged in any court. After special sessions of the assemblies of fifteen states had ratified the Bill on 28-29 July it received the president's assent on 1 August.

The endorsement of the proclamation of emergency was necessary under the law. But Mrs Gandhi was obsessed by the Allahabad judgement.

The "emergency council" at her residence had consulted some legal luminaries and had come to the conclusion that the law as existed could not but lead any judge to give a judgement different from that which Sinha gave.

The first priority was to ensure that it did not cast a shadow on her future. Mrs Gandhi's lawyers, even Palkhiwala before returning the brief to her, had told her that the Supreme Court would exonerate her from corrupt electoral practices. She had also the satisfaction that the Supreme Court's chief justice was A.N. Ray whom she had appointed out of turn. Hegde, one of the three superseded judges,[3] had said at that time that Mrs Gandhi was clearing the way for an appeal in case the judgement on the election petition against her was not in her favour.

Still she could not take chances. Gokhale prepared a draft Bill to invalidate the Allahabad judgement, and showed it to Sidhartha Ray and Rajni Patel, a "progressive" from Bombay who never drank anything other than the best Scotch whisky, Royal Salute. They were close to her and would often fly to her side whenever she wanted them for consultations. Sanjay however did not take kindly to them and was marking time to move against them.

At one time this "progressive" group suggested legislation to make the punitive period of debarment for a member of parliament

[3] See my book, *Supersession of Judges.*

run concurrently with the life of parliament. The idea was that in case the Supreme Court rejected Mrs Gandhi's appeal the prime minister could simply dissolve parliament and go to the polls. But not all thought alike. Sanjay was wildly opposed to the poll idea. Yunus would say that they should not think of elections for five years.

The government introduced in the Lok Sabha on 4 August a Bill to invalidate retroactively the ruling of the Allahabad High Court. The amendments proposed to the electoral law were many.

One, civil servants would no longer be prohibited from assisting political candidates during election campaigns in the course of their official duties. This meant condoning Mrs Gandhi's use of civil servants to build rostrums and to provide loudspeakers and electricity during her election meetings.

Two, publication in the official gazette was conclusive proof of the date of appointment, resignation, termination of service or removal of any central or state government servant. This was aimed at invalidating the second count on which Mrs Gandhi was convicted—that a civil servant, Yashpal Kapoor, acted as her campaign manager before he submitted his resignation to the government.

Three, for purposes of election expenses and "otherwise," the date of nomination should be the computing point. This was designed to ensure cn the one hand that the Supreme Court should not rule that Mrs Gandhi spent more than the permissible Rs 35,000 on her campaign and on the other that the declaration to fight the election was not the relevant date to consider.

Both PTI and UNI transmitted the full text of the Bill and its significance. But they withdrew the copy on orders from the censor office and put out another version which reduced the report to a brief summary making no mention of Mrs Gandhi.

The Bill was passed by the Lok Sabha on 5 August with an amendment. It provided that the case of every person disqualified on the basis of corrupt election practice should go to the president and that he should decide, after consulting the Election Commission, whether the disqualification should stay and for what period. In a way the authority of the election commissioner was to be wielded by the president. There was a point in this because the government later had an amendment to the Constitution to say that the president was "bound" to accept the advice given by the council of ministers. He would have no choice.

The Bill on disqualification was necessary but more essential was legislation to take away any dispute over the election of the prime minister from the purview of the Election Commission. As if such a thought were far from the government's mind, Mrs Gandhi and her advisers had it raised by a Congress party back-bencher. He said during the debate on the disqualification Bill that some elective offices should be immune from judicial scrutiny.

Gokhale "welcomed" the idea, gave it a legal shape within twenty-four hours and introduced on 7 August the Constitution (40th Amendment) Bill which provided a new authority, beyond the scope of any court, to deal with the election of the president, vice-president, prime minister and speaker of the Lok Sabha. The purpose was only to make doubly sure that no election petition would affect Mrs Gandhi. The others had to be included so that it would not look too obvious that the Bill was being introduced only to save Mrs Gandhi. Some chief ministers rang up New Delhi to try and see if they could be treated on par with the prime minister. There was no time to consider their cases.

Most of the Congress party's members as usual were smug and raised no objection to the Bill. Even if they had qualms of conscience, they showed no indication. But there were some who raised their voice against it. On behalf of the depleted opposition, Mohan Dharia declared, "It is to circumvent the judgement of the Allahabad High Court that this Bill is being introduced. Why this indecent haste to rush it through? Is it because the prime minister's case will be heard on 11 August."

Indeed, it was in unseemly hurry that the Bill was introduced in the Lok Sabha on 7 August at 11 A.M. and after overriding objections and suspension of the requirements of the minimum period of circulation for a Bill the government moved it for consideration at 11.08 A.M. The Bill was passed at 1.50 P.M. after clause by clause discussion and the required three readings. The Rajya Sabha passed it the following day in an hour without anyone speaking against it.

The state legislatures where the Congress had a majority were summoned on 8 August, the requisite ratification was secured the next day and on 10 August the president gave his assent—a day before the Supreme Court was to hear Mrs Gandhi's appeal.

But before the 40th Amendment Bill became law (officially it was the 39th) a few Congress MPs plugged another loophole. Suspecting that someone from the opposition might go to court and get a stay order on the Bill, they had the Rajya Sabha sit on 9 August and pass the Constitution (41st Amendment) Bill which said that no criminal proceedings might be instituted in any court against any person who had been the president, vice-president and prime minister. The inclusion of the president was incidental because the Constitution (Article 361) had already taken care of it. The Bill was really aimed at covering the prime minister. It was allowed to lapse when the election petition against her was taken up by the Supreme Court; the purpose had been served.

Now that the relevant laws had been passed, all attention was focused on Mrs Gandhi's appeal in the Supreme Court. The first thing to prevent was "undue and unfavourable" publicity. Chief Press Censor Harry D'Penha gave special orders to newspapers, news agencies and others not to put across any version of the proceedings without first clearing it with his office. All newspapers obeyed the order without any protest, except for a one-page daily, *Evening View*, subsequently banned.

The chief justice also did not object to the order of censoring the Supreme Court's proceedings—never done before in the court's history. In fact, he favoured he screening of even lawyers attending or listening to the proceedings. There was such a loud protest—and a threat to boycott the court—against the order that he did not enforce it.

A bench of five judges headed by the chief justice sat to hear the appeal on 11 August.

Shanti Bhushan, a lively lawyer who took up Raj Narain's case at Allahabad, pursued it in the Supreme Court; former Law Minister Asoke Sen took up Mrs Gandhi's. Sen asked the court to reverse the Allahabad High Court's judgement in view of the 39th Constitutional Amendment Act. Shanti Bhushan however contended that the court must first decide whether the amendment was constitutional. By placing certain persons above the law, the 39th Amendment had created inequality between one person and another on the basis of higher status; it was destructive of the concept of the rule of law, and parliament's declaration that the High Court's judgement was void was contrary to the principle of the separation of powers of the executive, parliament and the judiciary. He also held that all proceedings of the recent session of parliament were invalid, because several members had been illegally arrested and prevented from participating in the proceedings.

Niren De, the embarrassingly pro-government attorney-general, contended that a review of election disputes was not an essential feature of the judiciary and pointed out that in most Western democracies election matters fell exclusively within the competence of the legislature. He argued that in the Keshavananda Barathi *v.* State of Kerala case, the Supreme Court had held in 1973 that parliament had powers to amend or change the Constitution but without altering or destroying its "basic structure or framework."

Chief Justice Ray announced that the court would hear arguments on the merits and facts of Mrs Gandhi's appeal before ruling on the constitutional amendment.

Arguments in the Supreme Court did not worry Mrs Gandhi. What the constitutional amendments had left uncovered, her lawyers would take care of.

Her worry was the current happenings in neighbouring Bangladesh. Shaikh Mujibur Rahman and most of his family had been murdered in cold blood on 14 August. Neither RAW nor any other intelligence service had the faintest clue beforehand. They had failed Mrs Gandhi once again. In fact, from that day Sanjay started calling RAW the "Relatives of Wives Association." There were too many "relations" of top RAW officials in the organization. Mrs Gandhi did express to RAW Chief Ramji Kao her unhappiness over the lack of prior intelligence reports on Bangladesh. What worried her was that if the intelligence could fail her in Bangladesh, it could fail her in India as well.

Indeed, Mujib's death deeply disturbed Mrs Gandhi, particularly since both leaders had embarked on similar paths towards authoritarianism. When Mujib had assumed absolute power, scrapping the Constitution, JP had called in Delhi on 11 February a meeting of all opposition parties. He told them that it was probably a rehearsal for what they themselves might have to face in India. And they should be prepared for it. Ashok Mehta rejected JP's logic on the ground that such a thing was not possible in India. Morarji however did not rule out the possibility and if it did happen he would start an agitation in Gujarat. Charan Singh said "whatever she wanted to do let her do it," adding "what possibly could she do?" Raj Narain remarked, "At least she can put both of us in jail."

JP intervened to say that they were not serious; they should consider the possibility earnestly. He saw the end of civil liberties and the multi-party system. He said that they should agitate against the continuance of the external emergency.

Everyone wanted "something" to be done. No one knew what, but no one took JP seriously. Later, in Rohtak jail, where most opposition leaders were detained during the emergency, some did recall JP's warning. How prophetic it was!

However, there was no evidence of Mrs Gandhi learning any lesson from Mujib's murder. In hushed tones people talked about it and drew a parallel between the happenings in India and Bangladesh. The suggestion was that it could be repeated in India. Whatever the result, the security around Mrs Gandhi was further tightened; the portion of Safdarjang Road on which her residence was located had anyway been closed since the imposition of the emergency, but now traffic was restricted even on Akbar Road, skirting the bungalow adjoining her residence.

Someone floated the idea that she should not go to the Red Fort on 15 August to fly the national flag, a practice followed since India's independence in 1947. But she brushed the idea aside. She had practically stopped appearing in public but not doing so on 15 August would convince people that she was afraid to face the danger—a trait which had not been associated with her.

However, the ten-kilometre stretch between her residence and the Red Fort was heavily policed on 15 August morning; the residents of buildings in Daryaganj were ordered to keep windows giving on to the road shut. Policemen were posted on housetops on either side of the route. It was straight from the book, *The Day of the Jackal*, the story of police efforts to foil a plot to kill General de Gaulle. Only a few days earlier, on 8 August, a former captain in the army, Dhaja Ram Sangwan, who had been arrested with a telescopic rifle, told me in jail of a plot.[4]

Mrs Gandhi did not know of it when she rode in a closed car to Red Fort. Mujib's assassination was very much in her mind; this affected her style. She explained at length why she had imposed the emergency. She said that she had not done so with

[4]For details, see my forthcoming book, *In Jail*.

a happy heart. She had waited for a long time, but the situation was forced upon her. An extraordinary situation had developed and it needed extraordinary measures to take the country back on to the right road. She quoted her father Jawaharlal Nehru's famous words, "Freedom is in peril. Defend it with all your might."

These words could well be directed against her. She criticized the opposition for having resorted to agitations. A call had been given for launching Bihar and Gujarat type agitations elsewhere against the centre; students had been asked to give up studies. Indiscipline was made to spread in various ways and various groups, of whom some did not believe in democracy and non-violence, had come together to launch these agitations.

As if conscious of the excesses committed, she said that she had written to the chief ministers that there should be no injustice and high-handedness in getting orders implemented. Law-abiding citizens should be helped in all possible ways. The police and other officials should be like friends of the people. If mistakes had been committed they should be told of the proper manner in which they should act. She said that those who had been detained would be looked after well.

The "looking after" part was not correct. Living conditions in jail were appalling. The government was keen that the detenus should get treatment worse than ordinary criminals. During the early days, when the rules for interviews and other facilities were being finalized, Om Mehta was particular in making them as rigorous as possible and said so at a meeting of officials in the Ministry of Home Affairs. To begin with, there was only one interview a month for half an hour with two immediate relatives in the presence of a police official. The daily allowance was Rs 2.50 per prisoner. Initially, there was no radio provided to detenus; some did not even get the censored newspapers.

Since the number of the arrested totalled anywhere near a hundred thousand, jails were overcrowded. In the Delhi Tihar jail, meant for 1,200, there were more than 4,000. The meagre facilities were overstretched; the sewage in many jails overflowed and water was available for only a few hours.

B. K. Nehru, India's high commissioner, described conditions in Indian jails in a letter to the London *Times*, "The care and concern showered by the state authorities upon the welfare of the detenus who are well housed, well fed and well treated, is almost maternal." Bansi Lal said that the detenus had gained weight.

Conditions in jails were bad, but worse was the behaviour of officials. They had been particularly told to treat political detenus no "better than any criminal." At places there were regular chambers of torture. In Delhi's Red Fort, a very sophisticated room filled with the latest gadgets from abroad, was used to "extort" confessions. Floodlights were focused on a detenu for hours with sound effects in the background, to break him down. Intelligence officers would interrogate him for long and record all his movements and remarks through audio-visual tapes.

A few detenus died in jail, one of them was former MLA and trade unionist Bhairav Bharati, from Madhya Pradesh. Fourteen members of all political parties wrote to Mrs Gandhi, "We feel that in view of the hush-hush policy adopted by the authorities in regard to the death of an important worker under detention, the government should order a judicial inquiry into the cause of his death."

The stories of bad conditions in jails and the treatment meted out to detenus began appearing in foreign papers. Ivan Morris, chairman of Amnesty International said, "Mrs Gandhi's regime shows itself even less responsive to the principle of human rights than many other police states such as Chile, Taiwan, the Soviet Union and Korea."

A flame was lit at the foot of Mahatma Gandhi's statue in London to dramatize an appeal to JP and other political persons. The London *Times* ran on 15 August a six-column advertisement (worth £3,000), "Today is India's Independence Day. Don't let the light go out on Indian Democracy." Roughly 500 MPs and intellectuals, including Nobel Prize winners, from all over Europe signed the appeal. Yehudi Menuhin, the famous violinist, did not sign because he was in correspondence with Mrs Gandhi.

She was so irked by the intellectuals' call that she had a reply drafted by Chalapati Rau, editor of *National Herald*, the newspaper founded by Nehru, and sent it to them. She could not get many Indian counterparts to sign it though. Some who refused to sign it had to suffer harassment. Romilla Thapar, a historian at Jawaharlal Nehru University, was one of those who said No, and the result was that her income-tax assessments for a decade were reopened.

Indeed, reopening of income-tax cases and raids on business-men's and officials' houses by the income-tax enforcement branch of the Central Bureau of Investigation had become a government way of disciplining those who did not obey. Mantosh Sondhi, a bright engineer brought from a top position in the Bokaro steel plant to the Ministry of Industry, was troubled by the CBI at Sanjay's instance because Sondhi was a party to sending officers to the site of Maruti to collect some innocuous information for a reply to a question in parliament. Pai, then his minister, saved him by threatening to resign from the cabinet.

Harassment of people by raising the bogey of income-tax arrears had become worse after the bifurcation of the Finance Ministry. Income-tax, excise and banking had been converted into an independent department and handed to Pranab Mukherjee who was now a member of Sanjay's inner circle and would readily carry out his instructions.

The splitting of the Finance Ministry gave a heart attack to the namby-pamby Finance Minister C. Subramaniam, who had stood by Mrs Gandhi when K. Kamaraj, the tallest Congress leader in southern India, had sided with the old guard, which became the Congress (O). Subramaniam had told Mrs Gandhi that the Maruti project, as planned, would never come into being. In her presence he had spent hours with Sanjay to persuade him to associate the Birlas, one of the manufacturers of cars in India, with his project. Sanjay did not like Subramaniam's frank suggestions and had held a grudge against him, though much later Sanjay followed his advice to associate the Birlas with his factory.

With emergency rule a little more than two months old, a cult of personality began developing around Mrs Gandhi. Her pictures sprouted all over the country, her twenty-point programme began to be chanted like a mantra. "Indira-study circles" were organized by all major universities and the Indira Brigade gathered more volunteers.

And the portrayal of Mrs Gandhi as a goddess by Husain, a famous painter, was now being officially shown round the country. Mrs Gandhi of the emergency was the deity who rode a full-blooded roaring tiger, and not a lion as mythology depicted.

Socialist India, the Congress party's official magazine, carried a greater number of articles on Mrs Gandhi. "Why we should have complete faith and trust in Mrs Gandhi" was the title of one article. Articles eulogizing her appeared all over. And those published by foreign magazines and newspapers were circulated freely for reproduction. An article in a Canadian magazine said, "Prime Minister Indira Gandhi's wisdom is the wisdom of India."

Mrs Gandhi herself wrote an article for a Hindi magazine on "The Secret of my Success." She said that in her childhood when her teacher asked her what she would like to become she had replied, "I want to be like Joan of Arc." History will no doubt record what she finally became.

The majority of journals, particularly small publications, succumbed because of their reliance on government advertisements; newspapers turned themselves into virtual government gazettes or sycophantic supporters of Mrs Gandhi. However, when a few dailies like the *Indian Express* tried to stand up against censorship, the government brought pressure in various ways. The paper's proprietor, Ram Nath Goenka, a brave Marwari, was threatened that if he did not bend, he, his son and his daughter-in-law would be detained under MISA and his chain of papers auctioned. Goenka had to buy peace by reconstituting the board of directors of the *Indian Express* with the government's nominees in a majority. K.K Birla, quite close to Sanjay, became the chairman.

The *Statesman* was punished for not publishing a sufficient number of photographs of Mrs Gandhi on its front page. The newspaper was ordered to submit all page proofs to the censors for approval. The pages would be cleared only at 8 A.M., much after the newspaper's bedtime, purposely delaying the printing of the edition so that its sales would suffer.

In any case, the press was not much of a problem. The gagging was perfect. Sanjay's attention was focused on demolition of unauthorized structures or on the programme of Delhi's "beautification." All street hawkers had been banned from the capital. Even the little souvenir stalls near Jama Masjid were demolished. The traders, who had been there for decades, were asked to erect their stalls outside town—but there would be no customers.

The ousted traders of Jama Masjid approached Inder Mohan, a Ministry of Information and Broadcasting employee, who had given them a helping hand in the past. He was told that Sanjay was the man to decide. Inder went to Sanjay who did not offer any hope. The same evening eleven policemen entered

Inder's house, beat him up and dragged him away. When Inder asked the reason for his arrest he was told that the order for it came from "very high up." Later, he was beaten up again and after three days, a lawyer obtained his release.

What Sanjay wanted to prove was that nobody should come in his way and that he proved very successfully. Even the semblance of resistance against demolition crumbled, although it got built up in a big way in April 1976 when the demolition of the Turkman Gate locality started.

Slums in Karnal, Rohtak, Bhiwani and Gurgaon were razed to the ground without providing alternate accommodation to the slum dwellers. At least 10,000 structures were demolished in Lucknow, even the places of worship were not spared.

Probably, the anger against demolition around Jama Masjid had something to do with the pronouncements of the mosque's Imam who told his followers at his prayer meetings not to respect authoritarian rule. On 15 August, when Mrs Gandhi was speaking from the ramparts of the Red Fort, he had a running battle of words with her through the loudspeakers he had fixed on top of the mosque, opposite the Red Fort.

August was the month, eight weeks after the imposition of the emergency, when Sanjay began flexing his muscle; he thought he was a force to reckon with in his own right and he thought it better to record his views on many things.

To a New Delhi magazine, *Surge*, he said he was opposed to nationalization of industries and the concept of a controlled economy. He favoured tax cuts (which came true) and a greater role for the private sector to bring about economic viability. His rightist views were well known and he hated communists. He commented adversely on the Communist party and the manner in which non-communist parties had been functioning. He said, "I do not think you would find a richer or more corrupt people anywhere."

Chandrajit Yadav, a pro-CPI minister, told Mrs Gandhi the following day that the entire Congress party was agitated. Surprisingly, he suggested that Sanjay should openly join politics and that she should assign him some work in the party. She thought otherwise. She said that he was not interested in politics. She defended his interview on the ground that "he was a doer, not a thinker."

The CPI felt very hurt. Here was the party which was going out of its way to support Mrs Gandhi, keeping in view her close relations with the Soviet bloc, and here was her son who was not only adopting a pronounced rightist stance but also attacking the communists. The CPI protest to Mrs Gandhi had its effect. The full text of Sanjay's interview which was sent by Samachar to all papers was withdrawn; Sanjay issued a clarification to the *Indian Express*, which alone published the interview, on 28 August, to say, "I did not mean to make such a sweeping statement about an entire party. Obviously, in some parties like the Swatantra, the Jana Sangh and the BLD there are more wealthy people and there is also more corruption. I felt angry because I have heard that some individuals who call themselves Marxists and pose as being superior are in fact rich and also far from honest."

From that day, the CPI and Sanjay were at daggers drawn. Mrs Gandhi was conscious of Sanjay's antipathy towards the CPI but she would often tell him that if they wanted "to stay with us on our terms, what do we lose?"

Her worry was JP who had emerged as the moral conscience of India and the true inheritor of Mahatma Gandhi's passionate idealism. She thought of the last surviving disciple of the Mahatma and JP's political mentor, Acharya Vinoba Bhave, now eighty-one. She went to meet him at Paunar near Nagpur on 7 September. Baba, as they called him, expressed concern over JP's arrest and wanted his unconditional release. Breaking the vow of an year-long silence that he had taken, he told Mrs Gandhi that his last wish was to see a rapprochement between her and JP.

Bhave did not say anything in public except that the emergency was "an era of discipline." The government used this observation as a slogan to the extent of even defacing postal stamps with it.

He saw through the government's game and called at Paunar a meeting of *acharyas* (learned men). He told them to analyze the current situation in the country objectively and evolve "a discipline" to bring "happiness and peace."

It was indeed creditable that there was unanimity among members of this diverse group which included vice-chancellors, jurists, social workers and writers. The 1,000-word statement, issued after three days of deliberations, was clear, unequivocal and took a middle course. It did not apportion blame for past events. On the one hand, it appreciated a number of "constructive" developments in the fields of industry, economy and education that had taken place after the proclamation of emergency. On the other, it said that indefinite detention of a large number of social and political workers who believed in *ahimsa* (non-violence) and *sarvadharma samabhavana* (religious toleration) was not good for the health of the nation.

This statement of the acharyas annoyed Mrs Gandhi so much that Shriman Narayan who came to Delhi as Bhave's emissary was not given an appointment even in a week. Bhave did not join issue with Mrs Gandhi. Instead, he cancelled a bigger meeting of the acharyas and intellectuals which he had convened to find "an early solution to the present impasse."

A few intellectuals also staged a protest in another way. They assembled at Rajghat, Mahatma Gandhi's cremation ground, on his birthday, on 2 October, and shouted slogans against the emergency. J.B. Kripalani, the eighty-five year old Gandhite, was also one of the protesters. He was first arrested but then released. In Kerala, posters even in remote villages appeared on Mahatma Gandhi's birthday to urge the people "not to be cowards in front of injustice and tyranny."

That day one event really shook Mrs Gandhi. A man with a knife escaped the scrutiny of the security and sat near her at the Rajghat prayer meeting. Strong Shafi Qureshi, her deputy railway minister, captured the man. She ordered a high-power inquiry but, meanwhile, the strength of her security force was increased to 2,000.

The greatest blow to India on the Mahatma's birthday was Kamaraj's death.

The emergency had hurt K. Kamaraj the most; he had often said that she was on the way to becoming a dictator but had never suspected that she would really become one. His fear, as he expressed to me almost a year before his death, was that India might disintegrate and that north and south might come to a parting of ways if economic and political integration was late in coming. The emergency only swept this problem under the carpet, did not solve it. In fact, Kamaraj told a few close friends before his death that he had no role to play in the emergency, not even that of a mediator between JP and her because she did not trust anybody.

To JP he had once said that he did not trust Mrs Gandhi in the least. Being opposed both to the DMK and the ADMK, Kamaraj had little room to manoeuvre. As JP wrote in his jail diary on 3 October, "He knew that an unscrupulous politician like Mrs Gandhi would have no qualms about joining hands with the ADMK and he dreaded that eventuality. So, tentatively his position was to 'go it alone' at the next election."

Mrs Gandhi very much needed the south on her side. She knew that the emergency was unpopular in the north. After Kamaraj's death, she went all out to "prove" that the estrangement between the two had vanished and that the two had become quite close. This was not true but then who was there to check with Kamaraj? She said that he was in favour of a merger of the Tamil Nadu Congress (O) with Indira Gandhi's Congress. True, before the emergency, Kamaraj was willing to merge Congress (O) with Congress but on a national level, with all state Congress (O) leaders getting positions in the main Congress.

The fact that she flew to Madras specially for the cremation of Kamaraj impressed the people in Tamil Nadu, and some did come to believe that her story about Kamaraj joining the Congress was true, only if he had lived a little longer. This thinking helped her when the Lok Sabha elections were held later.

Another thing that happened on the Mahatma's birthday was a call to people by opposition leaders for a day's hunger strike to protest against the emergency. Political detenus all over the country responded.

In Delhi's Tihar jail, the jail superintendent marched into Ward 15 that night with three hundred officials and convicts and attempted to terrorize the detenus. The superintendent thought Mahatma Gandhi's birthday was the day to "reply" to the detenus' simple demands—better sanitary conditions, medical care and implementation of jail regulations regarding food, clothes and interviews and their refusal to be handcuffed when going to court or hospital. Tihar jail detenus continued their hunger strike on 3 October also. Charan Singh, Raj Narain and Nanaji Deshmukh lent support to their demands.

The government relented a bit and accepted certain demands of the detenus. But detention rules were made more stringent. MISA was further amended on 18 October in such a way that the government had no longer to disclose to anyone, including the judiciary, reasons for arrests carried out under the act. The ordinance was applied restrospectively from 29 June to keep persons already imprisoned from challenging their arrests. This step followed my release on 13 September, when the Delhi High Court ruled that the government had failed to satisfy the court that "Kuldip Nayar had been lawfully detained under the internal security laws." The news circuit of Reuter's, a British news agency, was cut on 9 October because it had put across this story and some others "in violation" of censorship rules. It took three months to get the circuit back.

The added stringency of MISA and the cutting of the Reuter's circuit strengthened the impression abroad that India was heading towards complete dictatorship. In the US, Indian students staged a "march of freedom" near the residence of Kaul in Washington. Kaul had gone out of his way to defend the emergency and even threatened that America would one day be sorry for not having accepted India's own version of democracy. He had written to the Education Ministry in New Delhi to withdraw the scholarships of those students who did not sing songs in praise of the emergency. He had the passports of a few students cancelled because they "were out to defame India."

In Chicago, about a hundred people, from different walks of life, representing professionals, businessmen and students, staged a demonstration, carrying a big ($10' \times 6'$) portrait of Mahatma Gandhi with his hands chained, signifying that he would have been in jail if he were alive.

Chavan who was in Chicago on 9 October had a rough time. His speech was interrupted several times; there were shouts of "shame, shame." When it was announced that the minister would only answer written questions from the floor the audience booed. Earlier, at a New York meeting, he had said, "Democracy has not only not suffered a demise in India, but is more living and throbbing than ever."

The World Council of Churches at Geneva urged upon Mrs Gandhi on 23 October to "restore the democratic right of the people for free expression." The council's general secretary also sent a letter to express "distress" over the detention of political figures without trial, asserting that the emergency powers of the government constituted a "very serious abridgement of human rights." Mrs Gandhi's defence was that the emergency was "in the correct order of priorities" as contained in the Constitution. The preamble mentioned social and economic justice first and only then referred to political justice, she said.

This did not convince many; but now she was on a stronger wicket. On 7 November the Supreme Court unanimously reversed her conviction of 12 June on two electoral offences by the Allahabad High Court. The High Court's ruling barring Mrs Gandhi from elective office for six years was also quashed.

The five-man tribunal's verdict was not based on the facts of the case, but rather on the election law amendment adopted by parliament in August. That in effect cleared her of her conviction.

The Supreme Court, by a 5-3 vote, also nullified part of a special constitutional amendment adopted by parliament in August that divested the courts of power to adjudicate on the election of the prime minister. This ruling upheld Raj Narain's contention that this sweeping power of immunity violated the basic spirit of the Constitution.

One of the five judges, who later became the chief justice of the Supreme Court out of turn, M.H. Beg, went into the merits of the case on the assumption that the case was to be decided on the basis of the law which existed at the time of the decision of the petition by the High Court. He came to the conclusion that the findings of the High Court were not sustaining. Beg said it appeared that "the learned judge was perhaps unduly conscious of the fact that he was dealing with the case of the prime minister of this country." He therefore, as he indicated in his judgement, seemed anxious not to allow this fact to affect his decision. Nevertheless, when it came to appraising evidence, "it seems to me that he applied unequal standards in assessing its worth, so as to largely relieve the election petitioner (Raj Narain) of the very heavy onus of proof that lies on a party which challenges the verdict of the electors by allegations of corrupt practices. . . . "

Mrs Gandhi's party held a victory celebration and said "the course of democracy has been fully vindicated. The judgement represents the triumph of democratic forces." But her opponents noted bitterly that the court's verdict had been based on the fact that parliament, as demanded by her party, had rewritten the election law, clearing her retroactively.

Soon after the judgement, the government requested the chief justice to review the Supreme Court's earlier judgement limiting parliament's power to amend the basic structure of the Constitution. Roughly 300 writ petitions were pending in various high courts challenging different laws and acts of the government on grounds that they violated the basic structure of the Constitution. A test case from Andhra Pradesh was selected. Niren De contended that the 1973 judgement had not clearly described the essential features of the Constitution and should be reconsidered so that parliament could know where it stood. Palkhiwala accused the government of acting with "indecent haste" in seeking a review of "the most momentous verdict handed down by one Indian court" only two years after it had been given.

After the third day of the hearing, the chief justice suddenly dissolved the thirteen-judge bench. He came to know that the majority of judges were not in favour of reviewing the case. It was a reverse for the government—the first in many months.

Dedicated lawyers enlarged the scope of their functioning, they filed thousands of writs for the release of detenus or for better living conditions in jails.

In the state High Court at Bangalore, Shanti Bhushan defended Advani, Atal Bihari Vajpayee, S.N. Mishra of Congress (O) and Madhu Dandavate, a Socialist. They were in Karnataka when the emergency was imposed. Shanti Bhushan said, "We are challenging the entire emergency and the measures the government has imposed and how they were part of what Mrs Gandhi called 'the gravely threatening conspiracy' that necessitated the emergency."

Two other lawyers who distinguished themselves in fighting gratis the cases of detenus were V.M. Tarkunde, former judge of Bombay High Court, and Solee Sorabjee from Bombay. Tarkunde also activated a body called the Citizens for Democracy. The body held many indoor meetings to ask for the restoration of fundamental rights. At Ahmedabad, it held a convention on 12 October, which was addressed among others by former Chief Justice M.C. Chagla of Bombay, former Supreme Court Chief Justice J.C. Shah, Tarkunde, Minoo Masani and some lawyers.

While inaugurating the convention, Chagla said, "Most people today in jails do not know why they are there and they cannot defend themselves, because where there is no charge, there cannot be any defence. They cannot go to any other tribunal because all that has stopped."

His speech led to grave trouble for a weekly, the *Bhoomi Putra*, from Baroda, and the Navjivan Trust press established by Mahatma Gandhi. The *Bhoomi Putra* press was sealed. The case went to High Court and the judges held some parts of the censorship directive void. The judgement itself was not allowed to appear till the High Court ordered its publication and said, "No decision of a court of law upholding the liberty of a citizen can ever cause any harm or prejudice to anyone."

The Navjivan Trust press, from where Mahatma Gandhi published his *Young India* and *Harijan* in his fight against the British, published a booklet on the *Bhoomi Putra* case. The police swooped down on the press, sealed it and kept it closed for six days. The press approached the Gujarat High Court. At one stage, it was suggested that if the Navjivan agreed to submit all that it printed for censorship, the government would not take action against it. Jitendra Desai, manager of the press, said it was the first time since independence that the government of a free India had sealed the institution which the Mahatma had created to win freedom for the country.

A few lawyers belonging to the Congress organized the Karnataka State Lawyers Conference on 8-9 November. It was advertized that it was in connection with legal aid to the poor. A sum of Rs 100,000 was granted by the state government. The real intention of the organizers was to pass a resolution in favour of the emergency. A large number of advocates who were openly opposed to the Congress were not allowed to become delegates. Only 600 out of 1,800 lawyers attended. Even then, when a resolution to congratulate Mrs Gandhi on her success in her appeal to the Supreme Court was placed before the conference it was found that only 10 votes were in favour and 490 against.

No doubt, this was an isolated incident in Karnataka. But the mood of lawyers all over the country was nasty. In the bar rooms they openly condemned the emergency and all that went with it.

Some lawyers, unmindful of consequences, went on fighting to uphold the rule of law. Many judges, mostly from high courts, also did not care about the persuasions of power. Mrs Padma Desai, for instance, sued for an interview with her father-in-law, Morarji, but the MISA Detenus Conditions of Detention Rules were never available for reference. The Delhi gazette had carried them but all copies were "exhausted." The spirited twosome of Rangarajan and Aggarwal heard her petition, insisted that secret executive orders could not supersede the law and struck down inhibiting clauses regarding interviews and correspondence. Mrs Satya Sharma, wife of S.D. Sharma, a signatory to Bhim Sen Sachar's letter, was rewarded with the ruling that executive action had to be justified by a valid law even during the emergency. Allahabad's Chief Justice K.B. Asthana, questioning the detention of a professor, said that only the government's *ipse dixit*—a dogmatic pronouncement—was not enough to justify arrests.

In Bombay, Justices J.R. Vimadalal and P.S. Shah struck down clauses relating to diet, interviews and medical treatment in the Maharashtra Conditions of Detention Order. They said "a detenu is not a convict and the power to detain is not a power to punish" and that "restrictions placed on a detenu must, consistently with the effectiveness of detention, be minimal."

Maharashtra's acting Chief Justice V.D. Tulzapurkar, struck down a police order banning a private meeting of lawyers to discuss civil liberties and the rule of law under the Constitution. He said, "No government which suppresses even peaceful and constructive criticism of emergency at a public debate, no government which preserves the freedoms only for the cringing and the craven, and no government which permits its police chief to perpetrate on its citizens the humiliation and indignity of being required to obtain prior permission for their normal, innocent and innocuous activities can have any moral right to proclaim to the world that democracy is alive in this country."

But these were isolated cases; the government tried its best to stand in the way of many others. At least 400 cases, including Mr Madhu Limaye's, were heard *ex parte* and "dismissed as withdrawn" without the plaintiffs being given an opportunity to make themselves heard. Stay orders by the Supreme Court were cynically timed only to prevent student prisoners from taking their examinations. Bombay's mayoral election was almost frustrated.

Obviously, the government's actions did not deter lawyers, at least in Delhi. When the emergency was at its "highest and foulest," on 7 April, the High Court Bar Association defeated Sanjay's favourite D.D. Chawla to elect Pran Nath Lekhi, who was then in solitary confinement in Tihar jail. The district Bar

Association elected Kanwar Lal Sharma, another rebel lawyer against a Congress candidate.

This was quite a challenge for Sanjay, who ordered the destruction of nearly a thousand chambers of district and sessions' court lawyers. Police kept vigil as bulldozers razed the structures to the ground.

Since it was a holiday, the occupants were away. But as word spread, panic-stricken lawyers arrived to try and salvage their property. They were rudely driven away and several sedate advocates, chased by the police, remained in hiding for over a month. Next day, a party of Bar Association members called on Delhi's Chief Jusitce T.V.R. Tatachari to protest; forty-three lawyers, travelling in the same bus, were promptly arrested, twenty-four under MISA and nineteen under the DIR. Union Minister of State for Works and Housing H.K.L. Bhagat told another delegation that "a lack of harmony" with the Delhi Development Authority (DDA) probably explained the demolition. Om Mehta assured a third group that there would be no further destruction.

But the DDA nevertheless demolished another 200 lawyers' cabins the following Sunday. The remaining 500 or so chambers were ruthlessly removed during the vacation. Similar official acts of vandalism were committed in the Shahdara and Parliament Street criminal courts. A total of fifty-eight lawyers were flung into jail; the only one to be released being Asoke Sapra, son of a deputy inspector-general of police (prisons), who was quietly bailed out at night.

But lawyers were an exception. Others had more or less begun to accept the emergency as a way of life, some even praised the "peace and discipline." Students who were the hope of JP were by and large quiet on their campuses.

They had protested. In Jawaharlal Nehru University at Delhi, students struck for one day in August and three days in September. The campus, like most other campuses, was full of intelligence men. When fifteen qualified students were denied admission, the president of the students union protested; the vice-chancellor expelled him. In Delhi University 500 teachers and students, including a young leader, Arun Jaitley, were arrested. Some students from Delhi were rusticated from their schools for two years; the High Court restored them to their schools. A few police inspectors admitted themselves as students.

A protest demonstration on 19 November in the National Stadium, New Delhi, was spearheaded by twenty-four boys between the age of fourteen and seventeen. Two of them seized the microphone and shouted, "Indira we will fill your jails but never bow before your tyranny."

But after brief protests, both students and teachers settled to a life which was not to their liking but was a stark reality.

A letter circulated by the underground at that time aptly described India:

It all depends on God. The situation in the country seems to be at its lowest. Self-interest has become limitless. There is no party now. It is the rule of an individual. All else are mere puppets now. The people as well as the higher and lower officials of the government have become mute and paralyzed. The people are groaning.

But who is there to listen to them and protect them? Perhaps no one had ever thought that this situation was possible. The fright of the emergency has submerged the people's consciousness. But now Indira Gandhi seems to be becoming aware of the situation she has created. Daily new ordinances are being passed. Now she herself and her son, Sanjay Gandhi, alone are running the government. The stage has come when each minister of the government acts only after he has got his instructions from Sanjay Gandhi. The reins of government are now in the hands of goondas. How the country will overcome this calamity one does not know.

Lakhs of people are in jail. The condition of their families worsens day by day. Large numbers of people have lost their jobs. The studies of many students have got halted. Large numbers of university and college teachers are now in prison. Even the old, the youth and the children are being terrorized. It is police rule now. Their cruelty and criminality are becoming unbearable.

Even economic gains were not there. Mrs Gandhi was yet to prove that poor countries like India needed benevolent autocrats to drag themselves out of poverty Economic mismanagement of the country, in fact, began with her regime in 1966 when she devalued the rupee.

Taking 1950-51 as the base year for the wholesale prices, which incidentally was the beginning of the planning era, the index went up from 100 to nearly 148, that is, by 48 per cent in fifteen years. Between 1966-67, the financial year in which Mrs Gandhi took over, and 1974-75, the wholesale price index moved from 148 to 351. In other words, prices went up more than 137 per cent during the nine years of her regime.

On the other hand, the money supply in 1950-51 was Rs 20,160 million; it had increased to Rs 45,300 million by 1965-66, a little more than double over fifteen years or so. But between 1965-66 and 1974-75 it moved up to over Rs 115,000 million, a steep increase by any yardstick.

So far as industrial production was concerned, it had reached 153 points by 1966. (On this scale the 1951 production was 55 points). In other words, the average rate of growth of industrial production was more than 6.5 per cent per year. Between 1965-66 and 1974-75 the index moved to about 208 points, indicating less than 4.0 per cent increase in industrial production. This was despite the respite provided by the green revolution.

Beginning from a low level of savings at 5.7 per cent of national income in 1950-51, the country had managed to bring it to 13.3 per cent by 1965-66. However, between 1965-66 and 1974-75 the rate consistently dropped and was never able to reach that level again; it hovered around 11 to 13 per cent. The peak investment was in 1966-67, when almost 15.3 per cent of the national income was ploughed back. The rate persistently dropped in subsequent years. In 1968-69 it was as low as 10.2 per cent and was not much higher until 1974-75.

Low savings, limited investment, sluggish industry, a steep rise in money supply and a sharp drop in agricultural production during the drought years of 1973-75 were bound to result in an economic crisis. And indeed the country witnessed it in 1974 and 1975. It appeared that her economic compulsions were such that she *had* to have something like the emergency.

What had helped Mrs Gandhi was record agricultural production, 120.83 million tonnes as against 99.83 million tonnes a year earlier (1974-75). Then there was the anti-smuggling drive which made the business of smuggling goods not only hazardous but also expensive. As many as 288 smugglers, including their top men like Haji Mastan and Yusuf Patel, were detained and the property of 177 was attached. An ordinance was issued on 1 July under which persons detained under the Conservation of Foreign Exchange and Prevention of Smuggling Activities Act need no longer be given the grounds for detention. If their detention was thought necessary in the interests of the country, their cases need not go to an advisory board. (Gayatri Devi was arrested under this act.)

The government also decided to "float" the rupee to encourage Indians abroad to remit money through official channels because the black market rate was no better. The remittances went up from Rs 800 million to Rs 2,000 million a year.

The fear of MISA also gave industrial peace. No strike was entertained and when there was one, the police intervened to "settle" it. This at least pleased industrialists, though not the trade unions, which in any case were simply afraid to do anything. Even when the Bonus Act was scrapped, making it no more obligatory for employers to pay compulsory bonus (8.33 per cent of salary) when they were losing money, trade unions by and large kept quiet; the CPI made some noise but only in newspapers.

The industrial peace and the government's efforts to show "some results" helped industrial units to harness their spare capacity. This created another problem—glut. Most industrialists complained that there were not enough customers to buy their goods which started piling up. The government did not do anything; its only concern was that there should be no closures or lay-offs. Nothing else mattered.

Was the emergency necessary for this? In fact, most of what had been achieved was because of the steps T. A. Pai, a business-minded minister, had taken after joining the Ministry of Industry in 1974. Even the anti-smuggling drive was as old as 1974 when Ganesh was the minister of state for finance.

The emergency had had little or no effect on bureaucratic sluggishness. Mrs Gandhi had gradually weakened the central ministries and state governments to give powers to her secretariat which, in turn, controlled the entire government machinery through special assistants, members of the Indian Administrative Service (IAS), and private secretaries, attached to ministers and ministries—S. K. Misra in the Ministry of Defence, N. K. Singh in the Ministry of Commerce and V. S. Tripathi in the Ministry of Information and Broadcasting. They slowly came to enjoy real power and lay down policies. Sanjay called them by their first names.

In fact, Mrs Gandhi had never been serious about administrative reforms. She first evaded them on the plea that the Administrative Reforms Commission, presided over by Morarji, had made certain recommendations which the secretaries to the Government of India were yet to process. When there was criticism against the slow pace, she set up a ministerial group comprising Mohan Kumaramangalam, D. P. Dhar and T. A. Pai to process the recommendations. Several papers and proposals were prepared only to be put into cold storage.

Her secretariat, the special assistants in various ministries, and RAW were all considered adequate to maintain and run the system. However, in her public speeches and in stray observations on files she continued to display interest and concern over the slow administrative procedure.

She wrote a letter to all chief ministers and cabinet ministers to tone up administration at all levels. She said, "We are passing through difficult times. It is natural that people should expect more of those in charge of administration. There is no place for indolence, indifference or indiscipline. Everyone should give of his best at his post of duty. Government servants of all ranks have rights. But there can be no question of right without obligation and responsibility. Effective leadership is important. . . ."

Though the letter was written on 10 March 1975, it spoke of "obligation and responsibility"—a theme which ran through Mrs Gandhi's speeches during the emergency.

Her letter brought in a flutter of surprise; for some time the corridors of the secretariat were rife with rumours about drastic changes and reforms. Every department and ministry worked out a drill in response to the PM's directives. Several cabinet ministers and chief ministers wrote back to the prime minister, giving more ideas and suggestions after paying tribute to her "vision and great understanding" of problems in the government—a ritual they had to observe.

Mrs Gandhi did not reply to any letter; she did not even read them. All were sent to her secretariat and cabinet secretary. No one heard anything of them later.

She however surprised all cabinet ministers and chief ministers by another letter on 25 April in which she reminded them about her earlier letter to tone up administration at all levels. She enclosed a rambling fourteen-page note prepared by L.P. Singh and L.K. Jha, both retired bureaucrats, on "improving efficiency in administration." She again wanted ministers to pay personal attention to improve administration and invited further suggestions to streamline and energize it. Again this letter became the talk of the secretariat. Each minister had several meetings with his senior officers and each secretary took all his officers into confidence. A fortnightly report on action taken was required to be sent to the cabinet secretary. The end product was the same— the administrative machinery stayed where it was, with all its cumbersome procedures and caste-ridden personnel.

However, in the name of the emergency, the government retired 200 officers at the centre and many more in the states. There had been a rule since 1960 that the deadwood could be weeded out after the age of fifty. This came in handy to punish some of those officers who refused to do illegal things. Many were victims of the vendetta of Sanjay, Dhavan or their counterparts in the states.

Mrs Gandhi was content to rule with her son and his henchmen. The relative stabilization of prices and the near absence of inflation on the one hand and the "responsive" administration on the other made her and Sanjay confident. They could now take chances.

This was the time when Mrs Gandhi thought of releasing JP temporarily. The news about his health was not good. If anything happened to him, people would not keep quiet. They would never excuse Mrs Gandhi and her government.

At one time JP's condition was so bad that even funeral arrangements had been made. Newspapers had prepared obituaries and for some reason Shukla had given instructions that the write-ups on JP should exclude any reference to friendship between Nehru and him.

Apart from his health, Mrs Gandhi had reason to believe that JP was in a dejected mood and blamed himself for what had happened to the people and the country. Her well-meaning Secretary P.N. Dhar who had succeeded Haksar, had, after consultations, sent Sugata Das Gupta, from the Institute of Gandhi Studies, to meet JP to know his mind. Dhar was of the view that JP and Mrs Gandhi had drifted apart because of a "misunderstanding" which could be "cleared." Gupta's impression was that JP was in a mood of retrospection. In fact, for the first time since his detention, JP got from Gupta a coherent picture of what had happened in the country and felt unhappy.

JP had also been wanting to go to Bihar to help the flood victims. On 27 August he had made a request for a month's parole to be able to do so. Instead, Mrs Gandhi had sent Balbir Vohra, secretary in the Ministry of Agriculture, to explain what was being done to render relief to the people of Patna. He did not say anything about rural areas and this disturbed JP.

But in a letter on 17 September, JP had not dwelt on floods alone; he had said, "Not only has the Bihar flood situation worsened, but there have also been floods in most parts of the country. There can be no question of anyone starting a movement or struggle at such a time. The political emergency, granting that it existed at any time, has passed and its place has been taken by an emergency of human suffering, calling for a national effort."

Mrs Gandhi read more into the letter than it was intended to convey. There was no doubt that JP was disappointed. But in no way did his determination to save the country from dictatorship weaken. Mrs Gandhi read too much into the reports that he was "disillusioned." She decided to release him first on a thirty-day parole and to watch him function.

Sanjay was opposed to his release but he saw little harm in the release on parole because then JP would be obliged to stay out of politics. However, JP had made it clear to the government that he proposed to resume active opposition to Mrs Gandhi.

JP was released on 12 November. The government allowed a bald announcement to this effect to appear in the press. The government did not give the terms of his parole. His political associates said that he had been freed to receive medical treatment; doctors had found him very weak with "a kidney infection."

Mrs Gandhi wanted to see how he—and the public—would react. The dice, after all, was loaded in her favour.

3. End of the Tunnel

JP NOTICED the fear on the faces of the people. Not many were present to receive him in Chandigarh. Intelligence men noted down the names of even the few people who were at Delhi airport, where he arrived two days later from Chandigarh by an Indian Airlines flight. The surveillance continued outside the Gandhi Peace Foundation building where he stayed.

If Mrs Gandhi thought that he had changed, she was greatly mistaken. He was like Wole Soyinka, the Nigerian poet and playwright who, after two years in prison, remarked about its effect on him, "You came out believing all the things you believed before you went in but much more strongly."

JP had told Sugata that Dhar obviously did not expect him, after all that had happened, to support or cooperate with Mrs Gandhi. If elections were announced, he would advocate ending of the confrontation with the government. Within a couple of days of his arrival in Delhi, JP held a press conference which only foreign correspondents attended; Indian reporters were afraid to go there lest they became marked men. The conference did not last more than fifteen minutes but JP made it clear that after he felt better he would continue to work for politics based on moral principles.

"This is what has been eroded by Mrs Gandhi. We have really not changed much from British days. I will do whatever I can to help unite the forces opposed to Mrs Gandhi," JP told the correspondents. "The middle class people are very demoralized, they don't know what to do. The opposition is in jail. The press is shackled. She must be afraid, she does so many things out of fear."

This was different from the government's own information. Intelligence men had reported that JP had lost his stamina. "JP is disillusioned and in a reminiscent mood," Dhar told me during those days. But he was mistaken. JP was still determined.

When Home Minister Uma Shankar Dikshit and Dhar went to talk to him, they did not find him in a relenting mood. JP stuck to his demand—there could be no dialogue unless all detenus were released, the emergency lifted, press censorship withdrawn and early elections ordered.

He told me more or less the same thing in Bombay where he went for dialysis because his kidney was damaged. How the kidney became damaged was a mystery. His impression was that it happened at the Post Graduate Institute of Medical Research in Chandigarh where he had been kept for treatment.

JP had heard rumours that he had been poisoned. In fact, he told the BBC that his health deteriorated after 27 September owing to "unnatural causes." Asked if it was engineered from outside, he told the BBC, "With full responsibility I must say that there is some doubt in my mind."

I could notice during my talk with him how the emergency and subsequent developments had affected him. He was indeed depressed and blamed himself for what had happened. But what gladdened him was the widespread reaction against the emergency. "One lakh of people is no small number to go to jail," he said. He was however disappointed that except for lawyers and judges, not many others "had shown courage."

He felt he was of "no more use" to the country; he said that as far as service to the country was concerned, he was finished. "My world lies in a shambles around me," he had written in his prison diary. But in this he was wrong. Little did he realize at that time that he would soon play a big role in restoring democracy in the country and that from the shambles would arise a new India.

The beginnings were already visible. A nationwide Satyagraha by the Lok Sangharsh Samiti was started on 14 November, the birthday of Nehru, who had once said that JP would one day play an important part in India's history. More than 100,000 volunteers signed a pledge to offer sacrifice.

In Delhi 108 volunteers, including 7 women and 6 teenagers, courted arrest in Chandni Chowk. Fifty Sarvodaya workers were arrested at Shantivana in the presence of Mrs Gandhi, who had gone there to pay homage to her father. The Satyagrahis shouted *Bharat Mata ki Jai* (Victory to Mother India) and *Tana*

Shahi Nahi Chalegi (dictatorship will not work).

Veteran freedom fighter and former MP, Tenneti Viswanathan, led Satyagrahis in Andhra Pradesh and all district volunteers courted arrest. In Orissa, Satyagraha was launched at Sambalpur and Cuttack; seven people were arrested on the first day.

In Kerala news of the Satyagraha call reached all district centres and other lower units through handwritten posters. In ten out of eleven districts, 280 volunteers courted arrest. Near Calicut the police lathi charged the volunteers.

Satyagraha was observed all over the country, and in every state there were some arrests. What distinguished this Satyagraha from that of 29 June, after JP's call at Delhi, was that this time many people turned out in the streets to watch the Satyagraha. Earlier, none dared to be seen. The pamphlets which the Satyagrahis were able to distribute were readily accepted. The behaviour of the police was also different in a way—they were more cruel than before as if they had no compunction or hesitation to lathi charge or to use force to disperse what they still considered a crowd.

The government was also becoming more and more authoritarian. Even though all fundamental rights remained suspended during the emergency the government issued orders specifically to suspend seven rights guaranteed by Article 19 of the Constitution—freedom of speech, freedom of assembly, freedom to form associations and labour unions, the right to move freely throughout India, and to live in any part of the country, the right to own property, and the right to pursue any profession, trade or business.

The order signed by President Fakhruddin Ali Ahmed, also barred appeals to courts to enforce Article 19. No reason was given for the additional curb against constitutional rights, the fourth since the imposition of emergency rule on 26 June 1975.

It was expected that Mrs Gandhi might start releasing people, but she went in the opposite direction. The popular response to the Satyagraha was probably the reason behind the government's cautioned crackdown against dissidents.

JP's parole was revoked on 4 December and although all restrictions on him were removed he was kept under watch. Intelligence men followed his movements, kept track of his visitors and examined his letters and sayings very closely. Just in case.

Otherwise, as JP told me, Mrs Gandhi was on top of the world. She was called Goddess Durga and at times she looked like believing that she had that *shakti* (power). She knew exactly how to act for the best effect. In a village she wore a plain dhoti, covering her head demurely. In Kashmir she dressed like a Kashmiri. In Punjab she wore a kurta and salwar and even said that she was Punjabi because her younger daughter-in-law, Sanjay's wife, Maneka, was from Punjab. She claimed she was the daughter-in-law of Gujarat, for her husband Feroze Gandhi was a Gujarati. All these things she knew went down well with the masses. And they did for some time.

The structure of "guided democracy" that she had built looked like having come to stay. A lot of people in the country seemed ready to accept the political solutions Mrs Gandhi offered. Many, particularly the elite, would say quite unashamedly, "We have always needed a master to make us do anything. We had the Mughals, we had the British and now we have Mrs Gandhi. Is it so bad?"

Sanjay had advanced both his political influence and his equivocal reputation under her benevolent eye. No chief minister thought his visit to Delhi was complete until he had met Sanjay. They all vied with one another in inviting him to their state and to show through government-sponsored rallies how popular he was.

Mrs Gandhi honestly believed that he was popular. Once when Chandrajit Yadav complained to her that most of Sanjay's receptions were sponsored ones, she took it as an offence and said, "Some people are jealous because Sanjay is really popular." Yunus would lend credence to her belief by repeating that he was a big draw. Yunus even wrote a special article, which was reproduced by many newspapers, to say that Sanjay was the man of the future. The fact was that the crowds that came to welcome Sanjay were all hired.

But what embarrassed Mrs Gandhi at times was that chief ministers started receiving Sanjay at airports. Sidhartha Ray had pointed this out to her. Through Barooah, she had instructions sent to them not to receive her son at the airport or railway station.

The chief minister however took the instructions lightly, for every time Sanjay went to a state, there was a Home Ministry circular to make "the usual arrangements" to receive him. All knew what the word usual meant. The ministry had also issued instructions on Sanjay's security—at the meetings addressed by him, the public should be kept beyond pistol range and the back of the dais should have a bullet proof screen; the intervening space to be filled by police and security men. This was in addition to the security men who had to be with him round the clock.

Sanjay would often travel to the states in an Indian Air Force (IAF) plane; officially it was a minister's trip but the real passenger was Sanjay. Om Mehta was generally the minister who requisitioned the plane. Before Mrs Gandhi's time, a minister of state for Home affairs was never entitled to an IAF plane; she extended the concession to him. Dhavan, and at times, Seshan, would arrange who among the ministers should requisition the plane. Once or twice the minister concerned did not go at the last minute; Sanjay went alone.

Most chief ministers had known from their experience that Mrs Gandhi wanted them to be in touch with Sanjay. Rajasthan Chief Minister Harideo Joshi was pulled up once because he had initially expressed his reluctance to meet Sanjay in connection with a state matter. He made up for it later by building 200 welcome arches for one of his visits to Jaipur. Mrs Gandhi had that visit cancelled because of the public indignation over the enormous waste on such preparations. But Joshi had proved his credentials.

Hitendra Desai, who was very close to Morarji but had now switched over to the Congress, did not take seriously Mrs Gandhi's hint to him to meet Sanjay. Desai had therefore to cool his heels in Delhi to see Mrs Gandhi till he started waiting on Sanjay.

For Giani Zail Singh, even Dhavan was Dhavan*ji*, a sign of respect. Once Sanjay dropped one of his sandals while boarding his plane. Zail Singh ran, like many others who were at the airport, to retrieve it for the young man.

Shyama Charan Shukla, who had replaced Sethi in Madhya Pradesh as chief minister, was at Sanjay's beck and call. Shyama had stayed in the wilderness for long and did not want to go back into oblivion. If attention to Sanjay was the price that

Mrs Gandhi wanted from Shyama Charan, he was only too willing to pay it.

For Sanjay, political management had come easily; he began to build up his own political strength through the Youth Congress which he joined on 10 December and which Barooah asked him formally to activate. He manoeuvred to throw out Priya Ranjan Das Munshi, a pro-CPI leader from West Bengal, from its president-ship and replace him with a dependable Punjabi girl, Ambika Soni.

But Sanjay's main worry was how to institutionalize the emergency which his mother would often say could not continue for ever and had to be replaced with something secure, depend-able and permanent.

Sanjay again began with the press. Shukla had reported that more or less all newspapers and journalists had come to behave and were no threat; they were acting as their own censors.

The Prevention of Publication of Objectionable Matter Act of pre-independence days was revived through an ordinance to prohibit the publication of "words, signs or visible representa-tion" which "bring into hatred or contempt or excite disaffection towards the government established by law in India or in any state thereof and thereby cause or tend to cause public disorder." Under the same law during the British raj, the person accused of writing "objectionable material" was arraigned before a senior judge and was entitled to trial by a special jury of persons in journalism or public affairs. But the ordinance empowered the government to judge, punish and hear the first appeal; only thereafter could the accused go to High Court.

The government was also empowered to demand cash bonds from printers, publishers and editors who were held responsible for publishing only "prescribed" material. The government could also close down the press that printed matter considered "prejudicial."

A set of convenient editors prepared a code of ethics for newspapers. It was a strange code; the more than 3,000-word exhortation did not once mention "freedom of press."

The government also withdrew the accreditation of more than forty newspaper correspondents. Journalists were permitted to continue to represent their newspapers, but were deprived of such privileges as admission to major news conferences and sessions of parliament. (I was listed among those who were to be denied accreditation if I were to apply.)

The ten year old Press Council of India, a body of journalists and newspaper interests to protect the freedom of the press, was dissolved. Here the pressure of Kishan Kumar Birla worked. He was very close to Sanjay because of the free advice and other help the Birlas provided to try and get the Maruti car on the road. K.K. Birla was the defendant in a complaint filed before the Press Council against the termination of the services of B.G. Verghese, editor, *Hindustan Times*, a Birla paper. It was contended that the action against Verghese was taken at the instance "of some members of the ruling party who were inimical to press freedom."

K.K. Birla had come to know from the discussions in the council that the judgement would go against him. It did, but it was never pronounced. However, the draft judgement prepared by the council's chairman on the basis of his informal discussions with the members indicated that Birla and one of his directors in the *Hindustan Times* would have been indicted.

The draft judgement said that the termination of the services of Verghese was clearly a violation of the freedom of the press and editorial independence. The Press Council also condemned the attempt by Birla to prevent the publication of the correspondence between him and Verghese. The verdict could not be delivered because the Press Council was abolished on 31 December 1975.

The immunity given to journalists to report parliamentary proceedings was also withdrawn. Sanjay was afraid that the press would splash all that would be said in parliament on the Nagarwala, import licence and Maruti scandals. He did not want dust kicked up again. Ironically, it was Feroze Gandhi, Sanjay's father, who had brought forward a Bill to help the press report the happenings in the two Houses of parliament freely. At one time Mrs Gandhi wanted the Bill to stay but Sanjay did not agree and he had his way. There was no room for sentiments in administration he said.

Even though the press had become a kind of government gazette—exerting self-censorship to the extent of not using even the health bulletins of JP without clearance by the government— Mrs Gandhi and her son were not happy. There was the chain of newspapers of the *Indian Express* group still not falling in line.

The only solution was to buy it up. And Ram Nath Goenka was asked to sell his publishing empire. But for him it was not that easy to part with an established set-up which he had built from scratch. He wanted to stall it by asking for time to come to a decision, hoping that the government would change its mind. Time was given but seeing that the government remained stubborn, Goenka climbed down and offered to sell the papers on one condition—he should get a fair price and that too in "white money." He knew this would not be possible.

Goenka was proving to be a hard case. He was too costly. The alternative was to have some control over the thirteen directors on the board. Sanjay thought it better to have the board of directors changed, with K.K. Birla as chairman, Kamal Nath, Sanjay's friend from Doon School days, as one of the six members, to give the government a majority. The first act of the new board was to retire compulsorily Mulgaokar, editor-in-chief, apparently on the pretext that he had reached the age of superannuation, but in fact because the government wanted its own man as editor. Two other senior members, Ajit Bhattacharjea and I were also to have been removed but Goenka stalled it.

The government still did not like the "tone" of the *Indian Express*. Shukla stopped all government advertisements and had his ministry issue a secret circular to all public undertakings and autonomous bodies to stop advertisements to the *Express* group of papers. The loss came to nearly Rs 1.5 million every month.

Despite a virtual control of the press, Shukla talked of "restructuring the entire press industry so as to make it accountable and answerable to the people, society and the country." This was all meant to have some permanent arrangement, not dependent on the powers available during the emergency.

For this purpose, the merger of the two major English news agencies, the Press Trust of India and the United News of India and two Hindi news agencies, Hindustan Samachar and Samachar Bharati into one was considered essential; it would mean only one point of control. Shukla used his known arm-twisting methods against newspaper proprietors and owners of news agencies to bring them to agree to one agency which later came to be known as Samachar. To break the resistance of some directors and top personnel, he tried to cripple the agencies by stopping the subscription of All India Radio, a substantial source of income for them.

Under the government plan, disclosed in the first week of January 1976, the President of India would nominate the chairman and fifteen members of the agency's first governing council. However, the president was empowered to "require the governing council to take appropriate measures" if "he is satisfied that the agency is not functioning effectively."

The government was aware that the measure would be understood as a curb on the freedom of the press, so it began explaining that what it was doing to the press was to "enable it to be truly free from vested interests." The agency formally came into being on 1 February.

While the reorganization of the press was continuing, Sanjay focused his attention on the more important issue of restructuring the government. He had always told his mother that left to himself, he would "change the entire government," and he had demanded the replacement of one-fourth of her fifty-four member council of ministers with members of the Youth Congress. Already he was scrutinizing senior appointments at the centre; officials were called to 1 Safdarjang Road, interviewed by Sanjay and Dhavan and then cleared or dropped.

But this was not enough. Sanjay wanted his men in the cabinet and in the states. That way he could ensure his instructions would be carried out in full. He had Bansi Lal, one hundred per cent loyal and committed, inducted into the cabinet. He would suggest a tough line in the cabinet—just what the household wanted. For obvious reasons Bansi Lal wanted the Defence Ministry and got it.

However, he did not want to be isolated from his principality, Haryana, and hence his successor, Banarsi Das Gupta (Bansi Lal himself had chosen him), was told that the "real chief minister" would continue to be Bansi Lal and that he should "listen" to him.

Mrs Gandhi also bowed to Sanjay's wishes to get rid of the eighty year old minister, Dixit. For her it was a big decision because as party treasurer since the 1971 elections, he had collected and distributed hundreds of millions of rupees on her behalf. Lately she was somewhat unhappy with him because his daughter-in-law was interfering in the administration. Mrs Gandhi had transferred Dixit's son, a civil servant, from Delhi to keep the meddling daughter-in-law away but she stayed back to help Dixit.

because he was not keeping his promises. He threatened to lock me up and I asked him to put me before a firing squad. 'Death is the same to you and me', I said.

Snehalata Reddy's was another heart-rending story. A frail girl, Snehalata Reddy, had been imprisoned on political suspicion in the Bangalore central jail on 1 May 1976.[2] No charges were specified. No questions were asked.

To the film-going public Snehalata was well known as the heroine of the multiple award-winning Kannada film, *Sanskara* (produced and directed by her husband Pattabhi). She was also a leading figure in the Bangalore theatre and world of arts.

But more than this she was known to people from all walks of life—Socialist leaders and intellectuals, theatre artistes from India and abroad, writers, painters, magicians, and above all, many young people still searching for a meaning and purpose in life. Her home was a home to friends at all hours of the day or night.

It was the range and warmth of her friendship which was to land her in prison. She had for a long time been a friend of George Fernandes. Under the changed circumstances, the mere fact of such a friendship led inexorably to tragic consequences.

Overnight her beautiful world collapsed and a nightmare of fear and uncertainty began. Her daughter, Nandana, was held for questioning on two occasions, and the family was kept under surveillance.

On 27 April, she and Pattabhi were to leave for Madras to arrange lights for shooting their new film. At 4 P.M., Nandana was picked up, from her house, to be questioned for the third time.

She returned only at 7 P.M. in the evening. No one had been informed, and the family was desperate with anxiety. Her sudden disappearance had upset their programme. It also left them disturbed. Eventually, they left for Madras at 9 P.M., leaving their son, Konarak, behind.

At midnight there was a knock on the door and a loud call "telegram." Konarak opened the door and was immediately seized by both arms, while a horde of policemen rushed into the house. On finding that the family had left for Madras, they dragged him off to the police station. Most of the policemen.

---

[2]Based on extracts from Snehalata's prison diary.

stayed back to ransack the house, endlessly questioning Sneha's eighty-four year old father and the servants. At 6 A.M. the next morning, the police finally left.

In Madras the first news the Reddys heard was that their long-time friend, Apa Rao, and his daughter had been arrested early that day, They immediately tried to telephone Bangalore. But their phone had been cut. Eventually, contacting a neighbour they learnt what had happened in the night. They decided to return to Bangalore and went to their hotel to pack.

On reaching Bangalore they were taken straight to Carlton House, where Sneha and her husband were held. The others were escorted home. Konarak's whereabouts were still unknown. Sneha and Pattabhi were in a state of extreme exhaustion, having driven the previous night to Madras, and returning the next day with hardly any rest.

All that night they were kept seated in a room, the only explanation from the guard on duty being "*Saibru eega bartare* (the officer is coming now)." Nobody came that night.

Eventually she and her husband were taken into separate rooms for questioning. The strategy of attrition—intentional or accidental—had its effect. Before a word could be spoken, or a question asked, Sneha herself said, "Bring back my son, release my husband, promise not to harass my daughter and I'll tell you everything I know."

Till this time nothing could be held against the Reddys, except their known friendship with a political refugee. But Sneha was too naive for the new world she had suddenly entered. Tired, sleepless, anxious about her son, she had been led to a seemingly incriminating statement.

Her family was elaborately brought into the room to prove their well-being. Then everyone was sent home and she was held alone. The next week seemed reassuring.

Sneha was often cross-examined but there wasn't much to tell. The family was allowed to bring her bedding, clothes and food. She was treated as a political detenu with visits from the family permitted.

On the evening of 7 May, when Pattabhi arrived with the dinner, the Carlton House was locked and deserted. Presuming that she had been taken elsewhere for interrogation, they settled down and waited. A 10.30 P.M. they returned home, but went back again at midnight. The place being still deserted, they returned home to make an endless round of futile phone calls. No one slept that night. Next morning a kind but anonymous caller told them that he suspected that Sneha had been taken to jail.

In the same pattern of deception as her first arrest, she had been tricked into jail, without the knowledge of her family. Late that afternoon, she was told that she was about to be released and asked to pack her things. The first stop was a magistrate's court.

The proceedings seemed routine, till she heard the words "commit you to detention." The magistrate said that as soon as her family raised the money for bail, she would be released. Sneha asked a policeman to phone her husband to inform him of her whereabouts. He went over to a phone, and went through the motions of making a call. But no call was made and the family remained ignorant of her plight till the next morning.

Meanwhile, papers were signed, orders passed. Sneha was taken back to Carlton House. By this time it was evening. In the despairing hours of the twilight of May, Sneha was taken to the grim, cold, stone prison which is the Bangalore central jail. On arrival she was put through the first of many humiliating experiences.

Her baggage was minutely examined, her signature and thumb impression taken in the inmates' register and she herself was stripped and searched.

Then she was locked up in a draughty cell, large enough to hold one person. It had a hole at one end in lieu of a toilet, an iron-grille door at the other. Fortunately she had still her personal bedding with her and passed that night on the floor. Her fear and depression were somewhat counteracted by indignation against her family, who had made no effort to release or even see her. She did not know of their all-night vigil, that the police never made the phone call to tell them of her whereabouts.

Next morning they found her in jail and went to the magistrate's house to apply for bail. He assured them that it would be given, if their lawyer applied in the proper form. The lawyer was not so confident, but went along to try. In private he was informed that this was a non-bailable case. The ordeal of imprisonment had begun. The case unfolded.

Sneha was charged under Section 120, 120A of the Indian Penal Code. Finally, unable to establish any of the charges, the state dropped them, but continued to hold Sneha in prison, this time under MISA. All possible discussion was stilled.

Gradually the reality of the prison began to dawn on Sneha. She became a physical wreck and had to be released on health grounds.

She died on 20 January 1977 after a heart attack soon after release from prison.

There were many other Lawrences and Snehalata Reddys. All of them had been victims of the excesses and tortures

Udaya Shankar, a student leader of Canara College, Mangalore, was taken into custody from his house without warrant. The police caned and kicked him in the Bunder police station. His body turned blue. He was not given water or food. Shrikant Desai of Hubli, a final year law student and state joint secretary of the Karnataka unit of the Vidyarthi Parishad was inhumanly beaten and put on an "aeroplane."

Rabin Kalita, a prominent worker of CPI(M) who was arrested under MISA, was hospitalized in the Gauhati Medical College hospital. His condition became serious. His relatives were neither allowed to meet nor attend on him. Even though his treatment was going on in the hospital, he was handcuffed. He breathed his last in the hospital with handcuffs on.

Hemant Kumar Vishnoi was arrested while on a picnic in Buddha Jayanti Park in New Delhi. He was hung upside down and beaten. Burning candles were applied to his bare soles. Chilli powder was put into his nose and rectum. Despite all this torture, he refused to confess to a non-existent "plot" against the prime minister. The police gave up.

Rajesh and Anil, aged fifteen and thirteen, who were picked up for distributing pamphlets with other boys at a function addressed by the president, were mercilessly beaten and made to sweep the entire floor of the big police station.

Two minor children named Sunil and Manoj were picked up from Jogiwara by the Hauz Khas police just to oblige some local Congress workers. They were beaten up till they finally broke down to make statements as wanted.

C.L. Lakhanpal, an advocate of Chandigarh, suffered a severe attack in jail. He was taken handcuffed to the PGI hospital and died within a few hours. The authorities had neglected his medical care.

The ire of the police was particularly directed against intellectuals. More than 200 teachers of Delhi University were arrested in the pre-dawn swoop of 26 June itself. One of them, O.P. Kohli, president of the Delhi University Teachers Association, who is physically handicapped, was made to stand for twenty-four hours at a stretch in the police lock-up while the policemen showered him with abuses and shoe beatings and pushed him around. Many a time he fell but was forced to stand up again.

Teachers were picked up while lecturing in classes. Many teachers who were released through some court orders were rearrested at the gates of the jail with a fresh chargesheet of the same crimes or no charges at all. Only the united protest of the academic community was able to stop the wave of rearrests.

The excesses against the Naxalites, extreme leftists, had been going on even before the emergency; now they were arrested without reason. The stories of so-called armed encounters between the police and the Naxalites were many, and it was impossible to believe that a few dozen Naxalites with a few old guns were engaging in open armed battles lasting hours with thousands of well-armed police.

Miss Mary Tyler who was released after six years of detention, revealed after release on 6 July how the allegations of "trying to establish a guerrilla base in Bihar" were concocted. The group were not guerrillas, she stated, but young left wing activists who were encouraging the people in remote rural areas of Bihar and West Bengal to resist landlords and moneylenders and bring about land reforms. Very few of them had known one another before they met in prison. After her arrest she had been kept in solitary confinement for a year at Hazaribagh, and later moved to Jamshedpur jail for court appearance. When she was released, she said the prison, designed for 137 prisoners, had contained about 1,200 as a result of the mass arrests which followed the declaration of emergency.

The problem of Naxalites was nothing new. It had been there since 1963 when the extreme leftists started a violent struggle at Naxalbari (West Bengal) near the Sino-Indian border to capture land by ousting the owners.

The authorities were more worried about the underground however; it was almost a year and George Fernandes had not been arrested. Mrs Gandhi called a meeting of top officials and took

them to task for not having arrested him. One of them said that
they had broken into his network and that their men were now
part of his set-up. He promised his arrest within a few days. And
this did happen. George was arrested on 10 June in Calcutta from
a house attached to a church. His arrest was a big blow to the
underground.

The underground was a mote in Sanjay's eye. The underground had circulated stories of the excesses he committed in the
family planning drive.

Indeed, Sanjay was following the programme ruthlessly. He
had set targets for the chief ministers who in turn had allotted
quotas to the bureaucracy. To please Sanjay, the chief ministers
vied with one another to meet his "wishes" on family planning.
Neither Sanjay nor Mrs Gandhi was bothered how the targets were
met as long as they were met or at least reported to have been
met.

For Sanjay the means were not the concern, it was the end that
mattered, and forced sterilizations were performed unchecked.

In Delhi, a glamorous girl, Ruksana Sultana, who considered
Sanjay a god, came to the forefront to push family planning.
Though she had no official position, she moved through the streets
of the walled city with heavy police escort, a jeep in front and
another behind her vehicle. Subsequently, she said in an interview
that she was proud that she got the opportunity to "associate
herself with the family planning programme—and Sanjay."

To appease him Uttar Pradesh raised the target of sterilization
cases to 1.5 million from 400,000 fixed by the Government of India
under the population control policy. All government departments
were allotted specific quotas. There were quotas for districts.
Teachers and the personnel of the health and medical departments
were denied promotions and increments for failure to achieve
their individual targets.

The drive was stepped up in July and gained momentum a
month later, resulting in 240 incidents of violence erupting from
resistance to forced sterilization. The average of 331 operations
per day in June rose to 1,578 in July and shot up to 5,644 per day
in August, when special camps were organized. In many places
people, irrespective of their age or marital status, were picked up
and forcibly sterilized.

The first major incidence of violence occurred in Narkadih

village in Sultanpur district of UP on 27 August when the divisional commissioner collected people to "motivate" them. The people opposed the programme and chased the officials out of the village. The police fired; as a result thirteen persons were killed and scores of others received bullet injuries.

The police, under orders of the district officials, virtually ran amuck in rounding up villagers for forcible sterilization. Terror stalked villages and people fled to take shelter in the fields to save the honour of their women and their own lives. Even during the legendary dacoits' days they never had to leave their houses but living in fields now became a pattern of villagers who were afraid to stay in their houses because of police raids.

The sterilization drive continued to a record 6,000 cases per day, only to result in another flare-up in Muzaffarnagar district on 18 October. In Muzaffarnagar family planning camps were organized by the district magistrate and people were forced to contribute large sums of money. In case of their refusal they were threatened with arrest under MISA or DIR. People were picked up from bus stands and railway stations by the prowling parties of policemen and forced to undergo sterilization.

From a particular locality people, married or unmarried, with children or no children, young or old, were picked up systematically for three days and were sterilized. Resentment mounted when eighteen such persons were driven to the family planning camp. A large mob, demanding their release, pelted stones. The police first burst teargas shells and when the mob stampeded, fire was opened on them. Twenty-five people were killed and eight reported missing. (They have not been traced since.) The incident was known as "mini Jallianwalabagh." Curfew was clamped and four persons were shot dead for violating it in another locality.

Despite censorship, news of the incidents spread by word of mouth and a protest procession was taken out in Kairana, about thirty-five kilometres from Muzaffarnagar. When the processionists, on the appeal of some public workers, began dispersing, the police chased them. When they ran for shelter into a mosque the police stormed in and opened fire resulting in the death of three persons.

In the village of Basti a block development officer, a panchayat secretary and a village level worker, who had gone to update the registers of target couples were hacked to pieces by a frenzied mob; this infuriated the police who terrorized and tortured the people with a vengeance.

In Haryana, a large number of people refused to get sterilized and resisted the officials who tried to force them into sterilization camps. They were arrested indiscriminately and subjected to various types of torture. A youth in Gurgaon district who was arrested for instigating his clansmen against sterilization was arrested by the local police and detained in a dark cell. During his interrogation his hair and nails were pulled out and when after a month he was released he had lost his hearing power.

A young government employee in Mehandergarh who refused to get sterilized because he had no issue was harassed so much that he became a mental case.

In Rohtak district an elderly school teacher was instructed by the district education officer to get two cases for sterilization to receive her salary. The grey haired widow could not get any. Ultimately she is said to have brought two insane beggars to the sterilization camp and thus got her salary.

The worst sufferers were the Harijans and other backward classes of the state. The government was not concerned whether they were young, unmarried boys, old widowers, impotent people or already sterilized ones; they had to undergo sterilization. The target was important, not the people or their sentiments.

For officials in Bihar the family planning campaign offered the easiest chance to show their "commitment." The tribals were perhaps the worst hit in the sterilization drive. The first deputy commissioner to earn the gold medal for good work" was the one posted in Singhbhum district, a part of the Chotanagpur tribal belt. The overlord at Ranchi, another tribal district, was not far behind. Excesses were also committed in Bhojpur district, but there it was not tribals who suffered most; everyone suffered equally.

There was trouble in east Patna. Police fired on a crowd angered by the forced sterilization, killing one and injuring several, but the censors ordered the press to publish only the official version which said that the police fired on people who were agitated over the eviction of pavements dwellers. Within twenty-four hours of the incident all the tents pitched by Youth Congress adherents along thoroughfares to propagate the virtues of family planning disappeared. These encroachers, of course, were not those that anyone fired on.

In the race for gold medals, Patna came from behind and took pride of place about two weeks before the Lok Sabha elections were announced. And against the target of 300,000 sterilizations fixed by the Union Government, Bihar achieved 650,000, which encouraged Health Minister Bindeswari Dubey to exhort the officials to reach the million mark before the end of 1976-77.

To observe the "good work" done, Sanjay visited the state four times. And the state Congress leaders and the government went all out to propitiate him. On his last visit to Bihar, before the elections, Sitaram Kesari the provincial Congress committee chief, said at a public meeting in Patna that Sanjay Gandhi was the new star on the political firmament and the leadership of the Congress and the country was safe for the next fifty years.

The VIP treatment accorded to Sanjay had cost one million rupees, at least half of which was borne by the state government on security arrangements and conveyance and crowd management; the other half reportedly came from captains of industry and commerce.

Punjab's enthusiasm for family planning was visible from the large number of eligible couples the state collected for sterilization at specially arranged camps. Some deaths were reported because of the operations.

No newspaper could print news of any family planning excesses. Nor was Mrs Gandhi's household prepared to believe them, although they knew that force was being used for sterilization. The intelligence bureau did learn of some excesses and sent reports both to the prime minister and her secretary. But action was seldom taken on them. Some force was inevitable, it was rationalized. Minister of State Shah Nawaz Khan at the centre, submitted to Mrs Gandhi a report on the Muzaffarnagar incidents and described how the police deliberately used force and indulged in brutalities. Her comment was that the account was exaggerated. Fakhruddin Ali Ahmed, who was also given a copy, was shocked. He complained against it to the prime minister and wrote about it in his diary which he maintained regularly.

Physical force was not the only method used; the government issued circulars to order the stoppage of promotions and increments to its employees if the employees did not either get themselves or others sterilized. Even the renewal of a driving licence was dependent on getting a minimum number of people sterilized.

The Delhi administration issued a circular that those employees eligible for sterilization would be paid their salary only on the production of a certificate of sterilization. The 10,000 teachers in the corporation's primary schools were given oral orders to motivate five persons each for sterilization. Headmistresses of schools were given the power to detain students until one of their parents got sterilized.

Some traders' representatives were summoned to the Delhi Raj Nivas. The lieutenant-governor told the traders to fix their quota of cases monthwise and motivate their employees and others for sterilization.

Many companies employing casual and contract labour had to close down because labour had decided to return to their villages rather than risk sterilization.

The government also announced a national policy on population. Sanjay was for limiting children to two per family but Mrs Gandhi and the rest of her family members favoured three children and this was accepted. The national policy envisaged the reduction of birth rate from the estimated 35 per 1,000 to 25 per 1,000 by 1984. By then the growth of population was expected to come down from 2.4 per cent to 1.4 per cent. The minimum age of marriage was raised to eighteen for girls and twenty-one for boys. Monetary compensation was offered for sterilization, male and female, but it was left to the states to legislate for compulsory sterilization if they so desired. (The population then stood at 615 million.)

Family planning apart, "beautification" of Delhi was also Sanjay's fad. He would daily tell Jagmohan, the DDA chief, what to do and assess the progress in slum clearance.

Following the unprecedented demolition of unauthorized structures the exodus of long-settled families had begun from many localities. One such locality was what was known as the Muslim Abadi. Turkman Gate residents, among whom were also non-Muslims, watched with concern the assembly of bulldozers outside their locality from 13 April, *Baisakhi* (harvest festival), which the Punjabis among the residents celebrated with abandon and enthusiasm.

On 16 April the residents met H.K.L. Bhagat who assured them that no houses would be demolished. How could they, he said, when these structures had been there for generations? But the bulldozers did not move away.

Suddenly on 19 April, the bulldozers started moving towards Turkman Gate. A group of people squatted in front of the freshly white-washed Dargha Elahi, just outside the locality, to stop the bulldozers. Many other residents joined in and the crowd swelled to several hundreds.

It was towards noon, when truckloads of riflemen of the Central Reserve Police (CRP) and Delhi policemen began to arrive on the scene. Within a few minutes pushing and shouting started, the policemen wanting to clear the passage and the people resisting them. At this time, a hail of stones came from the police side. Till then the demonstration was noisy but peaceful. The crowd ratialiated and stoned the police.

Around 1.30 P.M., the Daryaganj sub-divisional magistrate ordered a lathi charge which was brutal by any standards. There was a commotion in the crowd; the people ran here and there; some fell on the ground and many sustained injuries. Hundreds of them were arrested, including the injured. But then a regular fight started between the people and the police; women gave a helping hand and armed with kitchen implements, they got their menfolk released from the police.

This resistance angered the police who resorted at first to teargas and then to firing sporadically for almost three hours in the afternoon. As things got out of hand, curfew was imposed. And this was when the bulldozers, about fourteen, moved in. Roughly 1,000 houses were demolished; 150 people killed and 700 arrested. But that was not the end. The curfew continued for forty-five days. During this period, the houses were ransacked, almost one by one. Young brides were deprived of their jewellery; even the old and invalid were beaten up like animals and deprived of their possessions; people were picked up on suspicion that they had resisted the police.

The censors saw to it that not a word appeared in the press. But Delhi and gradually the entire country began to talk of the atrocities at Turkman Gate. The government was forced to admit a few deaths but the press note issued never told the truth.

At the time of clearing the Turkman Gate residents, the DDA

did not know what to do with the site. Three months later, a scheme was prepared to put up a fifty-storey commercial building.

The people forcibly ousted from their houses were dumped into a barren tract across the Jamuna, which did not have even drinking water, not to speak of any other amenity. When Sheikh Abdullah inspected the colony many days later, he described the Turkman Gate incident as *Karbala*. He was indeed unhappy and conveyed this to the authorities. When the residents waited in deputation on Sanjay—Mrs Gandhi was not available—to get better facilities, he said, "You have told lies to the Sheikh; you will pay for that." He said that the people would be punished for "attacking the police."

Slum clearance was not part of Sanjay's five-point programme (originally four) which was as much publicized as Mrs Gandhi's twenty-point programme. Sanjay's five points were: family planning, tree planting, ban on dowry, each-one-teach-one, and ousting casteism.

The programme was quite innocubus. But it created resentment because of the methods he used to implement it. There was yet another reason—every action of his had the stamp of extra-constitutional authority; people objected to the power he enjoyed and therefore suspected every move he made. Although many of them had reservations about him, they praised his "practical wisdom" and "sagacity." He, being the fountain of power, must be placated, self-seekers in Congress thought.

Sanjay did throw his weight about. This was not only in regard to Maruti, the five-point programme or the Youth Congress. He also tried to overawe and punish his critics. A contractor who had displeased him while building a part of the Maruti premises was arrested and Rajagopalan, then inspector-general of police, Delhi, was transferred to the border security police because he did not carry out Sanjay's wishes.

Sanjay's hand was visible in what happened to Air Marshal P.C. Lal, former chief of the IAF, who was inducted into the Indian Airlines as its chairman. This time Sanjay's pilot brother, Rajiv,[3] was also involved.

---

[3] An Indian Airlines Boeing 737 was hijacked to Lahore in September 1976. The Kashmiris responsible for this thought that Rajiv was piloting it. But he flew only an Avro, though on the same route.

Lal was due to retire on 31 July 1976; he wanted to put in his papers for retirement and go on leave. But he was keen to groom his successor. Next to him was V. Satyamurty, deputy managing director. Lal talked to his minister, Raj Bahadur, and the prime minister in September 1975 recommending that Satyamurti be appointed as managing director after his retirement and if they wanted he could continue as part-time chairman. Both Mrs Gandhi and Raj Bahadur agreed that Satyamurti could be his successor. Rajiv was said to be against him.

In October, Raj Bahadur told Lal that the prime minister wanted three pilots to be promoted. He replied that the pilots did not fulfil the criteria for promotion. Lal's No apparently irked the prime minister. Meanwhile, Raj Bahadur had changed his mind about Satyamurti and told Lal that he would not be appointed as managing director. Lal saw the prime minister—his last meeting with her—and told her that Satyamurti would make a good managing director. She said she had the impression that Satyamurti was not "quite honest," adding "I know everything that goes on in IA."

In December Lal made a series of transfers. But Raj Bahadur said no transfer or appointment should be made without his approval. He said he was under orders from Dhavan. However, Raj Bahadur promised in January 1976 that the IA officers on the board of directors would not be changed. But when, in February, the board was reconstituted, Satyamurti[4] was dropped and a junior officer was taken in his place. Lal protested to Raj Bahadur, who said that the prime minister was displeased with Lal's running of the airline.

Lal submitted his resignation in April and asked for leave. Raj Bahadur sent one of his joint secretaries to ask him not to go on leave. Lal withdrew his leave application. But by then Raj Bahadur had heard from Dhavan that Lal must go on leave. Lal vainly sought an interview with the prime minister.

On 13 April 1976, Lal saw plainclothes policemen posted outside his office and a DSP in the lobby. Lal was wanting to go on leave from 19 April, but the Civil Aviation Ministry had already sent a circular saying that Lal was on leave from 12 April. Later,

[4]P.K.G. Appuswamy, deputy managing director, Air India, was also dropped, probably to show that both managing directors had been dropped.

the ministry issued a letter saying that Lal's services had been terminated.

All transfers made by Lal were undone and the three pilots who were not "competent" by Lal's standards were promoted.

Lal and his brother were harassed by the income tax authorities, a familiar exercise. Lal later recalled how Mrs Gandhi told him once that in a country like Guyana if the prime minister did not like an officer, he was not allowed to enter his office. Lal now realized what it meant.

Sanjay was also creating scenes. He went to Bombay with Bansi Lal for a naval function on 11 January 1976. The coveted Nook, an MES bungalow, was already booked for the chiefs of the army and the air staff. The naval authorities arranged accommodation for Sanjay and Bansi Lal at another place—a suite and a double room. Bansi Lal gave the suite to Sanjay and occupied the double room himself. Bansi Lal told Naval Chief S.N. Kohli that he did not like the arrangements.

Then there was a rumpus over the seating arrangements at the ceremonial dinner. At the head table, there were seats for the president and his wife, the governor and his wife, Bansi Lal and his wife and two flag officers. Even the military chiefs had to be accommodated at the other tables, arranged in an E shape.

Sanjay was somewhat down in the order, with the naval officers. Bansi Lal wanted Sanjay at the head table. Kohli said it was not possible. Bansi Lal used foul language, as was his habit whenever his word was not heeded, before other naval officers. Kohli, who had only three months left for retirement, suddenly expressed his desire to resign immediately. Unprepared for such a statement Bansi Lal changed his tune. Since his wife did not attend the dinner he gave that place to Sanjay. The incident which left bitterness all around, reverberated throughout the country. And critical remarks could be heard, though in hushed tones.

Not that Bansi Lal was not known for his rough handling of situations. Only some time earlier, he had suspended Sukhjit Singh, a colonel in the military operations branch in Delhi. The matter related to the price of land in the Tarai area in UP which the colonel had "restored" to the owners. R.C. Methani, Bansi Lal's special assistant, called Sukhjit Singh to his office in the presence of the "ousted" party and insulted him. Bansi Lal went a step further, he "suspended" the officer. Sukhjit was removed from the military operations branch and given an unimportant post in Delhi cantonment. There was no inquiry and no protest by other officers who, down the line, gave in to Bansi Lal's pressure. Some amends were made subsequently when Sukhjit Singh, who was in the panel of brigadiers, was promoted and posted to eastern India.

Power had not gone to Bansi Lal's head alone; Shukla behaved in a similar manner. His favourite field of operation was the film industry and he used all types of methods to see that directors, producers and stars. would play to his tune. Kishore Kumar invited his wrath because the artiste expressed his reluctance to sing at a concert which the Youth Congress had organized in Delhi. Kishore's songs were banned from radio and TV. Many films had to wait for censors' clearance because Shukla wanted producers or stars to "placate" him. A.K. Verma, another police officer in the Ministry of Information and Broadcasting, was Shukla's operations man in this field.

The misuse of power had percolated to many in the household. Sonia, Mrs Gandhi's eldest daughter-in-law, Rajiv's wife, was an Italian; she had retained her Italian passport but had not registered herself under the Alien's Act which necessitated the registration of all foreigners with the police within ninety days. (The registration has to be renewed regularly.) She was once an agent of the government-owned Life Insurance Corporation but was now in the Maruti's consultancy firm. Mrs Gandhi's other daughter-in-law, Menaka, Sanjay's wife, had started a magazine, *Surya*, the advertisements were fatheted from all sources, through all methods.

Then there was Yunus who always talked in *pakar lo* (arrest them) terms. Before foreign journalists, he said that West Germans were "Hitler minded," the British "lunatics" and the Americans "indecent." He called President Ford "that football player."

However, Yunus was now in favour of relaxing press censorship as had been done in the case of foreign journalists.

In any case, press censorship was now used for party and personal ends. The censor would disallow news items or even statements by Congress or Youth Congress leaders simply because they did not suit Shukla who was always in touch with Dhavan and through him Sanjay. Whichever state Shukla visited, he told the censor and newsmen not to report on the internal quarrels of the Congress. The chief ministers used censorship to black out news against them and their group. In Punjab Mohinder Singh Gill, the Congress president, found it hard to get his statements published because Zail Singh had instructed the censor otherwise. Information Minister Subrata Mukherjee in West Bengal told the censor's office not to clear any news against his group.

Two English language journals that had been critical of India's emergency regulations were forced to stop publication. One, the weekly *Opinion*, was ordered to be closed by the Maharashtra state government because it had violated the Publication of Objectionable Matter Act and censorship rules.

The other periodical, the monthly *Seminar*, decided to cease printing voluntarily after it had rejected a 15 July government order to submit to censorship. The courageous couple, Ramesh Thapar and his wife, Raj, wrote in the final issue that *Seminar* "cannot surrender the integrity and right of free expression this way." No newspaper had printed the news of the closing of *Seminar* and *Opinion*.

The use of MISA for political purposes was now an accepted fact. The mere threat would bring round even conscientious objectors. For example, many leaders of the opposition Muslim League in Kerala were detained because they broke away from the ruling faction and turned against the government. While in detention they were induced to rejoin the ruling faction with the promise of release, but nothing came of it.

It was under the threat of arrest and imprisonment that the leaders of the Kerala Congress were made to break from the Marxist front and to join the ruling front. In fact, the Kerala Congress was a vocal critic of the emergency. But at the instance of Om Mehta, intelligence men forced K.M. George of the Kerala Congress and his colleagues to go to Delhi where they were plainly told that either they should join the ruling front, in which case places would be found for them in the ministry, or be prepared to go to jail.

Bansi Lal used MISA in Haryana to detain a factory manager who had made Bansi Lal's man resign his job because of embezzlement. Even when the complaint reached Mrs Gandhi, she did not do anything. All of them had autonomy in their own field of operation.

Despite the misuse of MISA, here and there people went on

courting arrest. The Janata Front in Gujarat organized on 15 August 1976 a march from Ahmedabad to Dandi, the destination of Mahatma Gandhi's march in Bulsar district of southern Gujarat in 1930. Though Miss Maniben Patel, Sardar Patel's daughter, led the march, she was not arrested while all her companions were. Delhi had given special instructions not to arrest her. She reached Dandi in twenty-two days.

Former Gujarat Chief Minister Babubhai Patel was also arrested during August under MISA.

Such arrests raised hopes abroad that there were still some Indians left who would fight for democratic values. Some foreign newspapers used these instances to attack Mrs Gandhi. The criticism did hurt her. In fact some people left India during the emergency to tell others abroad how freedom was being eroded systematically in the country.

The US granted political asylum on 24 August to Ram Jethmalani, chairman of the Bar Council of India. Facing possible arrest for an anti-government speech he had made in Kerala, Jethmalani left India by plane on 28 April for Montreal, Canada, and arrived in the US in May.

Jethmalani wrote to the Bar Council's vice-chairman from Wayne State University where he was a visiting professor of Comparative Constitutional Law: "I refuse to believe that your conscience is so dulled that you have begun to discover virtues in totalitarianism and tyranny. Do not tell me that you are impressed by the achievements which Mrs Gandhi claims. Both Mussolini and Hitler had much more to show to their nations than she can. . . . I assure you I am doing much more for India's freedom than I could ever have done from inside Mrs Gandhi's prisons. Some day you will know the whole truth. I have no doubt that her tyranny will not last and when the end comes each one of you who either passively acquiesce in the evil or actively support it will be adjudged criminal. The day of reckoning is not far."

Subramaniam Swamy, a Jana Sangh member of the Rajya Sabha was also accused of engaging in anti-government activity and fleeing from justice and the country. A warrant of arrest had been issued against him. His passport had been impounded. His family in Delhi were harassed. The Rajya Sabha voted on 2 September to set up a committee to investigate his case. He would cease to be a member if he absented himself from the House for six months. To retain his membership he appeared, with the connivance of the police, in the House in August but left the country again as mysteriously as he had come in. Later his membership of the Rajya Sabha was terminated.

Swamy's disappearance did give Mrs Gandhi's government a bad name. But it tried to retrieve the ground by indicting on 24 September an underground leader, George Fernandes, along with twenty-four others in a New Delhi magistrate's court on charges of conspiring against the government. The defendants were accused of sending from Baroda (Gujarat) tonnes of dynamite and plotting to "create countrywide chaos through large-scale sabotage of the railway system."

It was really Chimanbhai, a former chief minister, who had given Mrs Gandhi the information about the "Baroda dynamite case" people. He wanted to make up with her because it was she who forced him to resign from chief ministership in 1974.

Mrs Gandhi's reports were that the entire state machinery in Gujarat was slack and suffered from the "hangover" of the Janata Front government. She sent Petroleum and Chemicals Minister P.C. Sethi to report on the situation.

On landing at Ahmedabad airport, Sethi demanded to know why a guard of honour was not arranged for him. The police commissioner hurriedly got together a few policemen on duty for a token guard of honour. Sethi did not approve of this and ordered the dismissal of the police commissioner. After his departure the state authorities who knew the police commissioner to be an outstanding officer did not carry out his dismissal order. But by the time Sethi left for Delhi it was estimated he "dismissed" a few scores of police and other government officers in Ahmedabad and Baroda.

At a meeting organized by the municipal corporation in a labour area of Ahmedabad, Sethi began speaking in English. A Muslim labourer from the audience stood up and suggested that the minister speak in Hindi. Sethi's reaction was, "Why don't you arrest that man. Have I been called to be insulted?" With this he climbed down from the rostrum as Hitendra Desai and Mayor Vadilal Kamdar watched aghast. The mayor tried to explain to Sethi that no insult was meant to him. But like a street-brawler, Sethi pushed aside Ahmedabad's first citizen.

Hitendra Desai, as the PCC chief, was just getting into Sethi's car when he shouted, "Who asked you to come with me? Get lost."

Returning to Delhi, Sethi reported to Mrs Gandhi that there was no emergency in Gujarat. Om Mehta was sent to Ahmedabad and a round of arrests began which the president's advisers did not think was necessary.

A new wave of arrests in Gujarat spread the impression that the emergency was an endless tunnel. Many felt helpless and suffered silently. But Prabhakar Sharma, sixty-five years old, a worker in the Sarvodaya movement and colleague of Vinoba Bhave, immolated himself at Surgaon outside Wardha in Maharashtra on 11 October in protest against Mrs Gandhi's dictatorial methods of government.

Before immolating himself Sharma sent a letter to Mrs Gandhi explaining the reasons for his action. The letter said: "Forgetting God and humanity and arming itself with wide, brutal powers the government last year deprived the newspapers of their freedom of expression and attacked all those qualities of Indian living which can be decent, great and noble. This year it has shamelessly attacked the nation's spiritual and non-violent civilization.

"Your MISA rule transforms the bureaucrats into monsters and makes the people cowards. One who does his duties fearlessly will get interminable imprisonment. There will be no justice. The judges are your stooges. Under these circumstances it would be an acceptance of suppression to go to jail. I shall never tolerate your bullying me like a swine." Quoting Gandhi's *Young India* the letter said: "We must be content to die if we cannot live as free men and women." Sharma added: "I know writing such a letter itself is a sort of crime. Therefore, I do not intend to live under your sinful regime."

Vinoba had vainly sent word to Sharma to meet him. Vinoba, even though sympathetic to Mrs Gandhi, was himself depressed. The police and intelligence had raided his ashram on 9 June and seized 4,200 copies of his Hindi journal, *Maitri*, which carried the announcement that he intended to go on fast on 11 September unless a ban on cow-slaughter was imposed. (The government imposed the ban subsequently.)

The stories of excesses, and the feeling that there was no end of the turmoil, made even those who at one time saw some advantage in the emergency turn against it. They saw no respite from authoritarian rule, nor from the whimsical administration run by a caucus.

Two things alienated the people further—the amendments to the Constitution and yet another postponement of the elections. A nigh-power committee which the Congress had appointed on 27 February 1976 under the chairmanship of Swaran Singh submitted its report which the government adopted more or less in toto. "It would have been worse if I were not there," Swaran Singh told me. "We buried the presidential system once and for all," he said.

The proposed constitutional amendments aroused widespread indignation. Mrs Gandhi gave an assurance that the parliamentary system would not be destroyed and that the Constitution would undergo only "small modifications." But this did not allay fears and there was a demand, particularly from the intelligentsia, that there should be no constitutional amendment till after fresh elections. The Supreme Court Bar Association voiced a similar demand.

Nearly 300 educationists, artists and writers maintained, in a signed petition sent to Mrs Gandhi, that "the present parliament has neither the political nor the moral authority to effect fundamental changes in the Constitution." The non-communist opposition and the CPI(M) refused to have any discussion with the Congress party's committee on constitutional amendments and boycotted the special parliament session convened on 25 October to pass the necessary Bill.

Parliament passed by 366 to 4 the fifty-nine-clause Constitution (42nd Amendment) Bill on 2 November. The Bill, which became an Act after the ratification by half of the state assemblies and the president's assent on 18 December, gave precedence to the directive principles listed in the Constitution over the fundamental rights, enumerated for citizens a set of ten fundamental duties including compulsory national service, raised the term of the Lok Sabha and state assemblies from five to six years, authorized deployment of the central armed forces in any state to deal with a "grave" law and order situation, made the president bound by the advice of the council of ministers, banned "anti-national activity" and gave the president powers for two years to issue orders to remove any difficulty coming in the way of the amendments. It was also laid down that no constitutional amendment could be challenged in any court and that no central or state law could thereafter be declared unconstitutional until a two-thirds majority of at least seven judges had said so. The preamble of the Constitution was changed; the words "Sovereign Democratic Republic" were substituted by "Sovereign Socialist Republic" and "unity of the nation" by "unity and integrity of the nation."

Barooah said that the fundamental right of freedom of expression should be punishable, the "misuse" was to be decided by the government. Some proposed constitutional amendments were dropped at the last minute. Sidhartha wanted that the prime minister need not consult the council of ministers when advising the president.

All those people who had benefited from Mrs Gandhi's regime were pressed into service to justify the amendments. She always did that whenever she faced a problem.

Former Chief Justice of India and chairman of the Law Commission P.B. Gajendragadkar said in defence, "When Indian democracy embarks upon its missions of satisfying the legitimate but expanding hopes and aspirations of citizens and establishing a new social order based on social equality and economic justice, it may have to make suitable laws from time to time to achieve that purpose."

Opposition leader Ashok Mehta deplored that the government was "codifying the state of emergency [imposed in June 1975], giving *force of law* to concentration of power in [Prime Minister Indira] Gandhi's hands."

Most members of the opposition had stayed away when parliament convened on 25 October to consider the constitutional changes. A joint statement issued by four opposition parties said that the amendments would "eliminate the whole system of checks and balances provided in the Constitution and leave the arbitrary exercise of authority to the detriment of the citizen."

Mrs Gandhi lashed out at the opponents of the Bill by saying, during debate, that "those who want to fix the Constitution in a rigid and unalterable frame are entirely out of tune with the spirit of the new India."

There was criticism that what the government had done affected the basic structure of the Constitution—something which parliament, according to a majority Supreme Court judgement, could not do. Mrs Gandhi said that "we do not accept the dogma of the basic structure" of the Constitution which was "invented" by the judges. Pro-government constitutional experts said that the judges had never defined what the basic structure was.

It was really not difficult to list the basic features of the Constitution. Some were so fundamental—free and fair elections, accountability of the government to the people, judicial review exercised through an independent judiciary, rule of law which meant that a person would not be deprived of his life, liberty or property except by due process of law, equality before the law, a free press, secularism which meant freedom of religion and absence of discrimination on the ground of religion, and social justice.

It was not the basic structure of the Constitution which worried Mrs Gandhi or the ones around her. Their worry was that while almost everyone had more or less fallen in line, the judiciary had not. Some judges were still independent, and their judgements, which went against the government, always created a "problem" for the administration. They were an embarrassment; they had to be transferred and this would be a lesson for others.

Sixteen judges were transferred: S. Obal Reddy from Andhra Pradesh to Gujarat; C. Kondiah from Andhra Pradesh to Madhya Pradesh; O. Chinappa Reddy from Andhra Pradesh to Punjab; A.P. Sen from Madhya Pradesh to Rajasthan; C.M. Lodha from Rajasthan to Madhya Pradesh; A.D. Koshal from Punjab to Madras; D.S. Twetia from Punjab to Karnatak; D.B. Lal from Himachal Pradesh to Karnatak; B.J. Divan from Gujarat to Andhra Pradesh; J.M. Sheth from Gujarat to Andhra Pradesh; T.U. Mehta from Gujarat to Himachal Pradesh; D.M. Chandershaker from Karnataka to Allahabad; M. Sadananda Swamy from Karnataka to Gauhati; J.L. Vimadlal from Maharashtra to Andhra Pradesh (Retired); G.I. Rangarajan from Delhi to Gauhati; R. Sachar from Delhi to Rajasthan. Mrs Gandhi herself saw the file of transfers.

Legally, these judges could be transferred but at their annual conference in 1974, the chief justices themselves recommended that the transfer of a judge should be with the consent of the judge concerned. But the transfers were a punishment and hence there was no question of consulting the judges themselves.

Additional Judge J. L. Aggarwal of the Delhi High Court, who had pronounced judgement against the government in my detention case, was reverted as sessions judge. Both Law Minister Gokhale and Chief Justice Ray had recommended that Aggarwal be made permanent. But Mrs Gandhi rejected the suggestion. Om Mehta had told her that Aggarwal, like the transferred judges, had to be punished.

Gokhale told me that Mehta started meddling with the judges when he came to Home. Since the Home secretary was also secretary of the department of justice—transferred to Ministry of Law—Om Mehta could easily influence some decisions.

The transfer of judges did have some effect on the judiciary; judgements began to be more and more tailored in favour of the government. A Gujarat High Court judge challenged his transfer; and that stopped the transfer of forty-four more judges.

With the press and the judiciary "disciplined," Sanjay's mind was busy in finding ways to postpone elections. He came up with a proposal to convene a constituent assembly. And the present parliament could be converted into one. That would justify postponement of elections by two or three years.

Mrs Gandhi gave her oral consent. The Congress committees of Punjab, Haryana and UP passed resolutions that the constituent assembly was necessary to have a "threadbare" discussion on every aspect of the Constitution.

Mrs Gandhi asked Gokhale but he was opposed to the idea. He told her that it would reopen many questions like those of official language, state subjects, etc. and the very federal structure which gave parliament the power to amend the Constitution.

There was a hostile reaction in the country; even the pro-government CPI, opposed the idea. The opposition parties which were in favour of a constituent assembly wanted its members to be elected directly through adult franchise. Their argument was that the present parliament and state legislatures had outlived their life and hence had ceased to be representative of the electorate. The constituent assembly idea was not pursued.

The Lok Sabha extended by one more year its five-year term on 5 November; consequently, general elections, due in March 1976, were now due again it 1978.

There was no Madhu Limaye or Sharad Yadav to have resigned from the Lok Sabha as the two did when the Lok Sabha extended its term earlier. Madhu had written to the speaker, "I am of opinion that the extension of the term of the present Lok Sabha is a thoroughly immoral and unscrupulous act. I am deeply convinced that this government has no right to remain in office beyond 18 March 1976 without obtaining a favourable verdict from the electorate." In a letter to Mrs Gandhi, he had then written, "Well, I say, why stop at detentions? Why not go the whole hog? Why not abandon all republican pretensions and establish a monarchical or imperial constitution to ensure smooth dynastic succession on which your ambition seems to be focused? Perhaps the fascists among the Westerners would be happy to be confirmed in their long-held prejudice that we of the 'inferior races' of Asia and Africa are not worthy to enjoy the blessings of civil liberty and democracy."

The government defended the Lok Sabha extension on the ground that the "gains" of the emergency were yet to be consolidated. The second extension Bill was opposed by almost all opposition parties but it was passed by 180 votes to 34. Mrs Gandhi defended the postponement of elections on the plea that "we must rise above controversies or anything that could create chaotic conditions."

With the elections out of the way, Mrs Gandhi was now thinking of how to make Sanjay fit the large shoes he had started wearing. Already Sanjay was seeing cabinet papers; officials were coming to him for discussions; intelligence reports were being routed to the prime minister through him. (He often kept back information on Shukla's activities because Mrs Gandhi had warned the minister.) Most central ministers were consulting Sanjay or sending their secretaries for that purpose. Education Minister Nurul Hassan once told his secretary to find out Sanjay's views on a particular proposal. The chief ministers and even chief secretaries from the states waited upon him to know his mind.

But this was all *ad hoc*, vulnerable. She must give the whole thing a legal form. It had been suggested that he be brought to parliament, through the Rajya Sabha. But she did not accept this; it would look too obvious.

Probably, the best way for the time being was to strengthen the Youth Congress and defend Sanjay who was now being openly criticized even within the Congress party. Mrs Gandhi's first attack was on the CPI which had criticized Sanjay.

Sanjay made no secret of his dislike for the Communists and

their policies. He said more than once that they had betrayed the national movement in August 1942 by supporting the Soviet Union, the British and other Allied powers during World War II. Irked by the criticism, CPI General Secretary C. Rajeshwar Rao said that there was "a reactionary caucus" in the Congress party.

The reaction in the Congress party, now more loyal than the king, was equally strong and it regarded his statement as an interference in the internal affairs of the Congress. Mrs Gandhi took the same line.

For the first time in many years, she attacked, on 23 December, the CPI by name. She said "the Communists say that they support me but there can be no greater insult than to say that she could be influenced by reactionaries or anybody else." Defending her son, she said, "He is much too small a fry or a person because he is not going to be prime minister or the president or anything like this. All he can be is a Congress worker. Therefore, I think the attack is definitely on me."

Mrs Gandhi developed the same theme of defending Sanjay and his Youth Congress at the Congress annual session at Gauhati on 20 November. She said that the five-point programme, enunciated by Sanjay, was complementary to the twenty-point economic programme of the government and would help change the economic profile of the country. She expressed her faith that the future of India was safe in the hands of the youth who had accepted their responsibilities with a new sense of purpose.

The Gauhati session was really Sanjay's show. One after the other, the delegates praised him. Barooah compared him with Vivekananda, India's sage. Only A. K. Antony, a young, honest Congress chief of Kerala, struck a different note and emphasized that Congressmen must "correct" themselves and stay clean and above party politics.

Despite the chorus of praise for her son and herself, the Gauhati session disturbed Mrs Gandhi. It was "a silent non-cooperation." She noticed cynicism among the Congress delegates. Those very people who had silently accepted the emergency at Chandigarh a year before were now sullen. Mrs Gandhi did not want to be dependent on unwilling supporters. She would rather have a new crop of supporters. The nation was with her, she believed.

There was yet another reason for her wanting to have young

people. She wanted Sanjay to be established in his own right. Only the new and the young would be beholden to him.

Some day, when she quit the prime ministership, probably to become the Congress president, Sanjay should have enough strength in the party to succeed her. Most chief ministers were already his supporters—Mishra in Bihar, Tewari in UP, Zail Singh in Punjab, Banarsi Das Gupta in Haryana, Joshi in Rajasthan, Shukla in Madhya Pradesh, Vengal Rao in Andhra Pradesh, S.B. Chavan in Maharashtra and Madhavsinh Solanki in Gujarat.

The three chief ministers who were not "loyal" to Sanjay were Nandini Satpathy of Orissa, Sidhartha Shankar Ray of West Bengal and Devraj Urs of Karnataka. The first two were in fact considered hostile; Sanjay also did not like them because he thought they were communists.

Mrs Gandhi had them in mind when she said at Gauhati, "Just as each central minister has his own empire, we find the chief ministers also have their own empires and they are unmindful of whether their empire collides with other empires."

They had to be cut to size by depriving them of their empires. Nandini was first on the list. Akbar Ali, the state governor, who praised JP and had to quit, had written several letters to Mrs Gandhi accusing the chief minister of corruption and maladministration. He drew the prime minister's attention to a house she had built in Bhubaneswar at a cost for Rs 700,000. Akbar Ali alleged that PWD engineers supervised the building and that a lot of government material was used.

Through Vinayak Acharya, a minister in her cabinet, Sanjay had already prepared the ground to topple her. There were complaints that her son was playing havoc with the administration and Sanjay never liked him. Also, reports increased that Nandini was not paying full attention to administration and to the situation demanded by the drought in the state.

Some people told Nandini that Mrs Gandhi was against her but she did not rely on these reports. She did not want to because she had been loyal to Mrs Gandhi.

A.R. Antulay, general secretary of the AICC, who visited Orissa to make Nandini resign, said, "It is the sole democratic prerogative of Mrs Indira Gandhi, the supreme leader to decide who is loyal or not, loyalty is not divisible."

And Mrs Gandhi did not have the courage to tell Nandini

when the latter flew to Delhi to explain the situation in the state. The moment Nandini returned to the state capital and went on a brief holiday she was asked telegraphically to resign. And Nandini, even though she enjoyed the majority in the house, had to resign, on 16 December.

The loyalty of West Bengal's Sidhartha Ray to Sanjay was in doubt, in spite of the fact that he had tried in the past to make up with him by promising him at a business chamber's function his loyalty and by reminding him that he was the friend of the family. He had escaped by the skin of his teeth by playing one Congress group against the other—the basis of his strength from the very first day in the state as chief minister. Both Mrs Gandhi and Sanjay had him on their list of people who had to be removed. But Sidhartha again manoeuvred to play one group against another. He consolidated his position in West Bengal by parading his ability to defy New Delhi—a trait applauded by Bengalis.

Ray's group openly accused the Nehru family of never allowing Bengal leaders to come up the hard way. The anti-Ray group accused Ray of trying to stage a Bangladesh in West Bengal.

Ray privately said that the centre might try to stage communal riots or other types of civil disturbances to brand him as a failure. He argued that communal riots were staged in Ahmedabad in 1969 to ease out Hitendra Desai; the police revolt was engineered in UP to force out Tripathi; and now it was his turn.

Mrs Gandhi did not push out Ray, nor did she want to touch Dev Raj Urs. By this time, her mind had started working in some other direction.

If Sanjay was to be propped up and groomed to become the prime minister one day, the loyalty of chief ministers was not enough. Mrs Gandhi thought in terms of MPs who would have no qualms about the emergency and who would not differentiate between her and Sanjay.

Both the intelligence bureau and RAW had estimated that she would get more than 350 seats if she were to go to the polls immediately. Only CBI Director D. Sen whom she used to raid critics' houses, had struck a discordant note; he had emphasized that there should be a gap of six months between the release of detenus and elections so as to allow time for the halo around them to fade.

Mrs Gandhi's own Secretary Dhar was all for elections because this was the only way he could eliminate the disadvantages of the emergency? It might be easy to ride a tiger, but it was well-nigh impossible to get off from it. How did one do that? Dhar was also confident that the emergency had begun to be counter-productive and that economic problems would surface again.

The twenty-point programme had yielded a few results. Man-days lost between July 1975 and December 1975 were 4.5 million against 40.3 million in 1974; in the public sector, man-days lost before the emergency were 1.62 million and during the emergency 120,000. The rate of inflation in 1975-76 was 3.3 per cent against 23.4 per cent in 1974-75.

However, the reports of the failure of winter rains painted a grim picture of agriculture which affected the economy. (At this time the government decided to import 4.2 million tonnes of grain, part of which the European Economic Community and the US "Food for Peace" programme had supplied.) Labour was becoming restive and the old tempo of production was slowing down.

Reports were that the emergency and the extra-constitutional authority of Sanjay were openly discussed in military messes, particularly by junior officers. The jawans talked about the excesses committed through the family planning programme.

There were also commendable references to Bhutto for having announced elections[5] in Pakistan. And if Mrs Gandhi did not announce them, she would be attacked as not being democratic.

Then also, there was so much fear that it would deter voters from going to the polling booths to exercise their franchise. The emergency would only be relaxed, not lifted, and she would see to it that the cadre of the opposition parties would be released last.

The opposition parties were also far from united. No doubt, they had agreed on 16-17 December to form a single party, the Bhartiya Janata Congress, and had adopted their provisional collective symbol with wheel, plough and charkha embossed on it. But there was still the question of leadership. Mrs Gandhi thought it would be an insoluble problem.

In fact, the opposition parties wanted to hold discussions with

[5]When elections were announced by New Delhi, Bhutto said that the people in India should thank him.

her. They had adapted to Karunanidhi's suggestion of 15 December to open a dialogue with the prime minister and to find a way out to normalize the political situation in the country. JP also had welcomed the unanimous initiative to have a dialogue with the prime minister. The opposition parties had issued a statement, captioned "This we Believe," to underline their faith in nonviolence, secularism and the democratic way.

On the other hand, foreign criticism irked her; the West thought that she was an "illegal" ruler. She had to counter that. She chose France and arranged a trip in May to "talk" to the West from a Western country. By then she would have proved it to them that the people were behind her and what she did. It was not a question of legitimacy; she must prove that her hold over the masses was unquestioned.

These might seem good reasons on paper but they did not constitute practical politics according to both Sanjay and Bansi Lal. They were strongly opposed to the elections. Sanjay thought it was a "fuzzy idea" planted by the communists in his mother's mind. He was not very wrong because Barooah was in favour of elections.

Mrs Gandhi thought that Sanjay, Bansi Lal and others were unnecessarily concerned. The Constitution had been so amended that the emergency had been more or less institutionalized; parliament had accepted some months back, on 2 February, permanent press censorship after the lifting of the emergency. The judiciary, after the transfer of some judges, was beginning to face realities; and, in any case, Gokhale was working on a constitutional amendment to give the government the authority to dismiss a judge, instead of by a two-thirds majority of both Houses of parliament voting a motion of impeachment.

Sanjay's, opposition did make Mrs Gandhi ponder the point again. She talked to visiting chief ministers who dared not say that they could not win the elections. If the choice was between now and a year later, they thought it was better to hold them now; later they might have to make greater efforts to keep "discipline."

She also knew that the underground had come to be a force to be reckoned with. Their leaders talked over the telephone almost every day—sometimes on international lines—using codes and false names. When vulnerable urban printing presses were confiscated, clandestine newspapers were duplicated.

She asked the intelligence people to make another assessment of the mood of the people and they came to the same conclusion as earlier—that she would win comfortably. This time the seats given to her were 320, 30 less than before. Sanjay was still opposed to elections but she had made up her mind.

She also consulted many MPs but no one was in favour of going back to his constituency; the emergency had tainted their reputation. What weighed with her most was a study, by the Institute of Policy Research in New Delhi, which Dhar had brought to Mrs Gandhi's notice. The study showed that public opinion in Mrs Gandhi's favour had reached its apogee now. This looked like her best chance.

How wrong did she prove! All her timings in the past had been perfect but now her calculations were beginning to go wrong, for she had lost contact with the people. All that she had for information were intelligence reports doctored to her wishes. Sychophants around her would go on telling her that the emergency had done wonders and that the people had never been so happy before.

It was the intelligence men whom she first informed that she would hold elections in late March or early April and that they should be "prepared." She thought she was not taking any risk because she knew she would win.

Whatever Mrs Gandhi's compulsions, by deciding to go to the polls, she conceded that no system could work without the consent and concurrence of the people. In a way she paid tribute to their patience and suffering. Because they were the ones who finally won —the illiterate, the poor and the backward had won.

4. The Judgement

On 18 January 1977, Morarji had risen early as was his habit. He went for his morning walk, his daily routine for the past many months. It appeared like any other day.

Though a dull routine, it was better than what it had been when he was first detained at Sona. Then he was confined to a small, dark room, with closed windows. Following protests, he was allowed to walk around the compound after nightfall. Because of snakes and scorpions in the compound he decided to walk around his cot for exercise. He was literally kept in the dark and had no idea of what was going on outside. He had no access even to newspapers.

Only when he was shifted to a canal guest house, not far from Sona, was he allowed newspapers, and later interviews. That day, 18 January, he had seen a news item in the *Indian Express* that elections to the Lok Sabha might be held by the end of March. He did not believe it; he had his own doubts.

He looked up without interest when some senior policemen entered his sparsely-furnished room. They told him that he was being released unconditionally and that they would take him to his house in Dupleix Road. They had brought a car along.

By now the opposition leaders and most others had been released. The one-time figure of more than 100,000 detenus had come down to nearly 10,000.

On arriving at his house Morarji heard that Mrs Gandhi had decided to dissolve the Lok Sabha and have fresh elections. He was not surprised. "I always knew that she would release me only when she wanted to go to the polls," he told me later.

But there were others who were surprised. These included several cabinet ministers. They came to know of the decision only that afternoon when they were hurriedly summoned and informed about it. Mrs Gandhi told them that in a democratic system the government had to face the electorate periodically. She admitted that she had taken a risk.

No minister said anything. Bansi Lal, who knew of it earlier, was visibly disturbed; Jagjivan Ram and Chavan kept quiet. They had not been consulted about the elections, just as they had not been consulted about the imposition of the emergency. But they, like other ministers, suspected that they were coming after Sanjay had particularly told a public meeting in Bombay two days earlier that elections might be held shortly. Over the period, they had come to accept the fact that Sanjay knew best.

What they did not know was that most of them had been written off. Everyone in Mrs Gandhi's house said that Jagjivan Ram should not be made a minister after the elections. Sanjay had his own views on who should be in parliament and who should not. By then he had even a list of who were to be given the Congress ticket—and most of the sitting members of parliament were not in it. It would be futile for them to rebel and stand on their own.

Although the Congress party high command went through the motions and directed its state units to prepare their lists of candidates, most people soon knew it was only an eyewash. Sanjay had finalized most of the names and Mrs Gandhi had as usual approved what he had decided.

The opposition parties were happy over the elections but they knew they were at a terrible disadvantage. Their leaders had all been in jail til' a few days previously and were out of touch with the people; many of their workers were not yet released. They were pressed for time.

But they did not want to lose more time. The Congress (O), Jana Sangh, BLD and Socialist leaders met at Morarji's residence the day he was released. The discussion was exploratory. They again met the following day, by which time Mrs Gandhi had told the nation in a broadcast about the elections and the opportunity to "reaffirm the power of the people."

The opposition leaders had before them a JP letter which S. M. Joshi, a Socialist leader, had brought from Patna. JP had said that if they did not become one party he would dissociate himself from the elections. H: had telephoned a similar message earlier.

The problem before the opposition parties was not that of merger; their leaders had discussed and rediscussed this in jail and had come to the conclusion that one party was the only answer to the Congress juggernaut. The opposition leaders had felt the same way in their separate and collective discussions. In fact, Charan Singh was so disgusted with the merger talks that he had written as far back as 14 July 1976 to Ashok Mehta, the Congress (O) president that the BLD "is now fed up; even its motives have been doubted. So, it has decided to go it alone, free from the thought of any duty in this regard—except one, viz. if and when the three parties dissolve or decide to dissolve themselves in order to form an organization based, by and large, on the programmes broadly indicated by the Father of the Nation, the BLD will make haste to join."

What had really stalled the merger was the question: Who should be the leader? In the opposition leaders' meeting on 16 December, when Morarji was still in jail, Charan Singh looked like heading the party. Morarji had written from his place of detention that he was interested in merger, not leadership.

However, the way Morarji handled the discussions at the opposition leaders' meeting now, after the announcement of the poll, there was no doubting about the leadership. The parties agreed to have him as the chairman and Charan Singh as deputy chairman.

The mere instinct to survive had forced the four parties to come together and constitute an electoral party, a joint front—the Janata party, with one symbol for the election, and one flag. It was not possible to dissolve their individual entities without holding separate meetings of the parties; but that would take time and they had no time to lose. They knew that if they lost heavily, Mrs Gandhi and her son would take it as the people's mandate for dictatorship. But if they could get enough of their men returned to form a substantial group in parliament, she might not be able to claim a convincing mandate.

By joining hands they would ensure that the opposition vote would not be divided; earlier, it was the division that had made the Congress win although it had always polled less than 50 per cent of the votes and, even when it swept the polls in 1971, the percentage was only 46.2.

JP blessed the merger and put the choice before the people in simple terms; it was between democracy and dictatorship, between freedom and slavery. He said that a victory for Mrs

Gandhi would mean a victory for dictatorship. And this was what the Joint Front emphasized—not economic problems.

Mrs Gandhi told the people that her decision to hold elections clearly disproved the charge that she was a dictator. It was the opposition parties which had now formed a party of "obscurantist forces" that were responsible for the elections being postponed in the first place—they had created chaotic conditions to make her postpone the poll.

The opposition parties did not join issue with her on this point. They formally launched on 23 January the Janata party. A twenty-seven member national committee, the top decision making body, was constituted. JP had to work hard to bring about the several parties[1] with their conflicting interests and ideologies together; individual leaders had to be persuaded to sink their personal differences in the interest of the nation.

The opposition parties needed the men to carry the message to the people. But their most active workers were still in jail. The leaders met Om Mehta and later Mrs Gandhi to press for the early release of detenus. Both promised that they would be freed, but instructions sent to the states made it clear that they were not to act in haste—there was no general amnesty and each case must be considered separately; decisions should be referred to the centre before they were acted upon. The purpose was to keep as many opposition workers in jail as long as it was possible without seeming to be indulging in unfair election practices.

The relaxation of the emergency and press censorship was also halfhearted. The sword might have been lowered, but the government wanted to make it clear that it had not been sheathed; it should be seen and feared. And seen and feared it was, at least for a time. There was still such terror that the Jana Sangh went to the extent of saying that it might boycott the elections if the emergency was not withdrawn, detenus released and press censorship completely lifted.

There was endless discussions at Mrs Gandhi's house on the emergency and press censorship. Everyone was agreed that there was no question of lifting them; during the election they were

---

[1]The original idea of combining the regional parties into a single electoral party was that of Rajinder Puri, the renowned cartoonist, who initially became one of the general secretaries of the Janata party,

certain to inhibit a big turnout, not good for the Congress, and the press from open criticism. And after the election, which the Congress was sure to win, they could be reimposed quickly. Scrapping them now would mean that the whole rigmarole of debate and voting in the two Houses of parliament and approval by the president would have to be gone through again before they could be brought into force once more.

The relaxation of press censorship did not mean that the newspapers were free to publish anything they liked; there was always the Damocles' sword of the Publication of Objectionable Matter Act hanging. Shukla did not dismantle the censorship apparatus; the officers concerned were told to go round the country to meet editors and warn them that they had better behave. Most papers did "behave."

At the first press conference he had addressed at Morarji's house on arrival from Patna, JP felt that the Congress was bound to win, not because it was popular, but because the opposition parties had been given so little time to reorganize their cadre, raise funds and tell the people what was at stake. No doubt, JP's dream of having a viable alternative party to the Congress in the country appeared to have come true. But he was not confident of its success at the hustings.

The Janata party sent out feelers to the Akalis in Punjab and found them willing to join hands with it. The CPI(M) said that they would not join the new party but they would have an electoral alliance because without civil liberties no economic programme was possible.

This was the line Chandra Shekhar was taking while talking to the Congress partymen, once his colleagues, the Marxists and others. In a letter he said, "The option is very limited to join the (Congress) bandwagon and claim small personal gains and live in one's make-believe world, to remain silent observers to whatever is happening in society, or to choose to fight along with the forces which have made the basic freedom and civic rights an article of faith."

The DMK expressed its willingness to have an adjustment with the Congress (O) in Tamil Nadu. But all parties wanted to contest on their own election symbol, not the BLD's—a man with a plough on his shoulders, within a wheel—that Janata adopted because of the Election Commission's refusal to give it a new symbol.

The Congress also looked for allies and found them in the CPI and in the ADMK in Tamil Nadu. Sanjay did not want to have anything to do with the CPI, against which he had launched a campaign in the newspapers through Samachar, directed by Yunus, only a little earlier. But Mrs Gandhi reassured him that the alliance would be only on Congress terms.

The CPI cadres would be of some help, even if no help was actually needed, for the Congress party was sure of a victory. The fear instilled in the minds of the people over twenty months could not be shaken off in two or three; they would vote as they were directed to, for retribution would not be long in coming for those who turned against the party which controlled all the government apparatus.

But soon there were reports that were disquieting for the Congress. People were beginning to shed fear, they were talking against the emergency and did not mind being singled out. The crowds' mood against the Congress was clear from the response to the Janata's campaign launched on 30 January, Mahatma Gandhi's martyrdom day. There were mammoth rallies, much beyond the expectations of even the Janata leaders, in Delhi, Patna, Jaipur, Kanpur and many other places. The authorities were equally surprised by the response.

In Delhi the rally drew more than 100,000 people while officials had expected only 10,000 or at the most 20,000 to turn up. Morarji addressed it. The rally was on the same Ramlila grounds where, on 25 June 1975, only a few hours before the leaders were arrested and the emergency declared, JP had addressed another large crowd. That was in summer; now on a wet chilly January evening people listened to the leaders of the Janata party in pindrop silence and later many queued up to contribute money to the Janata election fund.

In Patna, JP administered a pledge to a vast crowd—to consider no sacrifice too great to defend the fundamental rights and civil liberties of citizens. This was his first public meeting after the Delhi meeting in June, and he broke down on seeing thousands of hands raised to take the pledge.

Charan Singh initiated the Janata campaign in Kanpur and Chandra Shekhar at Jaipur. The crowds were abnormally large. Intelligence reports reaching Mrs Gandhi the following morning did not make good reading. She was disturbed, though the reports tended to play down the significance of the vast crowds attending these rallies—it was natural that after the terrible months of emergency, when the only large meetings allowed were those to hail Sanjay Gandhi, people should have such "outings." She suggested that counter-rallies be held.

She also thought that the "old fogeys" in her party were losing their grip on their constituencies. It was time they were dropped, most of the MPs she knew were with her more out of fear than out of loyalty. This would also help Sanjay in politics because he would then have his own dependable men. The Youth Congress publicly said that it expected 150 to 200 seats to be allocated to its members. Ambika Soni said that the Youth Congress was the real Congress.

Mrs Gandhi indicated that she should be free to choose the candidates herself. One by one, the state Congress committees and their parliamentary boards unanimously passed resolutions to authorize the prime minister to select candidates on their behalf.

Sanjay began preparing the lists. More candidates queued outside his door or of those who had access to him than even the prime minister's. He consulted the intelligence bureau to determine each candidate's hold in his area—it also gave him access to much information to have a firm hold on these men. On an average there were 200 aspirants for each of the 542 seats.

Sanjay processed Haryana's list which Bansi Lal had prepared. Maharashtra's list was also announced. Everything seemed to be going according to Sanjay's plan.

And then the bottom fell out of the grand design. There was a political explosion. Jagjivan Ram resigned from the Congress and the government on 2 February. Nobody in the Congress was prepared for this.

Three days earlier, the intelligence bureau had passed on the rumour to Om Mehta that Jagjivan Ram was planning to revolt. But this was not taken seriously. Jagjivan Ram had himself met Mrs Gandhi a day before but had not mentioned anything. All that he told Mrs Gandhi was that he was against the continuation of the emergency. Subsequently, he told his friends that if he had said anything about quitting the party, he would have been arrested.

In the sprawling lawn of his residence, Jagjivan Ram told a crowded press conference on the day of his resignation that he wanted all Congressmen to join him to seek an end to the emergency and other "totalitarian and authoritarian trends that have of late crept into the nation's politics." He said that democracy inside the Congress organization at all levels had been not only abridged but also almost abolished. "Indiscipline within the Congress, both in the organizational and parliamentary wings, has not only been tolerated but instigated and encouraged from above."

H. N. Bahuguna, who had been forced out of UP's chief ministership, and Nandini out of Orissa's chief ministership sat on each side of Jagjivan Ram. They too announced that they had left the Congress party and so did K.R. Ganesh, former cabinet minister. All of them said, "We are not a new Congress. We continue to be the old Congress party." These were more or less the words which Mrs Gandhi and her supporters had used in December 1967 when they constituted a separate Congress party.

When I asked Jagjivan Ram why he resigned, he said that it was the result of many things that had happened over the months, they had had a "cumulative effect." He added, "I was under strain." For long Mrs Gandhi and her son had done everything that he disliked and he couldn't continue to be with them.

Probably true, but Chandra Shekhar and Bahuguna had spent many days trying to persuade him to take the plunge. It looked as if the Janata party's opening election rally in Delhi had confirmed his view that the people would throw out the Congress from many states.

While newspapers brought out special supplements to announce the news (though not the "committed" newspapers), Congressmen burst into a tirade against Jagjivan Ram and those who went out with him.

The Congress party's working committee unanimously passed a resolution condemning Jagjivan Ram's exit. Barooah characterized it as "one individual" defection. Mrs Gandhi said it was strange that he should have remained silent all these months; official information media, including Samachar, termed the resignation as defection.

The Congress leaders put up a brave front. Mrs Gandhi was deeply perturbed. For years she had been springing surprises on her colleagues; this time Jagjivan Ram had given her the shock of her life. While announcing the elections she had known that non-communist parties might form an alliance, but Jagjivan Ram's departure from her side was a terrible blow. His Congress for Democracy (CFD) could pull out all discontented men from her party, and she knew there were many.

She had reports that a number of her partymen had been unhappy with all that went on in the name of the emergency and the overbearing posture of her son and his Youth Congress. Fear and lack of an alternative forum had kept them in the party. She was afraid that many would follow Jagjivan Ram. Any sitting member not given the party ticket for the election would find that reason enough.

She could not longer afford to give up the "old fogeys." She had to depend on known and tried people. Sanjay Gandhi's lists had to be scrapped. The Youth Congress was the first casualty of Jagjivan Ram's exist. Most sitting members of the Congress party got the party ticket. "Stay with the old" became the slogan. And the joke going the rounds was that they all kept a portrait of Jagjivan Ram in their houses to bow to in fervent gratitude.

There was now a marked effort to placate the influential members lest they should leave the party. Typical was the story of how Sidhartha, once in the doghouse, staged a comeback. His list of candidates was not acceptable to his colleagues in the state cabinet or the state Congress. But he had his way by his threat that if he could not decide about the candidates, he would rather not continue as chief minister.

Jagjivan Ram's attack on "bossism" in the party also irked the Congress high command. Now every endeavour was being made to prove that the charge was wrong. Once again there was at least the semblance of discussion and consultation in the party. Persons like Chavan, Subramaniam and Swaran Singh were back in demand.

After the release of every list of candidates, the Congress spokesman would go out of his way to underline that it was the central election committee which had made the selection. One day the AICC secretariat hurriedly convened a meeting of local journalists to tell them that it was wrong to say that the selection of candidates had been left to the prime minister as reports from the states suggested.

The exit of Jagjivan Ram also affected the Congress collection of funds. Suddenly, the ruling party felt the pinch because most of the persons approached were not "available" and it was said that they had gone "abroad."

In a way, the Congress was sitting pretty. The party's souvenirs had collected Rs 300 million; all leading industrialists and businessmen had advertized in them. Another Rs 200 million had come from unaccounted cash contributions from private companies and businessmen. Both cheques for advertisements and cash contributions were delivered either to P.C. Sethi, or at 1 Safdarjang Road, Mrs Gandhi's residence.

The collection of advertisements was facilitated by a circular that T.P. Jhunjhunwala, secretary, Central Board of Direct Taxes, sent on 16 July 1976 (No. 203) to all commissioners of income tax with copies to chambers of commerce. The circular said, "A question has been raised as to whether an assessee can resort to publicity in more than one souvenir published by the same institution/organization. A businessman can advertize in more than one newspaper or magazine and also in more than one issue of the same newspaper or magazine. Expenditure on such advertisements will qualify for deduction. . . ."

For the first time, in 1973, the Congress party hit upon the idea of collecting funds in a big way through overpriced advertisements in souvenirs. This circumvented the law which prohibits political contributions from companies. The scheme was devised by Yashpal Kapoor and Dhavan. The interesting thing about the souvenirs was that no one ever got to see them except the advertizers themselves to whom voucher copies were sent to provide a legal facade.

The Congress thought that its resources would make up for the deficiency in popularity. The party had itself seen how the money bags were routed in 1971 against Mrs Gandhi's slogan: "*Garibi Hatao.*" Now the Congress had no choice but to use money to win people over. Sethi, the party's treasurer, opened his office at 2 Kaushik Road, New Delhi, where Justice Rangarajan was staying before the government transferred him to Gauhati. Sethi gave Rs 100,000 to every candidate, in addition to two jeeps.

The Janata party, on the other hand, unmindful of the lack of funds and depending on the election coupons which the party issued, plunged into the election campaign. CFD also lent it its voice—JP had brought them together to contest under one flag and with one poll symbol.

The Shahi Imam of Jama Masjid, Maulana Sayyed Abdullah Bukhari, who was quite popular among the Muslims, also threw his weight behind the opposition.

But the greatest boost to Janata-CFD morale came on 12 February from Mrs Vijayalakshmi Pandit, Nehru's sister and Mrs Gandhi's aunt, who threw in her lot against her niece. She said, "Democratic institutions which we had built up through the years of independence were smothered and destroyed one after another. The rule of law was undermined and the independence of the judiciary ended. Press censorship was imposed." She emphasized that the vital need of the hour was to put democracy back on the rails. "Erosion of our cherished values must be stopped and we must go back to the ideals to which we are pledged."

Indeed, for some time, there had been a gradual estrangement between Mrs Gandhi and Mrs Pandit and her family. Mrs Pandit had once to go to Mrs Gandhi to ask permission to travel abroad. Tara, Mrs Pandit's daughter, told me not long ago, "At one time even our dog was welcome at *Mamu's* (maternal uncle Nehru's) house; now even we are not welcome there."

Mrs Gandhi was disturbed by these developments. Though intelligence reports said that the Congress party would win, the estimate of the number of seats it was likely to get had dropped considerably. The reports also said that the intelligentsia had been further alienated by the supersession of Justice H.L. Khanna; M.H. Beg, junior to him, had been promoted as the Chief Justice of India. Gokhale told me that he tried to persuade Mrs Gandhi not to supersede Khanna but she didn't listen to him. Khanna paid the price for giving a dissenting judgement in the MISA case.

Since things were not going in favour of the Congress, rumours started that the elections would be postponed. The rumours were so strong that to set them at rest a notification announcing the dates for the elections had to be issued—they were to be held from 16 to 20 March.

Mrs Gandhi still thought that the Congress would scrape through with 280 seats; so did the intelligence departments. But she was beginning to see the danger. In her speeches she began to harp on internal and external threats to the country. The opposition groups, she said, were again trying to create instability—a theme with an ominous ring. She defended the emergency because of which, she said, the country had "progressed" in all fields, but the sullen attitude of the masses and the sparsely attended meetings made her take a defensive posture: "No doubt sometimes mistakes have been committed and for this we have taken action by suspending the officials responsible for them."

It was not one mistake; it was a series of them. The people had lost faith in her. So much so that when Fakhruddin Ali Ahmed died of a heart attack on 11 February 1977, there was a rumour that Mrs Gandhi had gone to his residence at 2 A.M., and that her pressure to make him sign an ordinance to bar MISA detenus from contesting the elections was responsible for the fatal heart attack. I checked with Mrs Ahmed who said that Mrs Gandhi never came to the house that night; the security men attached to the prime minister also confirmed that. However, Mrs Gandhi did ring up Mr Ahmed that night. She also denied, without provocation, that there were differences between her and the president.

Lack of faith in her was bad enough, but worse was the impression that she wanted Sanjay to be the prime minister. Even though she said that he had no "political ambitions," people thought otherwise, suspicions were confirmed when she nominated Sanjay as the Congress candidate from the Amethi constituency, next to her own, Rae Bareli. Thus, in addition to the slogan against her "Dictatorship *v.* Democracy" another was coined: "Dynasty *v.* Democracy."

In fact, during the entire election campaign Mrs Gandhi had to face the charge of authoritarianism. First she ignored the charge but when it was repeatedly voiced she said that "the Congress had not been a one-person party." She said, "I regard myself as the foremost *sevika* (servant) of the people and nothing else." But the charge of authoritarianism got stuck to her and the opposition party went on plugging the same point. She would say that the opposition had only a one-point programme, namely, to remove her. This was what she had said in the 1971 mid-term elections and had won a two-thirds majority in the Lok Sabha. But now

her credibility was zero and her performance in the economic
field hardly better.

The 500-word manifesto, which Mrs Gandhi released herself
said that the party's destination was socialism and that it would
step up its "war against poverty, disparities and social injustice."

The thrust of the Janata party manifesto was on the use of
Gandhian principles and policies to restructure the economy so
that the attention was focused on agriculture, unemployment and
decentralization of economic and political power. The CIP's
manifesto said that the party would "defend and extend"
democracy to create stable conditions for economic development.
The CFD said that it stood for the "commanding heights" of the
public sector and curbs on the monopoly houses, supply of all
essential commodities at fixed and stable prices within the reach
of the common man, full participation of workers at all stages of
industry, completion of land reforms within the shortest possible
time and so on.

But the manifestos never came to be discussed at the election
rallies. The parties seldom referred to them. Only two slogans
reverberated. The opposition would say that the choice was
between "dictatorship and democracy," while the Congress had
"democracy *v*. chaos."

The two sides also indulged in personal attacks. Mrs Gandhi
said that the opposition wanted "to encircle and stab me,"
Morarji replied "we have been stabbed too." Jagjivan Ram said
that the democratic functioning of the government and the
Congress was abridged. Chavan riposted that there were leaders
who failed to keep pace with the rank and file; such people
deserved to be ignored.

In this atmosphere of mutual recriminations, economic issues,
for that matter, all other issues, receded into the background.
Whatever the type of election campaign, elections looked like
being held for the first time in the country. Most seats had two
opponents: the Congress and the opposition. The Congress fielded
candidates for 492 seats and left 50 to its supporters—the CPI in
Kerala, Tamil Nadu and West Bengal, and the ADMK in Tamil
Nadu. The Janata party put up 391 candidates and left 147 seats
to the CFD, CPI(M), the Akali Dal in Punjab and the DMK in
Tamil Nadu.

In the 1967 elections, the Congress party polled 40.7 per cent votes and won 283 seats. A 3 per cent increase in 1971—43.6—gave the party 350, a two-thirds majority in the Lok Sabha. This time the opposition hoped to pull these votes so as to defeat the Congress.

On top of it, there was no Indira wave. In fact it was the other way round; the repressive rule since the imposition of the emergency in June 1975 had given the government a bad name. True, the people in villages did not understand the subtle difference between "bread and liberty" and "bread before liberty." But they were annoyed at the way some of the government programmes, particularly family planning, had been implemented. The policeman had wielded his stick in villages too often and too indiscriminately.

Intelligence reports received by the Home Ministry said that junior police officers were extorting money from villagers on the threat that if they did not pay they would be detained under MISA. The inhabitants of hundreds of villages, who spent nights in the fields or jungles to avoid the family planning teams, also "bought" the police to escape detection.

Mrs Gandhi tried to correct the impression while initiating the election campaign in Delhi. She conceded that her government had made mistakes in the implementation of the family planning programme and in the resettlement of slum dwellers at new places. But there were boos and derisive laughter in reply.

Respect for her word appeared to have taken a back seat. No doubt, she addressed twenty meetings a day for about a month—and she was the only one to draw some crowds because even leaders like Chavan could count the audience on their fingertips—but the impact was very little.

I covered her campaign at Phulpur, Allahabad. The prime minister arrived by helicopter to speak to a crowd which was far less than the one she had addressed at the same place during the UP assembly elections in 1974. Apparently the organizers who laid on transport for the crowd to reach the meeting place from Allahabad, a distance of forty kilometres, and from nearby places expected a bigger gathering, but many of the barricaded sections of the ground were empty and even the response to the slogans, raised from the fifteen-metre high platform, was feeble.

Mrs Gandhi's fifteen minute speech was laced with personal references: "We the Nehrus have a long history of sacrifices," she said. "My grandfather built a house, Swaraj Bhavan, which my father donated to the nation. Then we built another house, Anand Bhavan, which I bequeathed to the people. We do not want anything for ourselves. We want to serve the country even when some people are against us. Our family will continue to do so in the future."

Another personal note Mrs Gandhi struck was, "send those people to parliament who will support me and not stab me in the back."

The prime minister reiterated that the charge of her being a dictator was malicious because if she were one, there would not have been any elections, nor would have the opposition been allowed to say what it had been saying these days.

Long after Mrs Gandhi's speech was over the crowd stayed on till her helicopter, an amusing contraption in that part of India, flew away.

In comparison, even local leaders of the Janata or the CFD drew bigger crowds. People would wait for hours, often past midnight, just to hear them. People would not mind if the leaders came late because of other meetings and the delays that car or train travel could entail. Organizations supporting the opposition budded overnight; there was instant response to the call for volunteers and funds. The mood, at least in the Indo-Gangetic plain was reminiscent of the days before independence. At that time whatever the Congress said was carried out enthusiastically; now it was the Janata's clarion call that the people obeyed.

Any candidate that the Janata put up—at least in UP, Bihar, Punjab, Haryana, Rajasthan and Madhya Pradesh—was as good as elected; it was jocularly said that even a lamp-post on a Janata ticket would get elected. A candidate's merit or popularity did not matter; what counted was that he represented the Janata or its allies.

The Janata wave soon gathered force. People's anger over the nineteen months of authoriatarian rule made them a determined lot. Even the numerous admissions by government leaders that some mistakes had been committed did not mollify the people. It appeared that even before the elections were announced, they had made up their mind about whom to vote in.

Opposition leaders fanned the people's anger by telling them what they individually in jail and the nation collectively had gone through during the emergency. Instances of forced sterilization, slum clearance and tortures surfaced day by day. The newspapers which had by and large come to support the government and the emergency now vied with one another to highlight the horrors of the emergency. People wanted to ensure that "those frightful days" would not return and they could do so only by defeating the Congress.

The intelligence branch and civil servants, who in the past had shunned the opposition because it presented no alternative, went all out to oppose the Congress. The argument that the opposition was a motley crowd did not cut much ice. Even instability was preferable to the "stability" that the ruling party provided. The suffocation and denial of freedom gave birth only to robots. And they did not want to be automatons.

Indeed, things looked bad for the Congress. The Palace sent a message to chief ministers to announce concessions to win over the people. The chief ministers were too willing to empty the treasuries, most of which were in any case running on overdrafts from the Reserve Bank. The states distributed Rs 2,500 million in various forms—land revenue and agriculture income tax were lowered, irrigation levies cut, power rates reduced, house rent exemptions granted, and additional dearness allowance and rent and medical facilities were offered.

Apparently these concessions did not have any impact. Intelligence reports said that the best talking point that the opposition had was the emergency. Mrs Gandhi convened a cabinet meeting a few days before polling to discuss the pros and cons of lifting the emergency. The consensus was against it. Its removal might be misconstrued as a feather in the opposition's cap. In any case, even if it were lifted, many thought it was too late to get any advantage out of the act.

It was not the emergency alone that the people disliked; it was Sanjay they detested much more, it was Bansi Lal and in many ways it was Mrs Gandhi herself. She felt despondent but not defeated.

Most people thought, newspapermen were no exception, that the poll would be a very close race, with Mrs Gandhi's party having a slight edge over the opposition. It was difficult for anyone to imagine that Nehru's daughter, or for that matter the Congress which had been in power since independence, could be defeated.

Indeed this was the impression in the West. Though small Scandanavian countries did not lose hope in the Indian people reaffirming the faith 'n democracy, bigger nations were on Mrs Gandhi's side. At one time, West Germany had warned India that if ever any German correspondent was expelled from New Delhi, it would cut off aid. Now West Germany had changed; its envoy in New Delhi was convinced that Mrs Gandhi was the ideal leader for India. Privately he rationalized that if all Western countries were to turn against her, she would go over to the Soviet side.

The British High Commissioner Michael Walker told London that they had better accept Mrs Gandhi and forget democracy. His successor, J. A. Thomson, was only a shade better. His assessment for London was that reasons told him Mrs Gandhi might win but his instincts were against that.

The US Ambassador William B. Saxbe was all for Mrs Gandhi since the day she had accepted his private dinner party. She was the only one who stood between India and chaos, he told Washington. He was also friendly towards Sanjay, who had openly favoured free enterprise. Saxbe had arranged collaboration between Maruti and International Harvester, a US firm.

Of all big countries, the Soviet Union was not hopeful of Mrs Gandhi's victory. Russian officials informed the Indian embassy in Moscow that things did not look to favourable for her; they were worried.

Campaigning throughout was uneventful, except that Samachar put out, long after midnight when newspapers were not in a position to check the report, that Sanjay had been shot at but not hurt in Amethi, his constituency. All leaders including JP condemned the incident, although some wondered whether it was not a stunt to gain voter sympathy.

Mrs Gandhi returned to New Delhi on 18 March. By then most of the polling was over. The portents were ominous. Two meetings were held at her residence, on the 18th and 19th. Sanjay, Dhavan, Bansi Lal and Om Mehta were present. Among the senior officials were the Home secretary and the inspector-general of police, Delhi. They were told that the PM's house must be "defended at all costs."

They were also informed that the house would be protected by barricading the roads leading to it and that the Border Security

Force would be there to "act and defend." Already ten battalions (6,000 men) had been flown in from different centres by AN12, Russian transport planes which were at RAW's disposal.

The inspector-general in turn held a meeting of local police officials to convey the order. One DIG asked what was meant by "defend at all costs." The IG said it simply meant "at all costs," even people would have to be shot down. The DIG expressed the fear that he was not sure if his men would fire at people if ever that became necessary.

It was strongly rumoured that Mrs Gandhi, in case the verdict went against her, contemplated imposition of martial law, first with the help of the BSF—the Law Ministry said that martial law was possible without calling in the military—and later with the help of the three service chiefs. No confirmation was available of this; probably no confirmation could ever be possible.

However, it was a fact that there were conferences of army commanders and top naval officials in Delhi early in March. And the top military intelligence officer, Mani Misra was replaced by Hardyal Kaul, T.N. Kaul's brother.

The observations of the Chief of the Army Staff General T.N. Raina[2] at a Rotary meeting that the army was apolitical lent credence to the rumour that he had been asked by Mrs Gandhi "to help her rule" and that he had refused to do so.

It was not just a disturbance or riot that might get ignited after the results were out that worried Mrs Gandhi. Nor was she afraid that in case the Congress party was defeated, people might demonstrate outside her residence. She had something else in mind.

She thought she would get between 200 and 220 seats in the 542-member House and hoped to purchase some. She imagined it

[2]An American magazine, the *Nation*, had said in its May issue that between 5 and 7 March Gokhale ran "exercises" at his ministry to develop a legal strategy for using the Constitution to call off the elections. About the same time, according to the *Nation*, Mrs Gandhi was sounding Raina about deploying his forces in certain constituencies on the ground that public order required the presence of armed forces. Raina reportedly refused, whereupon he was ordered by the cabinet to deploy his forces as requested. Raina gave the appearance of doing so, but what he did, did not serve Mrs Gandhi's objectives.

I checked the veracity of the "exercises" to postpone the elections with Gokhale on 27 May. He said, "There is no truth in it."

should be possible for her to form the government with the help of acting President B.D. Jatti, who openly acknowledged his political debt to her. She had to stay in power and the use of force might become necessary if there was resistance to her plan to form the government.

Whatever her plans, they came to naught when she was defeated by her old rival, Raj Narain, in Rae Bareli a constituency in UP which had been her stronghold in all previous elections.

When this news and that of Sanjay's defeat were displayed on newspaper boards, thousands of people, including women, danced to the beat of drums. At one place an onlooker offered free tandoori chicken to all and sundry. Here was a person who was once at the pinnacle of glory and had now been humbled by the "ignorant" masses.

The departure of Mrs Gandhi ended an era which was neither altogether white nor black.

Her effort to keep the country secular and together was by no standard a mean contribution. She showed courage in fighting cant and convention, and even in political matters she took the path which most would fear to tread.

But courage was no substitute for good deeds or for the methods employed to achieve them. This had been the strongest and the weakest point in Mrs Gandhi's tenure of eleven years as prime minister. Methods to her were not important, results were.

Whether it was the split of the Congress party in 1969 or the imposition of internal emergency in June 1975, it showed that she would spare no weapon to win. It was success that mattered to her, not how she achieved it.

It was true that she believed in a left of centre programme, but ideology was primarily the means to an end. The nationalization of banks she effected in 1969 was a commendable step, but it was essentially meant to crowd her rival Morarji out. Ideology also gave her a progressive image which went down well with the masses. But in her time another 160 million people went below the proverty line, making an impressive total of sixty-eight per cent of India's population.

And as days went by, she convinced herself that she, and she alone, knew what was right or wrong for the country. This gave her a feeling of being indispensable and she built a strong secretariat which controlled every segment of government and a spy network which kept an eye on real and imaginary opponents.

This also cut her away from all advice because everything fed to her had to fit into her assumption that she was indispensable. Those who tried to place another point of view were motivated by the desire to oust her, she rationalized.

At cabinet meetings she would tend to behave like a school teacher and most ministers, fearing her displeasure, would not even open their mouths. She was the government and she left no one in doubt about that.

She did not care whether the concentration of power would expose her to the charge of dictatorship. She knew she had the power and she was ready to use it. The only role she set for the opposition was that of a scapegoat—for anything that went wrong with her government's policies or programmes. She wanted control, overt and covert, over every field.

For a particular matter, she would pick up somebody who knew the ropes. But later he was dropped. There was no permanent adviser. She would not trust one.

In this atmosphere, only the man who had no scruples, Bansi Lal, or the one she trusted most, Sanjay Gandhi, her son, could survive. They could do no wrong because they were the ones she depended on. It was tragic for such a courageous person to look for such wretched crutches. But she was confident that she could do away with them too when she so desired. This unfortunately did not come true.

And when she ordered the elections which proved to be her Waterloo, she thought that she knew best, not her son, nor Bansi Lal, both of whom wanted her to postpone the poll for many years to come. She felt she could win, and show them all that the people were behind her, no matter what she did. This would once again prove that she had not lost touch with the masses and that she was still courageous.

What she did not realize was that cut off as she was she had lost contact with the masses. But she could have one satisfaction —she did disprove those who compared her with Hitler or Mussolini. They never had free and fair elections; she at least had that.

Mrs Gandhi never expected to lose. The way the returning officer at Rae Bareli, Vinod Malhotra, was pressurized—Om Mehta phoned twice and Dhavan thrice from Delhi—to order a re-poll or at least a recount showed that if nothing else she wanted the fact of her defeat to be announced as late as possible. She probably thought that she could come back through a by-election if the Congress won a substantial number of seats.

But the people in all northern states of India rejected the Congress lock, stock and barrel. They asserted themselves to restore their personal freedom and all that they had lost during the nineteen months of the emergency. Their revolt was not only against forced sterilization but against the system which left them with no recourse to seek remedy against any kind of injustice— the police would not write a report, newspapers would not print their grievances, courts would not entertain their applications, and neighbours would not come to their help because of fear.

The defeat of the Congress was quite dismal. It managed to muster only 153 seats as against 350 in the 1971 elections. The Janata party and its ally, the CFD, won 298 seats. The Congress did not get a single seat out of 84 in UP, 54 in Bihar, 13 in Punjab, 11 in Haryana and 6 in Delhi. It won 1 seat in Madhya Pradesh, 1 in Rajasthan, 3 in West Bengal, 4 in Orissa and 10 each in Assam and Gujarat.

The percentage of votes polled by the Congress in different states (1971 percentages in brackets) was: West Bengal 29.39 (28.23), Uttar Pardesh 25.04 (48.56), Tamil Nadu 22.28 (12.51), Rajasthan 30.56 (45.96), Punjab 35.87 (45.96), Orissa 38.18 (38.46), Manipur 45.71 (30.02), Maharashtra 46.93 (63.18), Madhya Pradesh 32.5 (45.6), Kerala 29.12 (19.75), Karnataka 56.74 (70.87), Himachal Pradesh 38.3 (75.79), Haryana 17.95 (52.56), Gujarat 46.92 (44.85), Bihar 22.90 (40.06), Assam 50.56 (56.98), and Andhra Pradesh 57.36 (55.73).

While Janata swept the north, it did badly in southern India. It won one seat each in Andhra Pradesh, Tamil Nadu and Karnataka. Obviously, the Janata wave did not seep through the Vindhyas; it was apparent that the excesses in southern India were fewer and stories of torture had not come out yet.

The thundering victory of the Janata and the CFD, which fought on the plank of democracy and freedom, came as a great surprise to the intelligentsia in India and the people in the West—both cut off from the people. Little did they realize that the poor loved their liberty as much as anybody else. Their approach might not have been sophisticated or ideologically pure but their faith in what they considered democracy was unflinching. A vote gave them the power to select the people they wanted and they used it to prove that they were the real masters; Mrs Gandhi and her party had taken away that right. This was their judgement against such high-handedness.

A joke that went round those days was wherever Sanjay had gone, the Congress had lost. But Mrs Gandhi did not think so. In a press interview she said that it was an oversimplification to blame Sanjay for the party's election debacle. She said that the five-point programme propagated by Sanjay was the government's programme, it dated back to the 1950s, to the days of her father.

And she defended him even at the Congress working committee's meeting of 22 March, from which she first stayed away to know if she was still wanted and then allowed herself to be "persuaded" to attend it. "Expel me. Expel me," she cried when Sidhartha sought to expel Bansi Lal from the Congress for six years and to take action against the other members of Sanjay's caucus.

Mrs Gandhi could afford to talk like that. She knew the men sitting around her at 5 Rajendra Prasad Road could not do anything against her. These men had no courage, no guts. For eleven years they had succumbed to her dictates without a murmur, and had sung her praises. It was not surprising that the Congress working committee reaffirmed its faith in her leadership and postponed detailed discussion till 12 April. This gave her time to plan her next move to achieve her main objective— to retain her grip on the party and to protect her supporters.

What followed during the next weeks was an intense struggle to capture the party between Mrs Gandhi and her men on the one side and her pro-CPI[3] critics along with Dev Kanta Barooah on the other. Chavan and his supporters sat on the fence, as they always did in times of cisis, anxiously waiting for the final outcome and lending an occasional hand whenever it looked that the situation might worsen and lead to a split.

To divert the attack on Mrs Gandhi and her associates, her supporters began asking for Barooah's resignation. The charge against him was that he had not prepared the party to fight the

[3]When Subhadra Joshi, a pro-CPI former MP, went to call on Mrs Gandhi she was given a cold reception. Mrs Gandhi said that she had been let down by "insincere friends."

Lok Sabha elections. To counter this, a group of former MPs and some legislators from the states gathered at Chandrajit Yadav's house and demanded the ouster of Sanjay, Bansi Lal, Vidya Charan Shukla and Om Mehta.

In a move-counter-move atmosphere, Barooah was persuaded by Ray, Yadav and their friends to ask for Bansi Lal's resignation from the Congress working committee and the parliamentary board. This infuriated Mrs Gandhi who made it clear that she would not let anyone close to her be singled out for blame for the party's defeat. Her group retaliated by stepping up its demand for Barooah's resignation. They also asked for the postponement of the meeting of the working committee and wanted a meeting of the AICC to elect a new president in place of Barooah. The crisis deepened. The party was heading for a split.

At a meeting which took place at Mrs Gandhi's house one evening, Mrs Gandhi pulled out Bansi Lal's resignation letter from her bag and handed it over to Chavan, not to Barooah, but not before she had made everyone agree that the entire working committee should collectively resign, sharing the blame for the party's defeat.

This was a move to recapture the party. Chandrajit Yadav was the first to say that he was not a party to the move for collective resignations. Vyalar Ravi sent a letter to Barooah withdrawing his signature and said the move was aimed at preventing the working committee from analyzing the election results. Sidhartha sent word from Calcutta that the move for collective resignation was no longer valid. Barooah said Anthony, the Kerala pradesh Congress president, had also telephoned him from Trivandrum, asking how the working committee could shirk its responsibility of inquiring into why the party lost at the polls. Barooah summoned newsmen to his house to announce that in face of all these developments he had had "second thoughts" on the issue. The working committee meeting, he said, would be held as scheduled to carry out a postmortem of the party's debacle.

Mrs Gandhi threatened that she would not attend the working committee meeting, creating doubts whether the party would be able to avert the split. Barooah, meanwhile, enlarged the scope of the working committee meeting by inviting the chief ministers and pradesh Congress chiefs to its deliberations. On the eve of the working committee meeting Indira Gandhi made another clever move by sending a letter to the Congress president and other members of the working committee, owning up all responsibility for the party's defeat.

"As one who led the government, I unreservedly own full responsibility for this defeat," she said in her letter. "I am not interested in finding alibis or excuses for myself, nor am I interested in shielding anyone. I have no caucus to defend or group to fight against. I have never functioned as a group leader."

The working committee met on 12 April. With chief ministers and pradesh Congress chiefs having joined the meeting it was a huge gathering of disgraced men summoned to find out what exactly had gone wrong. There was no sign of Mrs Gandhi.

"How can we hold the meeting without her?" asked Sita Ram Kesri, one of her cronies from Bihar. There were others who made similar suggestions. "Let us all go to 1 Safdarjang Road and persuade Indiraji to come to the meeting," said some others. Confusion prevailed at the meeting for some time. Ultimately Barooah, Chavan and Kamlapati Tripathi came out of the meeting, dashed for a car, drove up to Mrs Gandhi's house and brought her along to the meeting. She was received with folded hands by one and all. She knew she had not lost her charisma.

The working committee discussion began on a calm note, but suddenly eyebrows were raised when the mild-mannered Haryana Chief Minister Banarsi Das Gupta unburdened himself with charges against his former mentor Bansi Lal. Banarsi Das said the state was being run from Delhi by Bansi Lal. His own job was to arrange rallies for the former defence minister; his orders were to collect by truck, bus or other means 100,000 people for every rally Bansi Lal addressed. And every rally which Bansi Lal addressed cost the Congress 10,000 votes. "Why did you not speak up earlier, Guptaji?" someone asked. "I was a coward," replied Gupta.

Mrs Gandhi did not defend Bansi Lal at the meeting but when in the evening Ray moved for Bansi Lal's expulsion she protested. One of her friends in the working committee suggested that Bansi Lal should be given an opportunity to resign within twenty-four hours. He was not. Next day the working committee met and decided to expel Bansi Lal for six years from primary membership of the party. Mrs Gandhi did not attend the meeting.

Others were virtually let off. Vidya Charan Shukla got away with a mild reprimand and not a word was mentioned about Om Mehta who had lobbied the whole day pleading for mercy. There was no question of any action against Sanjay, he was not even a Congress member. (It is said that Mrs Gandhi drove up to Barooah's house one morning and pleaded for her son. Barooah later confessed to a friend, "After all I am human.")

Mrs Gandhi herself got away. Not only did the working committee describe her as "our esteemed leader," but no one picked up courage to point an accusing finger at her.

The working committee accepted Barooah's resignation—as arranged earlier—and chose Swaran Singh as the party's interim president, much against Indira's wishes; she wanted Brahmananda Reddy elected as party chief. But she succeeded in that in May, and not without a contest. Reddy polled 317 votes and Ray 160. Karan Singh, another former minister was also in the fray, and polled a handful of votes. D. P. Mishra, a veteran Congress leader from Madhya Pradesh helped Mrs Gandhi to win—as he had done in 1969, against the Syndicate.

No such crisis faced the Janata, but since it was a combination of four parties, some signs of stress were visible. They had to choose the next prime minister. There were three claimants—Morarji, Jagjivan Ram and Charan Singh, particularly the first two.

The Jana Sangh and Congress (O) were in favour of Desai, while the Socialists and the Young Turks by and large preferred Jagjivan Ram. The Bharatiya Lok Dal wanted its leader, Charan Singh, to be chosen prime minister.

However, the matter was left to JP, who had emerged as the unquestioned leader after the elections. His faith in democracy, despite the cynicism of many, and his voice against the tyranny of dictatorship had prevailed. His concept of total revolution was taking shape. He personally wanted to stay away from the leadership election and had conveyed his wish to Ashok Mehta and Madhu Limaye. But he was prevailed upon to find out the consensus and declare the result. Acharya Kripalani was asked to help him.

The newly elected MPs—Janata party (271), Congress for Democracy (28), Marxists (22), Akalis (8), Peasants and Workers party (5), Republican party (2) and a dozen other members were asked to assemble on 24 March at the Gandhi Peace Foundation building. But before the meeting, Raj Narain, the BLD leader, handed over a letter from Charan Singh who was in hospital. The letter said that the BLD supported Morarji for the prime ministership. It had been thought that Charan Singh himself could contest; at least now he was not in the way.

The CPM did not take part in the process of assessing who, between Morarji and Jagjivan Ram, had the larger support. A few members of the party said individually that since they would be exposing "the misdeeds of the past government" in the twenty months of the emergency, it might be embarrassing for Jagjivan Ram if he headed the new government as he had been part of Mrs Gandhi's government during that period. However, the party's official position was that it would prefer Jagjivan Ram to Morarji.

As MPs began to assemble for the crucial meeting to decide the leadership question, printed ballot papers were brought into the hall. But before the consensus process could begin, Raj Narain suggested that the decision be left to JP, Madhu Limaye seconded the proposal. Both Jagjivan Ram and Bahuguna waited outside the hall. When they learnt that there would be no consensus they left the place. Their reaction was that the consensus proposal agreed to had been abandoned even before it was given a trial.

JP still favoured the consensus while Kripalani said there was no doubt that Morarji had the majority. So consensus was dropped and JP announced that Morarji was the leader.

Morarji was sworn in on 24 March as the fourth Prime Minister of India, a position which had eluded him at least twice before. Now his longtime dream had become a reality.

For days together, he could not announce the cabinet because he was waiting for the CFD to merge with the Janata party. Jagjivan Ram was willing to do so if he were made deputy prime minister. But Morarji had promised the office to Charan Singh. To have two deputy prime ministers would be odd. Morarji was in a fix. Charan Singh released Morarji from the bond and paved the way for Jagjivan Ram to enter. Jagjivan Ram did not like the way the leadership issue was decided. He announced that his party would not join the government.

When I asked him why he did not want to join the government, he merely said that he had not left the Congress party for the same ministership. "Nobody was ousting me from the ministry," he added. He made it clear, however, that his party would, while pledging support to the government, retain its separate identity outside parliament.

JP did not give up his effort to persuade Jagjivan Ram to join the cabinet. In fact, a small committee picked up the thread from where JP had left and brought about a compromise.

It was agreed that the major parties of the ruling alliance would have two members each in the cabinet—BLD represented by Charan Singh and Raj Narain, whose inclusion was made an issue by Charan Singh; Jana Sangh by Atal Behari Vajpayee and L.K. Advani; CFD by Jagjivan Ram and Bahuguna; Congress (O) by Ramachandran and Sikander Bakht; the Socialists by George Fernandes and Madhu Dandavate; the Young Turks and other interests by Mohan Dharia and Purshottam Lal Kaushik; and the Akalis by Prakash Singh Badal. There were thirteen names, an unlucky number.

The CFD would have joined the government but for the announcement of the ministers list which irked Jagjivan Ram. The announcement contained nineteen names instead of the thirteen agreed to earlier in the day. The six additional names were of H.M. Patel, Biju Patnaik, Pratap Chandra Chunder, Ravindra Verma, Shanti Bhushan and Nanaji Deshmukh. At midnight on 25 March, Jagjivan Ram rang up Morarji to express his inability to join the cabinet.

Jagjivan Ram had nothing against the new men but felt let down because he was not consulted. Both he and Bahuguna did not go for the swearing-in ceremony.

Fernandes, who had played a crucial role in bringing round Jagjivan Ram, also thought it advisable to stay away. Presumably, he calculated that by staying out he would be in a better position to persuade Jagjivan Ram to change his mind. Nanaji Deshmukh, also close to Jagjivan Ram, took a similar stand and proposed Brij Lal Varma's name in his place.

It was again JP who saved the situation; his message did the trick. He told Jagjivan Ram that he was not just an individual but a force "without which it is not possible to build a new India." Finally Jagjivan Ram with Bahuguna, joined the cabinet

without asking for a rank or portfolio. Fernandes who had
stayed out purposely also took the oath of office.

It was the end of the chapter in the ministerial drama, but the
curtain was not yet rung. For the CFD it was a "breach of
faith all along the line," for the Janata, it was "dictation by the
other side." The gulf between the two widened as the days passed.

The bitterness did not cause any difficulty in the government's
functioning. In fact some election promises were fulfilled quickly
—civil liberties were restored; external emergency, imposed during
the Bangladesh war in 1971, was revoked (the internal one was
removed by the Congress itself on 21 March when the opposition
got an absolute majority in the Lok Sabha). The setting up of
autonomous corporations for AIR and TV were announced. MISA
prisoners, who were still in jail, were released. So also were economic offenders. Only the Naxalites were denied this freedom.
(They later sought JP's intervention partly successfully.)

Fernandes, who was the main accused in the Baroda dynamite
case, was first released on bail and later the case itself was withdrawn, when CBI Director D. Sen, in charge of the case, told
Morarji that there was "nothing much" in the case. The other
twenty-four accused were also released.

But before the case was withdrawn, Fernandes had the last
word. He told the magistrate, "When the state-controlled radio
and the censored press were telling the world how the people of
India had accepted Mrs Gandhi's dictatorship and her dynastic
rule, I was engaged in organizing underground resistance against
her fascist dispensation. Those who joined me in this activity were
men and women who were fired with the ideals of freedom and
liberty, who were not willing to make any compromise with dictatorship, who were willing to stake everything in defence of human
rights, who were willing to pay the price of their convictions."

From the beginning it was known that the case had no substance,
that it was cooked up.

For the first time in a decade there was freedom of expression
when all restrictions on the press were withdrawn. Frankly, even
before the emergency, the press was too niminy-piminy, too nice,
too ready to oblige the government by leaving out embarrassing
reports.

The pressure on the judiciary was also off. It was announced
that all those judges who were transferred or demoted during the

emergency would be restored to their old positions. The acting president, in his first address on 28 March to the joint session of parliament also announced that the Janata government would remove the remaining curbs on fundamental freedoms and civil rights, restore the rule of law and the right of free expression to the press and would introduce legislation to ensure that no political or social organization was outlawed without independent judicial inquiry.

The government removed the ban on the RSS, the Jamaat-i-Islami and the Ananda Marg.

It also promised to repeal MISA, the Prevention of Publication of Objectionable Matter Act and the amendment of the Representation of the People Act affording protection to certain individuals for electoral offences. For the first time in thirty years the Congress party which had ruled the country uninterruptedly sat on the opposition benches, subdued and sullen.

The prime minister's secretariat was pruned and named as "office." RAW was trimmed and the family planning programme became a welfare programme. All those officials who had openly sided with Sanjay during the emergency were transferred away from Delhi.

On the other hand, the perpetrators of the emergency ran into difficulties. But they were not repentant. Mrs Gandhi said that her defeat was because she "mistimed" the holding of elections. Once again she criticized the press—an obsession with her—and blamed newspapermen for having given exaggerated versions of the excesses. Sanjay said that he would retire from politics but believed that he and his group would come back in a year's time. He said that the Janata should thank itself that Morarji was the prime minister; things would have gone worse if Jagjivan Ram had been there. Ambika Soni resigned from the Youth Congress presidentship and criticized Sanjay openly.

Dhavan submitted his resignation to Mrs Gandhi while she was a caretaker prime minister. He said that they had done nothing wrong and welcomed the inquiries. Yunus said that it would not be long before "they" would be back. He vacated the house in Willingdon Crescent, which was later allotted to Mrs Gandhi, and went to live in a private apartment in Delhi. Bansi Lal became hysterical but regained his composure after some time and said that his exit from the Congress was only part of "their tactics." Om

Mehta behaved as if he had never anything to do with the emergency. "Show me any order which is in support of what was done
during the emergency, he said." Shukla, retaining the same super-
cilious style, said that it was the press or information media to
blame. They volunteered to do things which even he did not like.
Sidhartha, though not repentant, considered it advisable to leave
Mrs Gandhi's camp to prove that he was not a party to the emergency and what happened during the nineteen months.

The officers, who were hand in glove with Sanjay, Dhavan and
others, denied their complicity. And all of them—Congressmen
were no exception—said that they never knew about the "heinous
things" that had taken place during the emergency.

There was not a person, except Mrs Gandhi and Dhavan, who
did not put the blame on Sanjay. "He was the villain of the
piece," even those closest to Mrs Gandhi said. The CPI, the sup-
porter of the emergency, which had won only seven Lok Sabha
seats, also blamed "Sanjay and his caucus."

However, this was a thing of the past. Now there was freedom
in the air. There was enthusiasm. There was jubilation. It was like
stepping out of the darkness into light. A different kind of fervour
was visible, a fervour not witnessed even when the country
attained independence from British rule in 1947. People were
willing to work hard and make sacrifices for the country's future.

The Janata-CFD government wanted to cash in on this atmosphere and wanted fresh assembly elections in those states where
it had swept the polls in March. This meant elections in all the
northern states—UP, Punjab, Haryana, Rajasthan, Madhya
Pradesh, Himachal Pradesh and Bihar, in addition to Orissa and
West Bengal. Chavan, who by this time was elected leader of the
opposition Congress parliamentary party, was approached for
cooperation. It was thought necessary because the Congress,
having a majority in the Rajya Sabha, could thwart the government's plan to amend the Constitution and revert the assemblies'
term to five years. (Every constitutional amendment had to have
the approval by a two-thirds majority of both Houses.) Chavan
consented to cooperate. A constitutional amendment (43rd) was
introduced in parliament on 7 April to reduce the term of the
assemblies from six to five years and thus restore the position
that obtained before the 42nd amendment. The government
wanted to pass it during that very session. This meant fresh

elections in all states except Gujarat, Kerala, Orissa, Uttar Pradesh, Manipur and Sikkim.

Chavan had not at first realized the implications, nor had he consulted his party members. There was long resistance by the Congress chief ministers. Chavan said that he had only agreed to the introduction of the Bill and not to its approval. He was prepared to go along with the dissolution of the assembly in Bihar—the state where JP's movement had the largest impact. Nowhere else.

The Janata was now in a fix; it did not want the wave on which it rode to victory to break into nothingness. Also, the election of a new president had to be completed before 12 August. The electoral college for the presidential election consisted of all elected members of the Lok Sabha, the Rajya Sabha and the state assemblies. The assemblies had quite a bulk of votes which could play a decisive roll. The cabinet decided to use the president's powers[4]—ironically under the chapter, "Emergency Provisions," in the Constitution—to dissolve the assemblies to have fresh elections if the Congress did not cooperate. There was heated discussion on the subject in the cabinet and a few ministers wondered how such a drastic step would be received by the people from the moral point of view. They would accuse Janata of doing exactly what Congress did—substituting government of a different kind.

Indeed, on the basis of the parliament elections, to dismiss the governments which still had their term to run could set a bad precedent; after all India's was a federal structure, and it could hurt the autonomy of states.

The cabinet's decision in favour of dissolution was announced by Charan Singh on 18 April at a press conference. He said he had advised the chief ministers of nine states—Bihar, Haryana, Himachal Pradesh, Madhya Pradesh, Orissa, Punjab, Rajasthan, UP and West Bengal—to seek dissolution of their assemblies.

Charan Singh justified the step on the plea that since the people rejected the Congress outright in the Lok Sabha poll, its governments in the states had no right to stay and he quoted some British constitutional experts to support his contention.

[4]Article 356 authorizes the president "to dissolve state assemblies on the recommendation of the governor or otherwise."

Apart from this, it was a moral challenge; those gover.'ments which detained their critics without trial, committed untold atrocities and hounded out members of the opposition could not stay. The chief ministers had become a law unto themselves and had used every conceivable method to curb dissent. How could ministers who had run amuck during the emergency be allowed to stay in power when they might misuse it.

But Home Minister Charan Singh went about it in the wrong way. He got himself entangled in a constitutional wrangle. It looked unseemly and the Congress did not lose the opportunity to use it to tarnish the Janata image.

JP thought that those states which had not completed their five-year term should not be dissolved. He had in mind UP and Orissa. Vajpayee, a senior minister (now in charge of external affairs) in the Janata government, wrote a letter to Morarji expressing his concern over the criticism against the dissolution of assemblies; he too preferred the dissolution of only seven out of the nine assemblies.

Some Congress state governments challenged the action in the Supreme Court which unanimously rejected on 24 April their plea for "injunctions and interim orders." But this did not clear the decks. Even as Mrs Gandhi was watching the drama from the wings, Jatti refused to sign the proclamation for dissolution. He had been "persuaded" not to do so many days before he actually said No. It was the brainwave of Yashpal Kapoor who thought that the acting president could stall the dissolution of assemblies. Mrs Gandhi had to be consulted and Kapoor moved through Dhavan because he (Kapoor) had been stopped from visiting Mrs Gandhi's house. Lately he had become a liability. Everyone swung into action, Mrs Gandhi as well as Chavan. Both talked to Jatti over the phone. The acting president met Gokhale, under the pretext of delivering him the invitation card for his son's wedding, to know from him the legal implications.

Jatti was stubborn; no amount of reasoning worked with him. Charan Singh, Shanti Bhushan and many other ministers drew a blank. Even the hint that he might be elected as the next president did not tempt him. Morarji and Jagjivan Ram felt that they had no option but to go "back to the people." Their idea was to hold another election to the Lok Sabha on this issue.

Little did they know that Jatti had thought of that eventuality and had decided to call Chavan to constitute the government in case the Janata-CFD government were to quit. The acting president had no intention to accept the advice for parliament's dissolution.

Fernandes got scent of his plan and vehemently opposed the idea of the government's resignation. "All that they (the Congress) have to do is to detain some of us to have the majority," he openly said. Gradually, everyone began to see through Jatti's reluctance to sign the proclamation. Everyone was sore; even the people reacted sharply and shouted slogans outside his house.

The cabinet met and approved the draft of a letter which said that if the acting president was not willing to accept the advice of the prime minister and his council of ministers, he should resign. The obnoxious 42nd amendment was quoted; it made amply clear that the advice of the prime minister and his council of ministers would be binding on the president. Tables were now turned on Jatti. The cabinet secretary delivered the letter. Jatti was cornered. He knew the consequences would be terrible and took no time in signing the proclamation. Another crisis had blown over and everybody was relieved.

The proclamation was issued on 30 April. Nine assemblies were dissolved and the election commissioner was asked to hold the elections as soon as possible, before the onset of the monsoon. The Janata, CFD and their allies hailed the proclamation, while the Congress described it as a "dictatorial act" and "a blow to the federal democratic structure" of the country.

Jatti's action in delaying his signature convinced Jagjivan Ram that Janata and CFD leaders should stay united and told Morarji that the CFD would join the Janata. This was almost a week before the CFD was to meet and decide on its future. The shrewd politician that he is, Jagjivan Ram knew that UP and Bihar could create a problem if the CFD and the Janata did not come to terms. However, for joining the Janata, Jagjivan Ram had another motive. He would be able to influence the election of its chief. He did not want anyone from the BLD to head the Janata. Chandra Shekhar, a clean person with leftist leanings, was unanimously chosen as the party's president.

The Janata and the CFD were now a unified force. Though it had taken more than a month for this process to be completed, it was welcomed all round as a good augury. It did alienate some opinion because people did not like the horse-trading and bargains which they had abhorred in the Congress now showing up in their new government.

Nor was the distribution of assembly tickets to their liking. Opening doors to defectors was bad enough, but what was worse was to see black marketeers, bootleggers, sycophants, time servers and communists at influential positions on the Janata side. Reports that money was being collected from big businessmen and industrialists—the way the Congress leaders did—disappointed the people further. Bureaucracy also seemed to be returning to its old, leisurely ways. How could this happen? the people wondered.

But JP had promised them people's committees, from villages up to New Delhi, to act as watchdogs. Would any government allow such close scrutiny? This is what is in the mind of the people today.

The Janata party has raised the moral tone of the country. After many years there is talk of values which Mrs Gandhi's regime had sedulously demolished. It is not that the people do not appreciate what the Janata does. It is that they are anxious to preserve the moral standards that the Janata had earlier set.

They are happy that the all-pervasive fear has disappeared—fear of the police, fear of the widespread secret service, fear of the official class, fear of oppressive laws, fear of detention without trial.

They are also happy that even the highest in the land will not be spared; Mrs Gandhi's bank accounts are already under examination and the commissions of enquiry are set to bring the guilty to book.

But they are equally keen that it should not happen again; a lesson should be learnt to prevent the recurrence of such a situation. One way to do it would be to give an economic content to democracy. An egalitarian society is possible and, may be, India can show the way to the rest of the world.

They also do not want the Janata to go the Congress way or its leaders to sink into the chairs vacated by their predecessors to become indistinguishable from them. The people's dilemma is that of values. They know that compromise helps and pays far more dividends than a wildgoose chase after ideals. But certain traits have come to be attributed to the Janata, and the people do not want them to be tainted.

No one expects any person or any party to undo in two or three months the wrongs committed over the years. But the manner and the speed with which the Janata has set about doing things has created some disappointment, if not disillusionment. The people have rejected the Congress which is still in control of the same old caucus. If the Janata disappoints them, what do the people do?

They are willing to wait. They think it is too early for them to give up hope and too soon to pronounce their judgement.

Maruti

THE IDEA to produce a low priced "people's" car indigenously had been mooted way back in the 1950s. Initially conceived by Manubhai Shah, the small car project had had a rather chequered career. On one occasion, the government had nearly signed a contract with Renault of France, following the recommendations of the Pandey Committee that this car would best meet the requirements. The contract was eventually shelved on account of Krishnamachari's strong opposition. For several years afterwards the project proposal was bandied about but no decision was taken.

Several private and public sector undertakings submitted tenders and prototype models of the projected car. One such application made by the Mysore State Industrial Development Corporation estimated that it would cost between Rs 5,000 and Rs 6,000 to manufacture their prototype on a commercial scale.

Two schools of thought dominated the government debate. One maintained that the car should be made locally with indigenous resources while the other felt it should be manufactured in collaboration with foreign car companies. At the time, Volkswagen, Toyota, Renault, Citroen and Morris were all keen to collaborate on this project.

It was at the height of this debate that Sanjay Gandhi returned to India after incomplete training at the Rolls Royce factory in Crewe, UK. It would not be wrong to say that once Sanjay entered the fray the issue was more or less automatically settled.

From the outset it was clear that Sanjay would get the licence. The delay in completing formalities was a result of the fact that Sanjay hoped to establish his credentials by producing a prototype for the public. This he did in a backyard garage in Delhi. Once that was done, it was only a matter of time before the letter of intent was issued. Finally, in November 1970, and in total disregard of the damning criticism that had been levelled against the prototype the licence was granted to Maruti Ltd to produce 50,000 cars annually. Maruti had been formed by Sanjay and he was the managing director, despite the fact that Sanjay's total shareholding in the company amounted to one share of Rs 100. Two main conditions stipulated in the letter of intent were: that the car should be built entirely from local resources, and it should be low priced. As is obvious, neither of these two conditions was ever likely to be met or could be met under the circumstances in which Maruti Ltd was destined to operate.

As far as Sanjay was concerned the first major hurdle had been crossed. With the letter of intent, Sanjay set about acquiring land and finance. Both these problems were resolved with the help of willing businessmen and ambitious and unscrupulous politicians.

With characteristic ruthlessness, Bansi Lal expropriated 445 acres of fertile land on the Delhi-Gurgaon highway evicting in the process inhabitants of villages Mahalada, Dhundera and Kheterpur. The villagers were paid the paltry sum of Rs 4.5 million as compensation at an average of Rs 10,000 an acre, at a time when adjacent land was commanding prices of up to Rs 35,000 per acre. Moreover, the site chosen violated the rule that no factory should be built within 1,000 metres of a defence installation—it was located right next to an army ammunition dump.

After the acquisition of land, Sanjay moved to the question of capital. The initial finance was raised through businessmen who had an eye on the possible favours that they could extort. By September 1974, the total paid-up share capital of Maruti Ltd was Rs 18,460,700; 2.2 per cent of this was owned by the UP Trading Company, 1.6 per cent by the Dharbhanga Marketing Company and 1.1 per cent by the Saran Trading Company. In addition, Maruti Ltd amassed a total of Rs 21,891,042 during the financial year 1973-74, from the sale of dealerships. Each dealership was sold for a fee ranging between Rs 300,000 and Rs 500,000 and mostly to businessmen who had no prior association with automobiles but nevertheless felt it prudent to invest, or were coerced into doing so.

Since its inception, the project has been an unmitigated failure. The first prototype was junked. The second turned turtle on its test run; and subsequent ones developed snags ranging from faults with the steering and suspension to overheating. At one stage, Sanjay abandoned the conditions laid down in the letter of intent and resorted to the use of imported equipment. Alas, even then Maruti Ltd failed to produce a roadworthy model. Meanwhile, as Maruti staggered along, Sanjay exuded confidence in public. At a press conference in December 1973 he said that the car would be ready in six months. He repeated this statement eighteen months later and said that by 1977 the factory would be working at its optimum capacity, producing 200 cars a day. Even as late as January 1976, at the Congress session in Chandigarh, Sanjay said that "by the end of March, the car will be available in selected showrooms."

With the consecutive failure of each prototype, Maruti Ltd sank so deep into debt that even Sanjay's sycophantic friends could not raise the resources to help. It was then that Sanjay turned to public financial institutions. Backed by his mother, nationalized banks were coerced into extending unsecured loans to Maruti Ltd. The Central Bank of India and the Punjab National Bank, each loaned Maruti nearly Rs 7.5 million.

Eventually, the Reserve Bank of India (RBI) was compelled to intervene. In a circular to all nationalized banks, the RBI warned that any further loans would undermine the basis of the country's credit policy. The imminent clash between the RBI and Sanjay was avoided by a fortuitous twist of circumstances.

Within days of the Allahabad High Court judgement, emergency was declared and absolute power vested in the hands of Mrs Gandhi. As a consequence, Sanjay was catapulted into political prominence.

One of Sanjay's first political initiatives was directed against those officers who had dragged their feet when Maruti Ltd had been desperate for finance. Dr Taneja, chairman of the Central Bank was sacked. He was followed by Dr Hazari, the deputy governor of RBI, who was replaced by a relatively junior officer, J.C. Luther, from the income tax office. The RBI Governor S. Jaganathan was retired and succeeded by K.R. Puri, formely chairman of the Life Insurance Corporation (LIC).

Eight months before Maruti Ltd was started, Sanjay set up the Maruti Technical Services Private Ltd (MTS). Out of a paid-up capital of Rs 215,000 Sanjay's share was Rs 115,000. The rest of the money came from Rajiv and his family. MTS was thus an entirely family owned concern.

In June 1972, MTS was appointed a consultant to Maruti Ltd. The contract stipulated that an initial payment of Rs 500,000 would be paid by Maruti Ltd and thereafter MTS would receive 2 per cent of the value of the sales by Maruti Ltd, subject to a minimum of Rs 250,000 per annum. MTS was thus guaranteed a 100 per cent return on the initial investment. It is estimated that by January 1975, MTS had earned a net income of Rs 102,000.

Another subsidiary of Maruti Ltd was the Maruti Heavy Works Ltd (MHW). Majority shareholding (59 per cent) was with the MTS. The rest of the shares were parcelled out between O.P. Modi (20 per cent), K.L. Jalan (13 per cent) and the Gandhi family (8 per cent). MHW had been registered as a small-scale company to manufacture road rollers. MTS was also appointed its technical consultant. Normally, none of these concerns would have made a profit; they were ill-equipped and staffed by ignoramuses. But these were not normal times. With the tremendous political clout of Mrs Gandhi to sustain him, Sanjay successfully inundated the Maruti companies with orders. Those who hesitated or questioned the capacity of these factories were given short shrift. And those who questioned the legality were harassed and suppressed. For instance, when questions were raised in parliament in April 1975 about the source of Maruti's equipment, the director in the Ministry of Industrial Development, Krishnaswamy asked PEC, a subsidiary of the STC and Batliboi, an agent for East European countries, to supply the needed information. It was through these two agencies that Maruti Ltd acquired machinery for the production of cars. Before any information could be divulged the directors of PEC and STC were summoned by the PM's office and reprimanded. They were told to stop the investigation. The two officials from the PEC, Cavale and Bhatnagar, involved with this investigation were transferred and suspended respectively. Krishnaswamy's residence was raided and after two bottles of liquor were found, he was suspended for contravening the excise rules.

Another example of official interference is highlighted by the Oil and Natural Gas Commission (ONGC) case. In January 1975, ONGC invited tenders for six road rollers. The Garden Reach Workshop (GRW), a public sector undertaking and two other companies submitted tenders. MHV also submitted a tender through a private company. The initial quotation of GRW was Rs 146,000, whereas that of Maruti was Rs 160,000. Maruti later reduced its quotation to Rs 141,000 but despite this the order was placed with the government undertaking. Two considerations determined this decision. First, GRW was a government undertaking and thus was entitled to a 10 per cent price preference, and second it had a far better reputation.

However, before the contract could be signed with GRW, the order was rescinded. The member for materials, Lahiri, called for revised estimates. Maruti lowered its price to Rs 125,000 while GRW stuck to its original price. Subsequently the contract was awarded to Maruti. Apart from exceeding his authority by calling for revised quotations, Lahiri also erred by disregarding the stipulation that a company's factory should be inspected before a contract is signed to assess its capacity. Furthermore, the order was processed at such a high level that even senior employees of the ONGC did not have the chance to object.

After the imposition of the Emergency the last shreds of legitimacy were removed. There was now no need to go in for competitive tenders. Sanjay had just to ask and there were many willing to comply. The *Washington Post* wrote in its 10 November 1976 issue, "The public believe a vast swindle is going on. The bureaucrats say they can do nothing. Sanjay calls up secretaries and says 'give the contract to so and so'."

Concrete manifestations of this trend were apparent from the sudden increase in the demand for road rollers by states and other public sector undertakings. Within a short while of the emergency, the Border Roads Organizations (BRO) had placed orders for 100 road rollers, Haryana for 50, Punjab for 40 and UP and NDMC for an undetermined number.

Without the necessary equipment or technical expertise to build genuinely new rollers, MHV sold as new repainted junk fitted with secondhand Ford and Perkin engines which had been bought for a paltry Rs 2,000. The price they charged (Rs 140,000) was forty per cent higher than any of the other rollers on the market. Needless to say, most were found unsuitable for the purpose for which they had been bought. The Border Roads Organization realized, much to their silent consternation, that none of the rollers supplied to them could function at high altitudes. They were thus kept at the BRO depot in Pathankot.

Another activity of MHV, and one into which they had only recently diversified, was the construction of bus bodies. Despite the fact that most states were fully equipped to handle demand for bus bodies, MHV was inundated with orders by state governments. MP, for example, not only placed orders for 100 bus bodies with MHV but paid them the grossly exaggerated sum of Rs 39,000 per body. To their own corporation they paid only Rs 27,813. Similarly, UP spent Rs 500,000 more than it should have to ingratiate itself with the Sanjay caucus. By the end of the emergency it is estimated that UP alone had placed orders for 499 bus bodies, MP for 180, Haryana for 307, Rajasthan for 152 and Delhi for 52. MHV is estimated to have made a net profit of Rs 10 million.

But perhaps the most scandalous examples of corruption and nepotism relate to Maruti's involvement with foreign multinational corporations (MNC). Soon after the emergency (some may have been before) Maruti became the agents for several MNC—in particular the International Harvester and Piper Co. of the US, the Man Co. and Demag Co. of W. Germany and the Shan Progetti Co. of Italy. Besides the products of these companies, Maruti were also agents for the supply of chemicals, pumping eng.nes, bulldozers and telephone cables.

In mid-1976 Sanjay Gandhi prevailed upon the Delhi Water Supply and Sewage Disposal Undertaking to utilize a water purifier called Quick Floc Polymix for the treatment of the city's water and sewage supply instead of the conventional alum.

The product was manufactured by MTS in collaboration with a friend of Sanjay Gandhi's R.C. Singh who was on sabbatical from the IIT, Delhi.

When some chemists at the undertaking expressed reservations about the use of the chemical, they were suspended. R.C. Singh was made a technical adviser to Municipal Comissioner B.R. Tamta and in this capacity he okayed the use of the product. The water supply undertaking started using Rs 10,000 worth of the chemical daily. Long after the polymix was being used by the undertaking, tenders were called for the product in an attempt to make the contract above board on paper.

The product has never been tested by the National Environment Engineering Research Institute, Kanpur, a prerequisite before being used for a city's water supply. According to chemists the monomer residue of the product can accumulate to toxic levels resulting in skin and eye infections. The monomer residue of the polymix is much above the limits laid down by the US Food and Drug Addiction Act. Abroad it is used only for treatment of sewage water and not for drinking water.

As agents Maruti received between 20 per cent to 25 per cent commission on the value of all completed transactions. At the risk of belabouring a pretty obvious point, government and private undertakings were coerced into placing orders with those companies for which Maruti were the agents. In the process, several ensuing contracts were quashed. For example, a contract between Indian Tube Company, a public sector undertaking, and ONGC, for the supply of big diameter pipes, manufactured by British Steel was revoked after a representative from Maruti, Jhunjhunwala, met the British Steel representative, Charles Gordon, and persuaded him that it would be in British Steel's interests to accept Maruti as their agents. Similarly, a contract with Poland for the supply of Harvesters was suspended after Maruti intervened on behalf of International Harvester.

In another instance, ONGC was compelled to place orders for twenty-four heavy trucks through Maruti. Twelve were to be supplied by International Harvester and the rest by the West German firm Man. The Maruti tender had been for Rs 5 million— twice as high as that of the nearest competitor. When tenders were invited by the ONGC for eight trucks with mounted mobile cranes of forty to forty-five tonnes, the lowest tender received was that of the Earth Moving and Machinery Corporation of New Delhi. They were offering American hoist cranes for Rs 15.8 million. The Maruti quotation was initially Rs 17.6 million but was later reduced to Rs 17 million. The contract was to be offered to the former company but after the personal intervention of K.D. Malaviya, it was awarded to Maruti. On another occasion, an expansion tender for the Trombay Phulpur plants was given to the Shan Progetti Company of Italy, as a result of which Maruti netted a profit of Rs 25 million in foreign exchange.

Maruti also engineered the collapse of the company Insov Auto Ltd. The purpose of this company had been to manufacture auto vehicles in collaboration with the Soviet Union. The agreement between the two countries stated that Prommash-Export, Moscow Ltd, would arrange for the supply of imported components for the production of 400 vehicles at a plant to be set up in Sandila in UP. Soon after the emergency, however, the Ministry of Industry wrote to the Soviets that since Maruti Ltd had all the necessary facilities to manufacture "light commercial vehicles," there was no need to set up another plant in India. Instead, the imported equipment should be supplied to Maruti Ltd, which would then manufacture the proposed car. This was followed by another letter which made it clear that the government would not sanction the creation of a new plant. As a consequence, the project was quietly shelved.

Perhaps the most well documented scandal is the one involving the aircraft. As agent for Piper aircraft, Sanjay secured orders for nineteen Piper planes. For each plane Sanjay received as commission Rs 500,000 in foreign exchange. From Piper, Sanjay acquired the agency for the Maule aircraft—an executive plane made by the Americans. Realizing that there were basic limits to the number of Maule aircraft India could buy, Sanjay put pressure on the Ministry of Agriculture to abandon the production of the Basant crop spray plane and replace it with the Maule. Fortunately, the end of the emergency forestalled a final decision.

As Sanjay's involvement with planes increased he created another company—the Maruti Aviation company. It was probably his intention to create a third feeder airline which could be run by private operators, assisted by the Indian Airlines (IA) and other government agencies. It is now known that he had persuaded IA to make a feasibility study of this proposal. In connection with his expanding interest in aviation, Sanjay made a bid to acquire the premises of Safdarjang airport. He ordered the IA to vacate all hangars and park their fleet of buses, station wagons and cars at the DTC depot at Indraprastha Estate. He intended to locate the workshops of Maruti Aviation at Safdarjang airport. Fortunately the end of the emergency also put an end to this crazy scheme.

As Sanjay and his caucus entered more lucrative pastures, plans for the commercial production of a people's car were quietly abandoned. To keep the employees of the Maruti Ltd occupied, they were set about to make pen-caps, nameplates, lock parts and other minor accessories. Occasionally the company would land a different sort of contract, such as the one in which they were asked to make bomb cap chambers for the Defence Ministry. Despite these occasional contracts, Maruti Ltd continued to flounder in debt. By the end of 1976, it had accumulated a loss of Rs 23 million, which was nearly equal to its initial paid-up capital of Rs 26.4 million.

It was rightly that people began referring to Maruti as *ma ruti* (mother crisis).

Censorship Guidelines

NOT FOR PUBLICATION (CONFIDENTIAL)

THE PURPOSE of censorship is to guide and advise the press to guard against publication of unauthorised, irresponsible or demoralising news items, reports, conjectures or rumours. To this end, these guidelines are intended to enlist the voluntary cooperation of all sections of the press in maintaining an atmosphere conducive to the maintenance of public order, stability and economic growth in the country.

2. Censorship covers any news, report, comment, statement, visual representation, film, photograph, picture and cartoon.

3. Censorship applies to the publication of news, comments or reports relating to the proceedings in Parliament, any Legislative Assembly or a Court of Law. The following should be kept in view for the publication of the proceedings of:

(a) Parliament and Legistative Assemblies:

    (i) The statements made on behalf of Government may be published either in full or in a condensed form, but its contents should not infringe censorship.

    (ii) Names and party affiliations of members speaking on a subject and their support for or against the subject may be mentioned.

    (iii) The results of voting on a bill, motion or resolution may be factually reported, and in the event of voting, the number of votes cast for and against mentioned.

    (iv) No extra-parliamentary activity, or anything excluded from the official proceedings of Parliament/Legislative Assembly, should be published.

(b) Court of Law:
  (i) The names of the judges and the counsels may be mentioned.
  (ii) The operative part of the order of the court may be published but in appropriate language.
  (iii) Nothing should be published which infringes censorship.
4. The following should be kept in view in publishing news, comments or reports:
(a) The factual accuracy of all news and reports should be ensured and nothing should be published which is based on hearsay or rumour.
(b) Reproduction of any objectionable matter already published is not permissible.
(c) No unauthorised news or advertisement or illustration should be published in regard to vital means of communication.
(d) Nothing should be published about arrangements relating to the protection of transport or communications, supply and distribution of essential commodities, industries etc.
(e) Nothing which is sought to be published should relate to agitations and violent incidents.
(f) Quotations, if torn out of context and intended to mislead or convey a distorted or wrong impression, should not be published.
(g) There should be no indication in the published material that it has been censored.
(h) No reference should be made to the places of detention and the names of the political personalities detained.
(i) Nothing should be published which is likely to:
  (i) affect India's relations with foreign countries;
  (ii) subvert the functioning of democratic institutions;
  (iii) denigrate the institutions of the Prime Minister, President, Governors and Judges and Supreme Court and High Courts;
  (iv) threaten internal security and economic stability;
  (v) cause disaffection among the members of the armed forces or public servants;
  (vi) bring into hatred or contempt the Government established by law in the country;

    (vii) promote feeling of enmity and hatred between different classes of citizens in India;

   (viii) cause or produce or instigate or incite, directly or indirectly, the cessation and slowing down of work in any place within the country;

    (ix) undermine the public confidence in the national credit or in any Government loan;

    (x) encourage or incite any person or class of persons to refuse or defer payment of taxes;

    (xi) instigate the use of criminal force against public servants;

   (xii) encourage people to break prohibitory laws;

5. Quotations from AIR broadcast, news agency reports and statements officially released by Government are permissible provided that such quotations give a true and faithful account of what has been stated and nothing is taken out of the relevant context or distorted in any manner.

6. Confirmation of any report picked up by Correspondents from a source which is not official or authentic can be obtained from the Press Information Officer.

7. If any report, comment or other matter, save and except editorial comment, is published in any newspaper, journal, periodical or other document which is contrary to the letter and spirit of these guidelines, and if it is apparent that it could only have been based on material supplied by the local Correspondent, responsibility for it shall be fixed upon the local Correspondent unless otherwise proved.

8. Copies of all press despatches not subjected to pre-censorship, should be filed with the Chief Censor for his information.

9. In case of any doubt about the advisability or otherwise of publishing any news, report or comment, the Chief Censor should be consulted.

NOT FOR PUBLICATION

Explanation I—Comments expressing disapprobation or criticism of any law of any policy or administrative action of the Government with a view to obtain its alteration or redress by lawful means, and words pointing out, with a view to their removal by

lawful means, matters which are producing, or have a tendency
to produce dishaimony of feelings of language or regional groups
or castes or communities, shall not be deemed to be objectionable matter within the meaning of this section.

Explanation II—In considering whether any matter is objectionable matter under this Act, the effect of the words, signs or visible
representations, and not the intention of the kepper of the press
or the publisher or editor of the newspaper or news-sheet, as the
case may be shall be taken into account.

4. To illustrate what has already been stated it is advised that
no news, reports and comments relating to the following shall be
published:

    (a) Matters which are grossly indecent or scurrilous or in-
        tended for blackmail;

    (b) Unparliamentary activities of proceedings for example
        dharnas, sitdown strikes, rushing to the dias, shouting,
        refusal to obey the Chair as they are not part of the
        proceedings;

    (c) Matters which tend to promote enmity, hatred or ill-will
        between different groups (regional, religious, racial, ling-
        uistic or caste);

    (d) Quotations from newspapers, journals, publications, books
        which are violative of censorship regulations;

    (e) Matters expunged by the Presiding Officer;

    (f) Matters which militate against the promotion of friendly
        relations with foreign countries;

    (g) Matters which infringe the requirements of security and
        integrity of the county;

    (h) Matters which tend to subvert the functioning of demo-
        cratic institutions.

NOR FOR PUBLICATION

Guidelines for covering the proceedings of
Parliament commencing March 8, 1976

Parliament is the sovereign body and, therefore, its deliberations
have sanctity. In no case, the image of Parliament as a voice of
the people and as a sovereign body should be allowed to be

impaired. Therefore, no news, report or comment attempting to defile the sanctity of the proceedings of Parliament or attempting to give an inaccurate or distorted version of the proceedings should be published.

2. News, reports and comments relating to the proceedings of Parliament are governed by Rule 48 of DISIR, 1971 and the statutory orders framed thereunder. The provisions of statutory order 275(e) dated June 26, 1975, and as amended on August 12, 1975 and February 2, 1976 under Rule 48 of DISIR are relevant. These cover news, comments, rumours or other reports, relating to:

(a) any contravention or alleged or purported contravention of any of the provisions of Part III rules 31 and 33 of Part IV, rules 37, 38, 39, 43, 46, 47, 48, 50, 51 and 52 of Part V, Part VIII and Part IX of the said Rules including orders made thereunder, or

(b) any action taken in relation to such contravention, or

(c) any action taken under the provisions of the Maintenance of Internal Security Act, 1971 (26 of 1971), or

(d) the proclamation of Emergency made by the President on the 25th day of June 1975 under Article 352 of the Constitution, or

(e) the Order made by the President on the 27th day of June 1975 under Article 359 of the Constitution, or

(f) any action taken under the provisions of the Defence of India Act 1971 (42 of 1971) or under the provisions of the Act as amended by the Defence of India (Amendment) Act, 1975 (32 of 1975) or under the rules and orders made thereunder, or

(g) any "prejudicial report" as defined in Clause 7 of Rule 36 of the Defence and Internal Security of India Rules, 1971.

(h) The proclamation, in relation to the State of Tamil Nadu, issued on the 31st day of January 1976, under Article 356 of the Constitution by the President.

3. Matters defined as objectionable in the Prevention of Publication of Objectionable Matter Act, 1976 should also be kept in view while covering the proceedings of Parliamentary Objectionable matter as defined in the Act is quoted below:

The expression "Objectional Matter" means any words, signs or visible representations:

(a) which are likely to—
(i) bring into hatred or contempt or excite disaffection towards the Government established by law in India or in any State thereof and thereby cause or tend to cause public disorder; or
(ii) incite any person to interfere with the production, supply or distribution of food or other essential commodities or with essential services; or
(iii) seduce any member of the Armed Forces or the Forces charged with the maintenance of public order from his allegiance or his duty or prejudice the recruiting of persons to serve in any such force or prejudice the discipline of any such Force.
(iv) promote disharmony or feelings of enmity, hatred or ill-will between different religious, racial, language of regional groups or castes or communities; or
(v) cause fear or alarm to the public or to any section of the public whereby any person may be induced to commit an offence against the State or against the public tranquillity; or
(vi) incite any person or any class or community persons to commit murder, mischief or any other offence;
(b) which—
(i) are defamatory of the President of India, the Vice-President of India, the Prime Minister, the Speaker of the House of the People or the Governor of a State;
(ii) are grossly indecent, or are scurrilous or obscene of intended for blackmail.

NDS 12. From Mirchandani to all UNI Centres and all subscribers

The following fresh guidelines were orally communicated to us by the Censor's office late last night. These are for your information, and should not be published:

No story relating to the following three cases to be issued:
1. Forthcoming Parliament Session business.
2. Prime Minister's Election Case in Supreme Court, and
3. Any statement by any representative of banned parties.

PRIO
DEL 65   GEN

*Editors Advisory: For your information only and not for publication.
Further to earlier advisory issued under DEL 4 this morning.*

The following guidelines for the coverage of Parliament pro-
ceedings have been provided by the Chief Censor:
  (A) The statements of Ministers may be published either in
      full or in a condensed form but its contents should not
      infringe censorship.
  (B) The speeches of members of Parliament paritcipating in
      a debate will not be published in any manner or form but
      their names and party affiliation may be mentioned. When
      publishing names of members who participated in a debate,
      the fact that they supported or opposed a motion can be
      mentioned.
  (C) The results of voting on a bill, motion, resolution etc.
      may be factually reported. In the event of voting, the
      number of votes cast for and against may be mentioned.

*Editors: We have been asked to circulate the following guidelines
issued by the Chief Press Adviser for your information (Not For
Publication).*

Guidelines for the press in the present emergency

Declaration of national emergency to meet the threat to the
security and stability of India by internal disturbance will point
to the need for extreme caution and circumspection in the handling and purveying of news and comments. The press requires to
be advised to guard against publication of unauthorised, irresponsible or demoralising news items, conjectures and rumours
and yet the press should be enabled to fulfil its obligation to the
public. One of the most powerful aids to the Government and the
people in an emergency is the press. In the manner in which
information is printed, published and disseminated there can be
an accretion of enormous strength to those who are posing a
threat to internal security.

In an emergency declared to meet an internal threat, the
concern of the government is mainly with the misguided and

subversive elements within the country which by their acts may try to prejudice peace and stability of the nation. In a democratic country in which citizens are fully conscious of their duties and responsibilities to the nation. The aim of the government is not so much to rely in every case on the wide and extraordinary powers confered on it. But as far as may be enlist the voluntary cooperation of all sections of the population in maintaining an atmosphere conducive to the fulfilment of the primary task of ridding the nation of the causes of emergency.

GENERAL GUIDANCE

1. Where news is plainly dangerous newspapers will assist the Chief Press Adviser by suppressing it themselves. Where doubts exist, a reference may and should be made to the nearest press adviser.
2. Where matter has been submitted for examination before publication. The advise of the Press Adviser should be followed.
3. When guidance is being given advising against the publication of news or comments relating to a particular matter, no mention of or reference to that matter should be made without obtaining fresh clearance for moderation should always be observed and all sensationalism avoided repeat avoided. This should be observed particularly in illustration of posters and headlines.
4. No publicity to be given for rumours.
5. When any document or photograph is officially issued, care must be taken to retain the sense of the accompanying caution or press motion.
6. No reproduction of objectionable **matter** already published in any Indian or foreign newspaper.
7. No news or advertisement or illustration to be published.
8. Nothing to be published about arrangements relating to the protection of transport or communications, supply and distribution of essential commodity, etc.
9. Nothing to be published which is likely to cause disaffection among the members of the armed forces or public servants.
10. Nothing to be published which is likely to bring into

hatred or contempt or to excite disaffection towards the government established by law in India.

11. Nothing to be published which is likely to promote feeling of enmity and hatred between different classes of persons in India.

12. Nothing to be published which is likely to cause or produce or to instigate or incite, directly or indirectly, the cessation or slowing down of work in any place.

13. Nothing to be published which is likely to undermine the public confidence in the national credit or in any government loan.

14. Nothing to be published to encourage or incite any person or class of persons to refuse or defer payment of taxes.

15. Nothing to be published which is likely to instigate the use of criminal force against public servants.

16. A prejudicial report means any report, statement or visible report, whether true or false, which, or the publication of which is an incitment to the commission of any of the prejudicial acts mentioned above.

GENERAL GUIDELINES FOR THE PRESS

Press is advised to keep the following main points in view while filing messages, news, stories and comments, etc.

1. Any attempt to subvert the functioning of democratic institutions.

2. Any attempt to compel members to resign.

3. Anything relating to agitations and violent incidents.

4. Any attempt to incite armed forces and police.

5. Any attempt promoting disintegration and communal passions by dangering the unity of the country.

6. Reports containing false allegations against leaders.

7. Any attempt at denigrating the instition of the Prime Minister.

8. Any attempt endangering law and order to disturb normal functioning.

9. Any attempt to threaten internal stability, production and prospects of economic improvement.

Phone from the Censor

Only the Samachar version of the occupation of the Syrian embassy by Arab students is to be published. No picture is to be published.
5.6.76

Mr Raghavan from Censors

No news regarding the transfer of Judges of the Andhra High Court is to be published.
June 8, 1976
5.30 pm

From Censor office

Mr Mehar Singh from censor rang up to say: Shri Jayaprakash Narayan is understood to have released a letter written by him to the Prime Minister regarding Prime Minister's contribution from the PM's fund for the purchase of a dialysis for JP's treatment. You are requested not to use the story.

Arya from the Censor room

Samachar would be issuing a story in this regard (JP's letter). It has been cleared for publication.

sd/
16.6.76   News Editor

Phone from the Censor's office (J.N. Sinha)

An agreement has been signed with Mizo delegation today in Delhi. The PIB has released an item on the agreement along with background. All critical comments on it may please be avoided.
July 1, 1976

Message from the Censor

If the MNF leader, Laldenga, issues any statement, it may be sent to censor.

sd/
2.7.76   News Editor

Telephone from the Censor

Nothing should appear in the newspaper about Charles Soberaj,

an international cheat who has been arrested in Delhi in a fraud-cum-poisoning case. The call was received by Mr Bhattacharjea.
July 6, 1976

Phone from Deputy Chief Censor Arya
Till July 14 no news, comments or pictures of the Israeli raid in Uganda is to be published. Particularly, there should be no eulogising or justifying the Israeli action.
July 8, 1976

Phone from Censor (Raghavan)
If there is any correspondent story about any walkout at the non-aligned pool conference, it is subject to pre-censorship.

10.7.76

sd/
News Editor

Message from Censor
Any news item emanating from Washington that the passport of Sri Kumar Poddar, a wealthy businessman of the US, has been cancelled should not be published.

July 14, 1976
CC: Editor

sd/
News Editor

Phone from Censor
News reports, comments or edit on the price situation in the country may please be submitted for pre-censorship.
17.7.76

sd/
News Editor

This does not cover reports about fall in prices (Mr Thukral from Censor)

Message from Censor
No news about JP is to be published.
20th July 1976

Phone from Censor (Mr Raghavan)
Kindly do not publish any adverse news or comments or

editorials about family planning programme and education levy in U.P.

sd/
News Editor

28.7.76

Instructions from the Censors

1. Nothing to be published about the Statesman's writ in the Delhi High Court against a directive of the Chief Censor.

2. No news or comment to be published regarding the validity of ordinances promulgated in Jammu and Kashmir.

sd/
News Editor

29.7.76

SERVICE NUMBER 2/8/7/2/1 (BGR/VIJ/MDS/BMY/DELH) HYDERABAD JULY 30

From Mr R. Srinivasan HYD to Shri T.R. Bangalore and copy to News Editors (all stations)

The following instructions have been received from the Censors in regard to the publication of news about the funeral of Mr T. Nagi Reddi:

"We regret you to be brief in publishing the report of the funeral of Late Sri T. Nagi Reddy without refering to post-mortem, his underground life, figure of persons who attended the funeral etc."

Phone from Censor (Raghavan)

Any report on Vinoba Bhave is subject to pre-censorship.

August 9, 1976

Mr Thukral from Censor's office

No news or comments regarding Mr Subramaniam Swamy, member Rajya Sabha, having raised a point of order today in Parliament or any other report about him relating to Parliament should be published.

10.8.76

Phone from Censor Pardhy

Nothing about Lok Sabha question relating to jail reform should be published.

sd/
Dy. News Editor

11.8.76

Phone from Censor

Jamait-ul-ulema-i-Hind has passed some resoluti on. One resolution is one Syria's intervention in Lebanon. This resolution is
subject to pre-censorship.

24.8.76

sd/
News Editor

Mr Raghavan Censor

Today's proceedings in Parliament will be subject to pre-
censorship.

September 1, 1976

sd/
News Editor

From Censor

All reports about Ram Jethamalani, Chairman, Bar Council
of India, who is in the U.S.A., are subject to pre-censorship.

6.9.76

sd/
News Editor

Phone from Censor

Mr Bilbagh Singh Daleke, State Minister for Transport, Punjab,
in a statement in the Vidhan Sabha on Punjab-Haryana transport
dispute has made a reference to a corridor between Ambala and
Chandigarh. All references to the corridor are to be dropped.

September 9, 1976
CC: Editor

sd/
News Editor

Message from Censor (Mr Raghavan)

No speculative story based on eye-witness accounts about the
identity, nationality and intention of the hijackers should be
published.

September 11, 1976
CC: Editor

sd/
GIRISH SAXENA

Mr Laxmi Chand from Censor

All news reports regarding Philips Petroleum Co. of U.S.A.
will be referred to censorship.

15. 9.76

sd/
A.P. SAXENA
News Editor

Mr Thukral from the Censor office rang up

Supreme Court proceedings on the writ petition filed by late Sri Nagi Reddy, MLA, Andhra Pradesh, against the Chief Minister of A.P., regarding contempt of court should not be published.

sd/
R. D. JOSHI
Chief Sub

September 20, 1976
CC: Editor
    News Delhi Bureau
    Desk

Phone from Censor (A.P. Singh)

New York Times correspondent William Borders had an interview with Kewal Singh. The interview or any story connected with it is not to be published.

sd/
TRIPATHI
Sub-Editor

September 20, 1976

Phone from Censor (A.P. Singh)

No news report on treasure search at Jaigarh Fort should be published without referring it to censors.

sd/
TRIPATHI
Sub-Editor

CC: Editor
    Bureau
    Chief Subs

September 21, 1976

Mr Lakshmi Chandra Censor

Please do not publish any speculative or sensational story about Dacoit Sunder as it may hamper the process of investigation. On this subject you are requested to publish only what is officially stated.

sd/
S.K. VARMA
Dy. News Editor

29.9.76

Message from the Censor

The External Affairs Ministry is issuing a statement on Indo-

Pak talks. You are requested to publish only official version without any comment or editorial.

sd/
A.P. SAXENA
7.10.1976   News Editor

Phone from K.B. Sharma Censor
Kindly do not use any news about a strike in the Dhariwal mills
in Punjab.

S.K. VARMA
6.10.1976   Dy. News Editor

Phone from Mr Rattan Censor
6 Congress leaders of Orissa, including J.B. Patnaik, Union
Minister, have made a statement in Puri on party affairs. This is
subject to censorship.

SIVADAS
12.10.1976   Chief-Sub

Phone from Censor
The report on Sheikh Abdullah's press conference must be submitted for pre-censorship.

sd/
A.P. SAXENA
12.10.1976   News Editor

Message from Censor Thukral
Any story on a reported bomb scare in Lusaka where the
Defence Minister, Mr Bansilal, was staying should not be pub-
lished.

sd/
SIVADAS
October 14, 1976   Chief-Sub

Lakshmi Chandra Censor
All news reports and comments including editorial regarding
sale of US arms to Iran will be subject to pre-censorship.

sd/
16.10.1976   News Editor

Phone from Censor

Any story on Govt. of India's imposition of restrictions on the Nepali citizens in certain restricted border areas and statements on this subject by the Nepalese Government and the Indian ambassador should be sent for pre-censorship.

sd/
A.P. SAXENA
News Editor

16.10.1976

Phone from Censor

News regarding the visit of the Naga Peace Council delegation to UK to see Phizo is not to be published.

sd/
A.C. SAXENA

20.10.76

Pillai, Deputy Chief Censor

There is to be the fourth Asian Badminton Tournament at Hyderabad from October 29 to November 7. The participation of the Chinese team need not be highlighted (either through description or exclusive photographs).

sd/
A.P. SAXENA
News Editor

21.10.1976

J.N. Sinha from Censor

On the question of swearing-in of new ministers of Jammu and Kashmir, which was scheduled today, only the Jammu and Kashmir Govt's press note and the statement of the Chief Minister may be published. There should be no commentative report.
October 25, 1976

Mr Raghavan from Censor room

Any story from the Gujarat High Court proceedings on transfer of judges should be submitted for pre-censorship.

sd/
A.P. SAXENA
News Editor

4. 11. 1976

Message from Censors (*Lakshmi Shankar*)

Speeches of Ambika Soni and Mahesh Joshi at the AICC session are not to be used.

Also, for the Prime Minister's speech please take Samachar copy as the model.

November 21, 1976

sd/
SIVADAS

Phone from Mr Raghavan of Censor office

In the MP first supplementary budget presented in the Assembly today any reference to subscription to the National Herald should be deleted.

30. 11. 76

sd/
S. BANERJEE

J.N. Sinha (*Censors*)

Only the official handout on non-payment of taxes by young entrepreneurs for industrial projects in colonies like Wazirpur in Delhi should be used.

4. 12 76

sd/
A.P. SAXENA
News Editor

J.N. Sinha (*Censors*)

No report or comment on Indo-UK air services talks now in progress in New Delhi should be published at this stage.

4. 12. 1976

sd/
A.P. SAXENA
News Editor

Message from Censor (*Pardhy*)

Any statement by Chief Ministers or Congress leaders regarding celebration of Mr Sanjay Gandhi's birthday on December 14 should not be used.

December 9, 1976

sd/
SIVADAS

J.N. Sinha (*Chief Censor's office*)

Kindly do not publish any news report on the supply of US

jet fighters skyhawk to India. Only official announcement may be used.
December 10, 1976
CC: Editor

From Lakshmikant (Censor)
No statement or speech on apartheid by Sri A.M. Moola, Chairman of the South African Indian Council, should be allowed to appear in your esteemed paper.

sd/
16.12.1976   News Editor

Mr Rattan from Censor
No news about intra-party rivalries and disputes and Congress vs Youth Congress should be published.

sd/
19.12.1976   A.C. SAXENA

Anand Pardhy's phone from Censor's office
The Pakistan Embassy has arranged some function on the occasion of the Jinnah centenary. One of the functions is today at India International Centre. Another will be the presentation of Jinnah medal to our President at Rashtrapati Bhavan on December 25. There might be some other functions also. Reports of these functions should be given in low key.

sd/
A.P. SAXENA
23.12.76   News Editor

Phone from Mr Mehr Singh (Censor)
Story and articles on insurgency in the North-Eastern region should not be published without clearance from the censor.

sd/
23.12.1976   News Editor

Pardhy from Censor
A statement of Dr Miss Hulgol in the dynamite case in the metropolitan magistrate's court should not be published.

sd/
23.12.1976   News Editor

Mr RNG does not want us to publish anything about the Tuli (PNB) case.

26.12.1976   News Editor

From Mr K.B. Sharma (Censor)

Nothing may kindly be carried about the collapse of the TV tower under construction at Raipur.

                                                         sd/
28.12.1976   H.D. JOSHI

From Chief Censor's office

The statements of Mr M. Moola of the African National Congress, who represents the aspiration of African people, may be fully publicised. He made at statement at Bhopal yesterday and was likely to make another shortly.

The earlier advice in respect of Mr A.M. Moola, Chairman, South African Indian Council, a stooge organisation of the South African Government, stands.

                                                           sd/
4.1.1977   News Editor

From Mr Arya (dy Chief Censor)

All stories on intra-party affairs in the Congress and Youth Congress including meetings of leaders may kindly be sent for pre-censorship.

                                                           sd/
January 8, 1977   S.K. VARMA
                                                         Dy. News Editor

Index

Abdullah, Sheikh, accord with Mrs Gandhi, 62; refusal to condemn JP, 62; reaction to emergency, 62

Administrative Reforms, lip service to, 101-102

Aggarwal, Justice, ruling of, 96

Ahmed, Fakhruddin Ali, opposition's *dharna* and plea to, 19, 20; on demand for Mrs Gandhi's resignation, 20; death of, 170; Emergency of June 1975 proclaimed by, 39-40; Mrs Gandhi's influence on, 39; rumour regarding death of, 170

Allahabad High Court judgement, conditional stay granted by Surpeme Court, 32-33; findings of, 3; hearing of appeal in Supreme Court, 81-82; Mrs Gandhi's anxiety before delivery of, 1-2; Mrs Gandhi's appeal against, 12, 13, 19-20, 28; qualified stay granted on, 4-5, 6, 9, 11; Supreme Court's reversal of, 93

Asthana, K.B., Justice, ruling of, 96

Bahuguna, H.N., 166; ouster from UP's chief ministership, 113-114

Bansi Lal, 57, 112; advice to Mrs Gandhi, 24; braggings of, 38; criticism of Inder Gujaral by, 25; in Mrs Gandhi's caucus, 7; knowledge of proposed emergency proclamation, 35; power abused by, 142-143; party action against, 182; role of, 27; role in Emergency Council, 53

Bar Associations, protest on emergency, 46

Barooah, Dev Kant, 109; as Mrs Gandhi's henchmen, 7; as peacemaker between Feroze Gandhi and Mrs Gandhi, 7; "Indira is India" slogan coined by, 8; on Jagjivan Ram's resignation, 66; progressive measures proposed by, 60; reaction to Allahabad judgement, 4; resignation of, 183; role of, 15; subservience to Mrs Gandhi, 29

Basu, Jyotirmoy, premonition on emergency proclamation, 36

Beautification of Delhi, Sanjay's fad of, 138

Beg, M.H., 123; on reversal of Allahabad judgement, 93; as Chief Justice of India, 169

Bhagalpur Jail firing, blackout on, 48

Bharati, Bhairav, death in detention, 85

Bhave, Acharya Vinoba, Mrs Gandhi's annoyance with, 90; Mrs Gandhi's visit to, 89; interpretation of emergency by, 89

Bhinder, P.S. (Special intelligence branch), role of, 38, 54

BKD, reaction to Allahabad judgement, 10-11

Bhoomi Putra, action against, 95

Bhutto, Z.A., comments on developments in India, 51; remark on Mrs Gandhi's poll decision, 156n

tion moved in Lok Sabha by, 66; Congress leadership's assessment on, 15; fears of, 44; income-tax arrears of, 14; line with young Turks, 18; meeting with Mrs Gandhi, 165; Mrs Gandhi supported by, 33; neutral zation of, 43; on Mrs Gandhi's right to nominate successor, 18; post-emergency intelligence on, 44; press conference on resignation day, 165-166; relations with Mrs Gandhi, 13-14; resignation from the Congress, 165; role of, 20; surprise at emergency proclamation, 41; tact of, 29; Young Turks disappointment with, 34; *v.* Mrs Gandhi, 19

Jagmohan, DDA chief, role of, 138

JP, arrest and detention of, 41; assessment of Mrs Gandhi by, 56; Bihar movement of, 11; blessing to the Janata party, 161; call for opposition merger, 11; Chandra Shekhar's 24 June dinner for, 34; contemplated detention of, 38; criticism of Mrs Gandhi by, 22; crusade of, 11; Delhi's appearent peace shown to, 57; doubts about kidney ailment, 105; increasing popularity of, 22; election campaign launching in Patna by, 164; Indira meeting, 11-12; kidney ailment of, 103; letter from prison to Mrs Gandhi, 56, 103; Lok Sangharash Samiti announced by, 36-37; Mrs Gandhi's propaganda about, 58; 1942 escape from prison, 57; on Mrs Gandhi tactics, 107; on Mujib's assuming dictatorial powers, 82; at opposition rally of 25 June 1975, 30,36; opposition's message to, 11, 12; parole revoked, 106; planned action against, 26-27; planned arrest of, 27; press conference after release, 104, 163; remark at the time of

arrest, 41; Sikh-Hindu amity enforced by, 45; Socialist International delegation refused permission to meet, 55; support for Jagjivan Ram as PM, 14, 14n; total revolution, plan of, 12, 48-49; treatment in detention, 56-57; truth about appeal to armed forces, 37

Janata Party formation of, 161; common programme of, 161-162; election campaign launching of, 164-165; electoral alliances with Akalis and CPM, 163; lack of funds, 168-169; manifesto of, 171; Morarji's election as prime minister, 183

Journalists' accreditation, curbs on, 108-109

Kapoor, Yashpal, Allahabad judgement on role of, 3; Dhavan's relations with, 8; Mrs Gandhi's explanation on role of, 21; role in ouster of Bahuguna, 113-114

Khanna, H.R., 123; dissenting judgement in MISA case, 169; supersession of, 169

Kishan Chand, Lt-governor of Delhi, Sanjay's influence on, 28; knowledge of proposed emergency proclamation, 35; role of, 38

Lal, P.C., rough handling of, 140-142

Limaye, Madhu, *ex-parte* hearing and dismissal of care, 96; information on smugglers asked by, 60; resignation from the Lok Sabha, 151, 152

Maintenance of international Security Act (MISA), abuse of, 144-145; amendment of, 38, 91, 92, 120, 122; assurance on use of, 38; Mrs Gandhi's assurance on use of, 60; misuse of, 49; political use of, 41; selective use against smugglers, 61